ROUTLEDGE LIBRARY EDITIONS: JEWISH HISTORY AND IDENTITY

Volume 5

THE SPIRIT OF JUDAISM

THE SPIRIT OF JUDAISM
Sermons Preached Chiefly at the
West London Synagogue

MORRIS JOSEPH

LONDON AND NEW YORK

First published in 1930 by George Routledge & Sons Ltd

This edition first published in 2020
by Routledge
2 Park Square, Milton Park, Abingdon, Oxon OX14 4RN

and by Routledge
52 Vanderbilt Avenue, New York, NY 10017

Routledge is an imprint of the Taylor & Francis Group, an informa business

© 1930 Morris Joseph

All rights reserved. No part of this book may be reprinted or reproduced or utilised in any form or by any electronic, mechanical, or other means, now known or hereafter invented, including photocopying and recording, or in any information storage or retrieval system, without permission in writing from the publishers.

Trademark notice: Product or corporate names may be trademarks or registered trademarks, and are used only for identification and explanation without intent to infringe.

British Library Cataloguing in Publication Data
A catalogue record for this book is available from the British Library

ISBN: 978-0-367-44247-7 (Set)
ISBN: 978-1-00-300850-7 (Set) (ebk)
ISBN: 978-0-367-90374-9 (Volume 5) (hbk)
ISBN: 978-0-367-90380-0 (Volume 5) (pbk)
ISBN: 978-1-00-302404-0 (Volume 5) (ebk)

Publisher's Note
The publisher has gone to great lengths to ensure the quality of this reprint but points out that some imperfections in the original copies may be apparent.

Disclaimer
The publisher has made every effort to trace copyright holders and would welcome correspondence from those they have been unable to trace.

THE SPIRIT OF JUDAISM

SERMONS PREACHED CHIEFLY AT THE
WEST LONDON SYNAGOGUE

BY

THE REV. MORRIS JOSEPH

LONDON
GEORGE ROUTLEDGE & SONS, LTD.
NEW YORK: THE BLOCH PUBLISHING CO.
1930

TO MY FRIENDS
CLAUDE GOLDSMID MONTEFIORE
AND
PHILIP SAMUEL WALEY
IN AFFECTION AND GRATITUDE

PREFACE

My two volumes of sermons, "The Ideal in Judaism" and "The Message of Judaism," having been out of print for some time, I have decided to comply with the suggestion of a few of my friends, and issue a third collection. I have come to this decision not without hesitation. What response, I ask myself, can ideas and teachings, largely coloured by nineteenth century training and associations, expect to draw from the present generation? Yet I prefer to be optimistic, comfortable as it is, though not altogether egotistical. I should like to believe that this book may find some acceptance, and justify both my kind publishers' venture and my own hope that these sermons may be of service in deepening the reader's respect for Judaism as a living creed, and as an effective inspiration to faith and duty.

MORRIS JOSEPH.

London, September, 1929.

CONTENTS

	PAGE
THE IDEAL SYNAGOGUE	1
THE SYNAGOGUE AND THE WORSHIPPER	10
THE JEWISH SPIRIT	16
ANTI-SEMITISM	23
"BEARING THE NAME IN VAIN"	29
ISRAEL'S ANCIENT VIRTUES	35
HAVE THE JEWS A MISSION?	41
LEADERSHIP	52
ISRAEL A NATION	58
PALESTINE'S FUTURE	64
THE HEBREW UNIVERSITY	70
THE PSALMS IN JEWISH LIFE	76
HOPE (PASSOVER)	89
THE GARDEN OF THE SOUL (PENTECOST)	95
A HAPPY NEW YEAR (NEW YEAR)	102
ONCE IN THE YEAR (KOL NIDRE)	108
PLANNING THE NEW LIFE (NEILAH)	115
THE SUCCAH (TABERNACLES)	123
ON RAIN (TABERNACLES)	129
ABOUT TOYS (CHANUKAH). FOR CHILDREN	135
OLD TIMES AND OLD FOLKS (CHANUKAH). FOR CHILDREN	141
THE FRAGRANT LIFE	147
SPIRITUAL EXPERIENCE	152
THE UNSEEN WORLD	157
THE POWER OF PRAYER	165
THE FIERY CHARIOTS	171
THE REVELATION OF THE DIVINE	177

CONTENTS

	PAGE
FRIENDSHIP, DIVINE AND HUMAN	183
THE FEAR OF GOD	188
THE CRY OF RELIGION	193
THE WAR AND RELIGION	199
THE WAR AND THE FUTURE	207
CHRISTMAS AND WAR	214
PEACE AND GOODWILL	220
THE POWER OF THE BIBLE	226
MORALITY AND RELIGION	233
FAITH AND REASON	239
CHARLES DARWIN	245
SUPERSTITION	251
OPTIMISM	258
MAKING THE BEST OF THINGS	263
GOD'S TREES	269
THE HALLOWING OF KNOWLEDGE	274
THE CHILD	284
PARENTS AND CHILDREN	290
MANLINESS	296
THE ETHICS OF WORK	304
ABOUT "WHISPERING"	311
ILL TEMPER	318
GIANTS	324

THE SPIRIT OF JUDAISM

THE IDEAL SYNAGOGUE

" In that day will I cause a horn to bud forth unto the house of Israel, and I will give thee the opening of the mouth in the midst of them, and they shall know that I am the Lord."
EZEKIEL xxix., 21.

THESE are the concluding words of the *Haphtorah* read this morning. The Prophet foretells the various destinies of the nations—among them Israel, who though brought very low, is to rise again, with the Prophet himself as a power in his midst. He shall preach God's message to His people, and preach it to responsive hearts. "In that day will I cause a horn to bud forth unto the house of Israel, and I will give thee the opening of the mouth in the midst of them, and they shall know that I am the Lord."

The days of the Prophet are past, but his gracious message still retains its ancient force. Despite ages of suffering, Israel lives, and is bidden to hope. The Prophetic promise is till cherished in his heart, and he is for ever looking forward to the time when his horn, token of renewed youth, shall bud forth. The future may present itself to each of us in different shapes. We may be Zionists or anti-Zionists. But one common bond unites the members of our race all the world over—the unalterable conviction that Israel's work is not yet done, that he is still reserved to accomplish the Divine purpose in the world.

Nor is this all the promise. Ezekiel prophesies to himself as well as to his people. A happier time is coming for him also—a time when he will speak for God, and find men to listen. How is this prediction to be fulfilled in these prosaic days? Who is to be this eloquent, this soul-winning Prophet in an age when Prophecy is dead? My friends, he is to be found in everyone, however lowly his station, however humble his intellectual gifts, who gives himself with heart and soul to the service of the Most High. For every good life that is inspired by Judaism is a witness to the God of Israel. It is, in the best sense of the word, a prophetic life. And if one noble life can be thus mighty, how much more powerful will be a union of such lives, when in the words of the liturgy for the New Year Festival, "they are all joined together into one band to do the Divine will with a perfect heart." It is upon such holy brotherhoods, as well as upon the individuals that compose them, that Judaism counts for the fulfilment of the high destinies that await it. A congregation of good men and true, of Israelites conscious of their sacred character as "a kingdom of priests and a holy nation," and earnestly striving to be faithful to it—the ideal congregation—what a power this will be in the world, nay, what a redeeming force in Jewry itself! How mightily may its example set other hearts aflame with religious ardour! To it will indeed be given "the opening of the mouth in the midst of Israel." For many a congregation shall hear the gracious doctrine, and seek to live by it.

The ideal synagogue! Here is a programme for you —yes, for you, small in numbers and not over rich, though you are.[1] Will you not accept the alluring mission? You have some special qualifications for it.

[1] Preached to a congregation of working tailors.

In certain respects you are a unique body. You have a synagogue whose importance, greater than your intrinsic strength, is for that very reason ever beckoning you on to the ideal. You enjoy a measure of independence denied even to more influential communities. You have won the sympathies of some of the best representatives of English Judaism. Nay, you have already evinced a religious energy and a spiritual breadth to which small congregations cannot always lay claim. Your horn has begun to bud; why should it not reach its full pride? Why should you not be the ideal congregation, to whose message your brethren at large shall listen, whose witness to God shall help to sanctify Him among the Gentiles? It is an attractive mission; nor is it an impossible one. For it has ever been by a few that Israel has been saved—ever by the humble that God has been vindicated. Gideon, about to fight the enemy, is warned by the Divine voice that the men with him are too many. "Be tender," cry the Rabbins, "with the children of the poor, for from them goeth forth the Law." And in like manner it is from congregations such as yours, children in growth, lowly of spirit, doing their Master's bidding meekly and trustfully, that the persuasive teaching which is to capture many a heart may go forth in these our times.

What are the characteristics of the ideal Synagogue? I have already suggested them in general outline. But what are the details? To answer this question let me remind you of a truism. Every congregation has a double character. It is a body of worshippers and a body of workers. It has two spheres of action—the Synagogue and the World. In each of these spheres the ideal congregation will shine resplendent.

First, then, as to the Synagogue. It is necessary to start with a right idea of its purpose. It is first a place of prayer, not of gossip, or mechanical routine, or indifference, or inertness. When you come here you must pray. You must come as sons of God who desire to seek their Father's face, to tell Him of their hopes and their griefs, and in the very telling find comfort and strength, to get His blessing on their work ere they turn to begin the worldly struggle anew. Therefore pray; be devout. That is the great essential. Let your service take what shape seems best to you. Let it be as orthodox as you please, so long as it helps you to worship in sincerity. God wants our prayers; the form they are to take He leaves to us.

Pray, then, with all your hearts. I think that even the most orthodox Rabbi will tell you that it is not necessary to repeat every word of the Service, but only as much as you can say with devotion. He will tell you that, as regards the rest, all that one need do is to listen quietly and reverently. For quantity is nothing, quality is everything. The shortest prayer may go straight to Heaven, while the longest may miss the way. Though this is not the same as saying that the longest can never find it. As the Rabbins are fond of pointing out, five words of Moses once healed his suffering sister—" O God, heal her, I beseech Thee "; and yet on another occasion he prayed on the Mount for forty days and forty nights.

But the Synagogue is something else besides a House of Prayer. It is Israel's meeting-place. This it was in former times; for it was the centre of Jewish life, religious, but corporate too—the fount at which the Jew would slake his spiritual thirst, and feed at the same time his racial consciousness. And this the Synagogue is, or ought to be. It is the spot where the living Israel meets in spirit the Israel of the Past, and from that impressive communion catches some of the religious, the courageous, the self-sacrificing temper that made the Past glorious. Here, inspired by the memory of the illustrious dead who bore their witness for Judaism in both life and death, the congregation renews its covenant with the Supreme—the ancient covenant of Sinai by which Israel vowed to hearken to God's voice and to keep His commandments, whatever might betide. Nay, the congregation worships as Israel, as the visible representative of the Lord's people, heirs to all the mighty hopes that have sustained it, pledged to all the splendid obligations that have uplifted it. Thus it is that we pray in the Synagogue as an historic brotherhood, and not only as individuals, thus that we ask less for private boons than for collective blessings, especially for blessings that will bring help and salvation to the race, and crown with success God's great cause. It is as if the people who were ransomed from Egypt in olden days, who sat at God's feet to receive His Law, who fought for Him in the heroic Maccabean days, who have suffered exile and insult and bitter oppression for His sake, lived again in us, and spoke again in our prayers.

It is an inspiring thought, seeing that it opens to us a realm of service far wider than the Synagogue itself. For the ideal House of Prayer is one in which the worshipper's heart is steeped in pious feeling, which, outlasting itself, overflows into the daily life and sanctifies it. It keeps him awhile in God's company, so that, uplifted and purified by that holy fellowship, he may bear himself the more worthily when in the company of men. It gives him a glimpse of Heaven, in order that, encouraged by the vision, he may tread bravely and undefiled the lower places of the earth.

And if this is true of every House of Prayer, it is especially true of the Synagogue, where to the exalting influences wrought by all worship are added the specific influences of Jewish worship. For a double motive summons the Jew to the good life—the intrinsic beauty of it and the obligation of keeping untarnished the religious heritage borne to him from God by the hands of successive generations. Every time, then, that a Jewish congregation comes together for prayer its members are admonished that they owe the duty of rectitude to their historic as well as to their moral conscience, that they owe it to their religion, which their rectitude will defend and vindicate, even as their fathers' self-renunciation defended and vindicated it. Here it is that we reach one of the most characteristic and the most fertile ideas in Jewish theology. The Jew must be upright, honest, pure because to be otherwise would be a *Chillul Hashem*, a "profanation of the Divine Name," because, in other words, it would bring Judaism into contempt, and so dishonour its Divine Author. No Biblical writer uses this conception more freely or more effectively than our Prophet, Ezekiel. He speaks of Israel exiled among the nations, and by the very fact of his exile profaning God's Holy Name, "in that men say of them: These are the people of the Lord, and yet are gone forth out of His land." To the onlooker among the Gentiles God's hand seems to have waxed short, seeing that it has not availed to save His chosen people from the calamity of banishment. And the idea retains its force to this day. Every time one of us sins, or as a great Jewish writer, Bachya, points out, even *seems* to sin, he profanes the Name. For such is Jewish solidarity that men say of the whole race "These are the Lord's people, and yet they have been banished out of His land"—exiled from the goodly land of righteousness into which an ennobling religion had led them. And remember that this deadly sin, though it is a sin against God, though it is the worst betrayal of Judaism, does

THE IDEAL SYNAGOGUE

not spring from a violation of *Jewish* precept only, though such a violation sets our neighbours marvelling at our irreligion. Every offence against the moral law is equally a *Chillul Hashem.* " Swear not by my Name falsely, lest ye profane my Name," says the Almighty in Holy Writ. Every deception in deed or word, every sordid act, every departure from the standard of seemly living that prevails among our neighbours besmirches the fair fame of Israel, and thus is a *Chillul Hashem.* It drags the good name of Judaism through the mire, for it inevitably provokes the question : " What good can there be in a religion whose followers have fallen so low ? This God's chosen people ?—the idea is a blasphemy ! "

The ideal congregation will keep this conception steadily before it, and make it fruitful. Its great aim will be to sanctify the Divine Name—to sanctify it by self-consecration, by a deep-lying holiness which, stimulated by outward and symbolic purity, by the hallowing of Sabbaths and Festivals, by wholesome restraints upon eating and drinking, yet reaches its highest and fullest expression in cleanness of life— cleanness of act and speech and thought.

Nor is the picture complete even yet. The true Jew will look within as well as without. The men and women of the ideal Synagogue will see that it is broad-based upon peace and brotherly love. The friendly aspect they show to the world will but mirror the kindly feeling for each other that reigns in their own hearts. Cherish this truth too, I beseech you. " Seek peace and pursue it "—peace in your Synagogue councils, in your private, everyday lives. In this respect, almost above all, be a pattern to other small congregations. For strife is the poison that most surely kills the religious life. All your efforts after the establishment of the goodly

Synagogue—your fine House of Prayer, your devoutness, your religious school—all will be useless if dissension rend you asunder. "Even if Israel worship idols," so the Rabbins, in their bold fashion, represent God as saying, "I cannot harm them so long as peace reigns in their midst." For creed is naught, severed from conduct; and no real hurt can touch a community that is held together by love. It is a little thing, but mighty. You know the old Talmudic story which tells how a Rabbi, meeting Elijah the Prophet one day in the crowded market-place, asks him to point out those among the busy throng who are surest of Heaven. For answer the Prophet indicates two men of homely garb and mien. Thereupon the Rabbi goes to them and says: "Friends, tell me what are your good qualities." "We know of none," they reply, "except this, that when people are in trouble we comfort them, and when they quarrel we make them friends again. That is all." Yes, that was all; but it fitted them for eternity. For the simple virtues are the materials of the higher life. And so if you would be a model community, you can get your wish not by restlessly striving after great achievements, but by doing the little acts of goodness that offer themselves to you every day.

Finally, if you are to be an ideal Synagogue, let this holy House be a wellspring of all gracious influences. Let it be the rallying point of all your best energies, religious and moral, but intellectual as well. Let it animate you with a love for sacred study—study of the splendid literature and the moving story of our race—but with a love, too, for every kind of culture that may lend grace and completeness to life. For the ideal Synagogue is only symbolised by the visible fabric of brick and stone. As for that glorious fabric itself, no hands have raised it, nor eye seen it. It is built up out

THE IDEAL SYNAGOGUE

of the finest activities of the human spirit—out of gentleness and prayerfulness and high endeavour, out of enthusiasm for all things that are true and beautiful. Ezekiel, to refer to him once more, sees in a vision the Temple of the future, the Temple of his hopes. From it issues forth a stream which, as it flows, swells into a mighty river that brings healing and life to every creature in its neighbourhood. I pray that your Synagogue may in some measure fulfil the vision. From it let the vivifying waters go forth that may be bought by each of us " without money and without price "—the waters of faith and trust which heal every hurt and fill the drooping heart with new life. And so your witness to the saving force of Judaism, to the beauty of the good life, nay, to the wonders that can be wrought by a Synagogue founded in a single-hearted desire to glorify God, shall reach and move many a soul. To you, too, God will give "the opening of the mouth" in the midst of your brethren, and through you " they shall know that He is the Lord." And so I say, Press on—on "like the stars, without haste, without rest "—on to the goal. For, few though you be, yours will be as the voice of a multitude, seeing that God's voice will speak in it. Verily to you the Prophetic promise is spoken :—" The little one shall become a thousand, and the small one a mighty people ; I the Lord will hasten it in its time."

THE SYNAGOGUE AND THE WORSHIPPER

> "One thing have I asked of the Lord, that will I seek after;
> that I may dwell in the house of the Lord all the days of my life,
> to behold the graciousness of the Lord, and to seek Him in His
> temple. For in the day of trouble He will keep me secretly in
> His booth; in the covert of His tent will He hide me; He will
> lift me up upon a rock."—PSALM xxvii., 4, 5.

THIS 27th Psalm is the Psalm chosen by the Synagogue for daily recital during the Penitential Season. The ancient Rabbins, as we read in the Midrash, saw in its opening words "The Lord is my light and my salvation," an allusion to that solemn period of the year. On New Year's Day God is our light, our sure and trusty guide through the darkness that shrouds the dawning year; He is our salvation on the Day of Atonement which, under His grace, will redeem us from the grasp and the shame of sin. But the entire Psalm, especially the first half of it, is happily attuned to the message of the Penitential, nay, of every consecrated season. It is one of the most mystical utterances of the Psalter. It voices that vivid realization of the presence of God, that intense yearning to be at one with Him, which is the very quintessence of mysticism. The Psalmist is beset by enemies, but he cares not, for the Almighty is the strength of his life. To be sure of this, to be sure of God, is all that he needs. He would steep himself in the sense of the Divine; and where can he best attain his desire save in the Sanctuary? "One thing," he cries, "do I ask of the Lord, that do I seek after: That I may dwell in the house of the Lord all the days of my life, to behold the graciousness of the Lord, and to seek Him in

His temple." There, in the hallowed place, so remote from the strife and turmoil of the world, his soul may hear the heavenly voices; in its clear atmosphere he may see God more clearly, hold Him faster and closer, realize His graciousness, His beauty, His sweetness. For all these shades of meaning are to be found in that elusive Hebrew word noam. It stands for that condescending, yet most intimate and most loving attribute of Deity which draws the child of clay nearer to the great Heart of all things, and draws out from Him an answering love. "The sweetness of God!"—it sounds like the utterance of some medieval devotee. But it is as old as the Bible, which again and again speaks of the Highest in terms of human relationships. And yet there are people who say that Judaism is deficient in spirituality, and the Jew lacking in the deeper experience of the things of God. And there are people, too, who charge the God of Israel with being a far-off and a fearsome God, whereas the Psalter clearly pictures Him as very near and loving.

In the Temple, then, in its peacefulness and its sanctity, the inspired singer would come into closer touch with the God of his life. That fellowship is his one desire, and the very place helps him to attain it. It is a refuge where sorrow cannot find him, a safe hiding-place past which cares speed on, and touch him not. "For in the day of trouble God will keep me secretly in His booth; in the covert of His tent will He hide me; He will lift me up upon a rock." Like the keeper of a vineyard in his shade-giving hut, like some fugitive sheltered from his pursuers in a Bedouin tent, like some wayfarer who has climbed from treacherous ground to a high rock and its firm resting-place, so this disquieted soul finds rest and security in God—in the House of God. It is a sanctuary for him in both senses of the word—a holy place whose very holiness is his protection. We speak sometimes of a sanctuary for birds, where the timid, famished creatures are sure of food and safety. Even so, in the house of his God, the fluttering spirit of this Psalmist finds sustenance, strength and peace amid life's turmoil and alarms.

The text tells us all this. Perhaps, as has been conjectured, it tells us still more. Perhaps the poet's idea, centring at first in the material sanctuary, widens its bounds, and envisages a spiritual temple not made by human hands. The very graciousness of God, His all-encompassing presence, becomes a cherished refuge for the soul, a shrine whence the Supreme speaks to His aspiring child as He did from the mercy-seat in the old Mosaic days. If this be the true interpretation, then the text can be matched with kindred utterances from the Psalms. "O how great is Thy goodness which Thou hast laid up for them that fear Thee, which Thou hast wrought for them that trust in Thee before the sons of men! In the covert of Thy presence Thou hidest them from the plottings of man; Thou keepest them secretly in a booth from the strife of tongues." And again :—" How precious is Thy lovingkindness, O God! The children of men take refuge under the shadow of Thy wings. They feast on the rich things of Thy house, and Thou makest them drink of the stream of Thy delights. For with Thee is the fountain of life; in Thy light we see light."

Certain it is, at any rate, that the Psalm utters a longing for that nearer communion with the Supreme for which the house of Prayer offers an almost unique opportunity. We ourselves—some of us at least—have felt its power in this respect. We know that, in the synagogue, if only we yield ourselves to its influence— to the influence not only of the worship, but of the fane itself—we can get that deep consciousness of God, with its resultant peace and joy, for which the Psalmist yearned. The fane itself, I say ; for prayer, the incense, leaves behind some of its fragrance to perfume the very altar ! I have known devout hearts who have purposely come here on Sabbath eve some little time before the service has begun in order that, in the solemn atmosphere woven partly by the stillness and the twilight, partly by the moving associations and memories wrought by the genius of the places, they might draw peace into their souls. God, as they have said, has been very near to them in that mystic hour. And what has been possible for them is surely not impossible for others. Why do we not more abundantly avail ourselves of the precious boon thus proffered to us ? For to refill the springs of the spiritual life which the hot and dusty world so quickly dries up, to find God again, after all but losing Him in the week's preoccupations—surely this is indeed a boon, one that we may have " without money and without price."

It is wonderful to think how this love of God's house has persisted in Israel in all generations. " O Lord, I love the habitation of Thy house and the place of the residence of Thy glory "—so one Psalmist exclaims. " How lovely are Thy tabernacles, O Lord of Hosts ! My soul longeth for the courts of the Lord ; my heart and my flesh cry out unto the living God "—so exclaims another. Nor is attendance in the holy place a mere duty ; it is a privilege. For the Israelite of old appearance before God in the Sanctuary was less obedience to any pious feeling of his own than a sign of the divine grace. " As for me, in Thy great lovingkindness I come into Thy house "—with these words of the Psalmist we still, to this very day, open every one of our services. And in the same spirit the later teachers thought of the synagogue and of its worship. "When thou comest to pray," one of them exhorts us, "say to thyself how honoured am I in being permitted to offer a crown to the King of Glory!" "Who am I," so runs one of the many private prayers included in old manuals of devotion, "who am I, sinner that I am, that I should dare to pray to Thee, O great and majestic God? But out of Thy abounding mercy and lovingkindness Thou takest pleasure in the supplication of Thy servant." And in another prayer of more mystical tenor, God, invoked as "The beautiful One, the splendour of the world," is asked to answer the cry of "the soul sick for love of Thee." "O God," it proceeds, "heal her, I beseech Thee, show her Thy glory and graciousness; then will she be whole and strong, and have everlasting joy."

These beautiful prayers are supplemented by directions concerning the right attitude towards the House of Prayer itself. Even when worship is not being offered it must be held sacred. One must not speak aloud, especially not call to another person, in it. We are to hasten to it at prayer time; but having reached it, we must pause at the door, and then enter slowly and reverently, as beseems us when drawing near to the shrine of the Most High. The synagogue, moreover, must be scrupulously tended. It must be kept free from every particle of dust; and it was the pride of members of the congregation, even of great Rabbis, to perform this pious duty with their own hands.

All this is equally far from the old-fashioned familiarity with the synagogue, which bred unseemly irreverence, and the frigid decorum which is the boast of the up-to-date congregant. Having rightly rid ourselves of the levity which marked the attitude of the uninstructed Jew towards his place of worship, we have still to recapture the devout fervour of his more spiritual-minded brother. More than ever do we need that fervour—we whom the world holds in yet stronger grip, for whom life is more than ever a battle, and God harder to find and to hold. O ye faithful remnant, true to the holy house where you have so long worshipped, keep your faithfulness to the end, and let it yield you an ever clearer sight of the Divine, an ever-growing spiritual strength, an ever deepening joy, "For by these things men live, and wholly therein is the life of the spirit." But if we are to have these boons we must prepare ourselves to receive them. We must throw open our souls to the inspiration of the place and the worship. We must help God to come to us—help Him by striving after fervour, by being no mere audience, but a worshipping, a praying, a singing congregation. For God "is near unto all them that call upon Him in truth"—in earnestness, that is to say, as well as in sincerity.

THE JEWISH SPIRIT[1]

"And the boys grew; and Esau was a cunning hunter, a man of the field; but Jacob was a quiet man, dwelling in tents."—
GENESIS xxv., 27.

A quiet man—the marginal rendering of the revised version gets very near to the meaning of the Hebrew original. Esau is of a restless disposition; he is fond of the chase, fond of something new. Jacob is the quiet man, the "steady" man, the stedfast man. He looks at home for his joys; he seeks them in his own soul. We may admire the elder brother without disparaging the younger. Each has his faults and his virtues. Esau has the qualities of his defects; he is generous and forgiving and affectionate. The Rabbins pay lavish tribute to his love for his father. Jacob has a far less winsome personality; he is a schemer, too, and none too "straight." If Esau is a cunning hunter, Jacob—and here I part company with the Rabbins—is a trapper of men. And yet the old Jewish instinct, the still older Scriptural tradition, which give the palm to the younger brother, are right after all. "Jacob I loved; but Esau I hated." For Jacob, taken altogether, is the finer character. He schemes to get the birthright, but at least he values it; Esau barters it away for a passing gratification. Unlike Esau too, Jacob knows what he wants, and toils for it unremittingly; the drought by day, the cold by night, Laban's shifty devices, are powerless to deter him. He is stedfast, with a soul which, beneath the material advantages of the birthright, can

[1] Preached to Jewish members of the University of Cambridge.

THE JEWISH SPIRIT

get some glimpses of its spiritual glory and blessing. And so he is the stronger of the two, though he does not seem to be so. He can wrestle with gods and men, and prevail. And he does it all by virtue of that indomitable will, that steady determination to conquer, which are his most distinctive characteristics.

The two brothers are everlasting types. Men, all the world over, and through all time, have conformed to one or other of them. There are the ease-loving, with little fixity of purpose, who drift through life, who "eddy about here and there . . . are raised aloft, are hurled in the dust, striving blindly, achieving nothing"; and there are the dour, determined natures that set duty above pleasure, principle above popularity. At the University there are the idler and the reading-man; in the world outside there are the slack and the self-indulgent on the one hand, there is the self-denying worker, eager for service, on the other. We know with whom the ultimate victory rests—the victory over gods and men, the victory that is attested by divine approval and by human homage. In Jewry likewise these two opposing types are found to-day, as they have been found in every generation. There are those who, having Jacob for their progenitor, seem rather to have been created in Esau's likeness. Their Judaism sits lightly on them; they heed but little, if they hear at all, its plaintive, its inspiring appeal. Their cry is assimilation; their policy is virtual fusion. Their birthright, religious and historic, is of small account, set against the gratification which social advancement and personal comfort promise them. Or, "blown about by every wind of doctrine," they plane down their Judaism so as to minimise its points of divergence from Christian thought and practice, or they trim it into correspondence with the latest deliverance on theology, or criticism, or science. There are others of nobler mould who are Jews first, and all else afterwards. For them no sacrifice is too great that will keep the old religion alive and intact. It is their one sacred possession, which it is a point of honour with them to preserve inviolate, which, though it rightly develops always by a slow and orderly process of evolution, must still essentially remain unchanged, finding the elements of growth and expansion within itself.

It is with the latter class of Jews that we shall range ourselves. During the night of the recent Day of Atonement an obscure synagogue in the East End of London was burnt down. Nothing dismayed, the congregation worshipped all the next day among the ruins. That little house of God, charred and disfigured and wrecked, was as dear to them as ever; and though it was—perhaps *because* it was—the most solemn day in the year, they felt that they could not forsake it. And so they determined to pray as heretofore in the beloved precincts, heedless of the discomfort it entailed. It is a touching, an instructive incident. What a fine determination it betokened! What loyalty on the part of the congregants to the things they had! What a power of transfiguring their ruined synagogue, and making it a worthy shrine for the most momentous of supplications!

Theirs was the true Jewish temper—the temper that has preserved Israel through the ages, and that will preserve him through ages yet to come. For they say nowadays—our newspapers are always saying it—that Jewry is ailing, that there is something wrong with the community. There is nothing wrong with either. There is something wrong, undoubtedly, with individual Jews. But greater than individual Jews is Israel, and when the Jew, here and there, has perished of spiritual inanition, Israel will still survive. Again and again has he been saved by a remnant. Moreover the prevailing uneasiness

THE JEWISH SPIRIT

about the religious condition of Jewry, the familiar talk about apathy, and spiritual deadness, and want of leaders, is not a bad sign, but a good one. It shows that the communal conscience, or at least the conscience of some of us, is awake ; and the awakened conscience is a symptom of moral health, of moral vitality. There is hope for the sinner who recognises his sin, who is uneasy and ashamed because of it ; it is only the hardened transgressor who is lost, for in his case repentance and redemption—redemption in this life—are impossible. Religious torpor, too, is no new thing in Israel. The Bible and the Talmud teem with examples of it ; and it was the constant theme of lament and denunciation for the medieval teachers, though we usually deem their age one of general religious conformity. The truly disquieting feature would be universal acquiescence in a decline of the Jewish spirit. If no voice were raised to deplore it as a shame and a danger, then we might indeed despair of Judaism.

It is reassuring to discern signs of this awakened conscience in these latter days—especially reassuring to discern them among our younger brethren. A friend of mine, who has recently left the sister University after a distinguished career, spoke to my Synagogue Association a short time ago about the difficulties which the Jewish undergraduate has to encounter. He is set in a pronounced Christian atmosphere, all the more alluring because of the historic associations that go to the making of it ; and the simple services of the plain brick structure that does duty for a synagogue present a glaring contrast to the impressive form and environment of the public worship of the University churches. The contrast and its consequent handicap are real enough, and my friend was justified in dwelling upon them. But there is only one way of facing these disadvantages, and that is to make up one's mind not to be defeated by them. What the Jewish member of a University has to do is to imitate the spirit of the little East End congregation of which I spoke just now, and to resolve that the less impressive the old form of worship seems to be, the less inviting the place in which it is carried on, the greater shall be his loving attachment to them, and the more firmly will he persist in upholding them. This has been the temper of the faithful Jew in every age. He has had to pray at times in dark underground cellars, while the followers of the dominant faith have had stately cathedrals to foster and intensify their fervour. But the dark cellar has been for him the house of God, the house of the true God, and the thought has amply sufficed for him.

So must it be with the Jew to-day. Whether it be at a University or in the world of affairs he has to hold fast to the holy things he inherits in order to counteract the disabilities which inevitably spring from the clash of Judaism with the conditions of modern life. Between this meeting hall, with its unpretending services, and your University churches, with their ornate form of worship, how great is the gap! But this synagogue, like all synagogues, has a grandeur far transcending mere chance or outward splendour in that it is the lineal descendant of the primitive *Beth Hakeneseth* which existed centuries before Christianity was born, in that, too, you assemble here as Israelites, the custodians of a sublime religion, heirs to the traditions of the Patriarchs, spiritual children of the Prophets and the Psalmists. Your religion differs sharply from the religion of the great mass of Englishmen; it is a silent protest against it. In that difference you will see no stumbling-block, no reason for vacillation, and in that protest you will find your pride, for it is a protest on behalf of the truth, and to make it is to place yourselves in line with the

Patriarchs and the Rabbins, and all the martyrs of your people. In the ordering of your daily life you must needs be now and again at variance with your neighbours; for whatever be the complexion of our Judaism some differentiating ritual is demanded of us if we are to have any Judaism at all. But you will be strengthened in this separatist practice, exacting at times, as I own it to be, by the thought that it is the condition precedent to the fulfilment of the Israelite's mission—that of enriching the world with his exalted ideals, with his inspiring example, with the culture which, through all the long centuries of suffering, has kept him a living soul.

Well, it is a sort of obstinacy, I suppose; but it is a glorious obstinacy, the obstinacy that makes the weak strong, and gives the victory to the seemingly vanquished. In one of Beaumont and Fletcher's plays, as Emerson reminds us, a rough tyrant tells some mariners who are at his mercy: " Why, slaves, 'tis in our power to hang ye." " Very likely," is the reply; " 'tis in our power, then, to be hanged, and scorn ye." This is the source of the everlasting triumph of the weak over the strong: their noble stubbornness, their will to suffer, their resolve, that, do what fate and the world may, they will be mightier than the world and fate. " The Lord is with me," cries the Psalmist; " what, then, can man do unto me ? " It is the one supreme lesson for the Jew. Let us have faith in ourselves, faith in the truth that we have been appointed to keep, faith in our star, to use the great Napoleon's phrase, faith in God, the ordainer of events, Israel's Creator and Redeemer, and all our disadvantages are as nought. Nay, they are transformed into advantages; for they are a challenge to our courage, the metal on which our determination sharpens itself.

To Jeremiah, when but a youth, the word of the Lord

comes appointing him a Prophet unto the nations. It is his first call, and his heart misgives him. "Ah, Lord God, I cannot speak, for I am but as a child." But swift the answer comes : " Say not so ; for to whomsoever I shall send thee thou shalt go, and whatsoever I command thee thou shalt speak. . . . Be not dismayed, lest I dismay thee before them. For, behold, I have made thee this day a defenced city, and an iron pillar, and brazen walls, against the whole land, against the kings of Judah, against the princes thereof, against the priests thereof, and against the people of the land." Brazen walls against king and princes and priests and people !—one lad against a world ! It is a hard task, but a glorious one. It is the task of the Jew, the task especially of the Jewish youth, who, going forth to face life with fresh hearts and with high courage, with a reverence for the birthright, with a deep consciousness of its splendour and its obligations, are determined, in the fine old Scriptural phrase, to " be strong and of good courage, and do."

ANTI SEMITISM

> "Commit thy way unto the Lord; trust also in Him, and He will bring it to pass. And He will make thy righteousness to come forth as the light and thy vindication as the noonday."—
> PSALM xxxvii., 5. 6.

THE Psalmist rebukes an impatience which is as common to-day as it was in his far-off time. The world moves too slowly for us. Its ills are very slowly redressed. Wars are as frequent and as cruel as ever. Social ailments, equally with physical disease, are being overcome all too tardily. Sin and vice still offend the conscience of good men as of old. "Truth for ever on the scaffold; wrong for ever on the throne"—so we cry with the poet, and sigh for the power to make a full end of all these evils. We would outstrip Providence. For God moves and works, though sometimes we are tempted to doubt it. His mills grind slowly; their very slowness, we may be sure, is essential to the stability of the better order which is in the making. For the Eternal the triumph of right and of goodness is everything, time nothing. A thousand years in His sight are but as yesterday; enough for Him that His work prospers, and for us that we have some small share in making it prosper. So to the soul in every age the Psalmist's exhortation comes home with unabated force:—"Commit thy way unto the Lord; trust also in Him and He will bring it to pass." Our eyes may not see the dawn; but through the long night the presage of it quiets and sustains our hearts.

The message is for the community as well as for the individual. Patience, born of faith in the ultimate vindication of right and truth, in the ultimate vindication of Israel, is one of our prime needs as Jews. Detraction and calumny are the outstanding residue of the age-long persecution which has incessantly tortured our race. When we think of them as persisting in these days, marked by a deepening passion for justice, by a growing liberality of thought, by an increasing rejection of theology which divides, for religion which unites, we are disappointed and sad. "When," we ask, "will these relics of dark ages disappear? When will Israel be free from his oppressor, fully cleared in the sight of mankind? What can we do to speed that consummation?" But again the Psalmist steps in with his wise admonition :—"Commit thy way unto the Lord, and He will bring it to pass. He will make thy righteousness to come forth as the light and thy vindication as the noonday. Be patient, and your very patience will achieve your desire. Commit your cause to the Higher Powers who are working for you, and the better time will come as surely as the day-spring follows the night and, slowly spreading, reaches at last the farthest point of the heavens." Patience—there is no better way, none half so good.

The newspapers have lately been acclaiming a deed of heroism performed at the battle of Bourlon Wood. Two names have been especially associated with it—why should I not mention them here?—Captain Stone and Lieut. Benzecry; the one a Christian, the other a Jew. Their company held an indefensible position, and was ordered to retire, leaving only a covering rearguard. Both officers elected to remain. "The rearguard," says the official report, "was seen fighting to the last. There was no survivor. Captain Stone saved the situation at the cost of his life; Lieut. Benzecry continued to fight until he was killed." The story of the war contains few finer episodes, and it is only natural that we should remember with pride that one of the chief actors in it was a Jew. Let us reverently salute his memory. But while we gratefully think of his Jewishness, we are not going to trumpet it forth to the world, to "make a song about it." Otherwise we shall seem to imply that Jewish courage is so rare a thing that when we meet with a specimen of it we must needs invite all other men to come and applaud it. Moreover, we shall lend indirect approval to the tactics of the anti-Semite who, having discovered some real or imaginary example of Jewish shortcomings, at once lays them at the door of the entire race. The Jew, generally speaking, is as brave as his average Christian neighbour—no more, and certainly no less; and when a particular Jew has shown himself especially brave there is no more necessity to emphasize his Jewish descent than there is, in a like case, to emphasize the Christianity of a Christian hero. Let the *man*, in each instance, speak, rather than the religionist. Let the credit go to the account of our common humanity; and if Judaism profits incidentally in the process, as no doubt it will, so much greater the gain.

We may be sure that it is only in this way that it will profit. The reputation of Israel is built up not by noisy testimonials to the surpassing excellence of the Jewish character, but by the silent influence exerted by that character upon general opinion. An unalterable conviction that truth and right will come into their own by the very force of things—this is the one weapon with which to meet the attacks of our enemies. There is much virtue in a dignified silence. "They say; what do they say? Let them say." This is not the prevailing attitude. Now and again Anti-Semitism lifts its head even in this country. An individual or a newspaper breaks out into vile accusations of the Jew; he is a warmonger, a shirker, a bloated profiteer, a parasitical pauper. And straightway some well-meaning, but misguided people on our side launch out into fiery objurgations and indignant arguments. All such efforts are either useless or superfluous. They are useless because Anti-Semitism, if genuine, is an irrational prejudice which obviously cannot be reached by argument, and if artificial, is a mere crafty, fraudulent pose not to be overcome by any appeal to truth or justice. Anti-Semitism is often a trade, and falsehoods are the goods it deals in. It deliberately aims at hurting us. So that when it is hurled out of one trench it establishes itself in another, and the angrier we are, the more sensitive we show ourselves, the more clearly are we hurt; and that is just what the enemy desires. If there are to be protests and articulate vindications let them come from others; they will be far more telling because obviously unbiassed and disinterested. This week Mr. Gerard, lately American Ambassador in Berlin, publicly declared that almost the only remaining representatives of real culture in Germany are the Jews, and this is true, he says, whatever branch of culture one thinks of, whether medicine, science, music, journalism. It is a remarkable assertion, and because it is so remarkable, all the more powerful as a witness on behalf of the Jew. Could any testimony from our own camp equal it in effectiveness? And so it is with regard to the yet higher culture of the character and the spirit.

No; the proper way to deal with the Anti-Semite is to let him severely alone. Let him roll himself in the web he spins so cunningly. One day, perhaps, it will be a trap for himself. But whether it be so or not matters little; the main point is that we should trust for our justification to the force of truth and enlightenment, which one day will assuredly master the minds of men. It is a slow business, but let us not despair or grow weary. If the light seems never to be coming, or to come too slowly, we may be sure that Eternal Wisdom has so ordained it. The other day we were reading the Book of Esther, with story so romantic and so instructive. Mordecai, the Jewish hero, detects a plot against the king's life, of which the only result is that the conspirators are put to death. Mordecai gets no reward for his loyalty—at least not then. In like manner, Esther, asked by Ahasuerus to prefer her dearest request, lets slip the opportunity of pleading for the lives of her doomed people, and merely invites the king and Haman to a second banquet. But, between those two banquets, so much happens that the whole situation is suddenly changed. Mordecai's services to the royal person are revealed ; Haman, but yesterday the favourite, has deferentially to parade his enemy, for whom he has built a specially high gallows, through the streets, and to proclaim him the man whom the king most delights to honour. And thus the way is paved for Esther's successful intervention on behalf of her people. See, then, the uses of a timely delay, a wise reticence. In recognising those uses lies the art of the dramatist, borrowing something from the boundless insight of the Divine Shaper of events. One day too soon, and the result would have been destruction, not salvation, for the devoted objects of an implacable enemy's fury.

Patience, then. "In quietness and in confidence shall be your strength"—so the Prophet cries to his brethrem when they would rush into a disastrous war ; and the monition is always in season. But with the quietness must go a dogged persistence in rectitude. The inevitable victory of right and truth must be prepared by the integrity of those who would taste the blessedness of it. There is only one force that can impede the justification of the Jew; it is his own unworthiness. The antagonisms we have really to fear are the antagonisms of just men, and these obviously are only made possible by our own defects. Upon those defects let us fix our gaze, and not upon the foolish or cunning enmities of prejudice or hatred. Let the justice of our cause be enhanced by the evergrowing strength of our personal integrity; let us achieve our justification by meriting it. We have to live down calumny—to live it down in the best sense of the words by opposing to it the argument of our personal lives. " Trust in God," cries the Psalmist, but he adds, " do good; be faithful; be staunch." Let us trust to time and to the Lord of it, but to our own righteousness also. And then we shall get our "heart's desire"; for God and men will have joined to fulfil it. Nothing can withstand these world-forces, any more than one can stop the march of the dawn which slowly beats back the night. It is the powers of light arrayed against the powers of darkness. Can the issue be in doubt? Our righteousness will assuredly come forth as the light and our vindication as the noonday.

BEARING THE NAME IN VAIN

"Thou shalt not take the name of the Lord thy God in vain."—
EXODUS xx., 7.

THIS is the accepted and doubtless the true rendering of the Third Commandment. But the Rabbins give another and a figurative interpretation of it with the object of enforcing a striking ethical lesson. Justified by the literal significance of the Hebrew original, they translate the Commandment :—" Thou shalt not *bear* the name of the Lord thy God in vain " ; " and it teaches thee," they say, " that thou shalt not put on thy *tephillin*, thy phylacteries, and then go and sin." For, they add, the performance of the rite of the *tephillin* must have, as its indispensable accompaniment, even as its necessary antecedent, purity of life. The *tephillin* are inscribed with the Divine name ; and he who binds them about his body, yet scruples not to defile both body and soul by violations of the moral law, makes a mockery of holy symbols, nay, dishonours God Himself. He bears the name of the Lord in vain.

It is, I say, a striking thought—striking less in itself than in virtue of the form in which it is expressed. For the idea, in its general purport, is familiar to every student of the Talmudic literature. Legalists the Rabbins may have been, but formalists, in the sense of exalting the ceremonials of religion above the religious spirit, they certainly were not. There is as much enthusiasm in Talmud and Midrash for what Christian writers call "inwardness" as there is in the Gospels. Unfortunately the general impression—and there are

Jews who share it—is the direct opposite. The Gospels are open to all, so that he who runs may read; the Rabbinic literature is accessible to but few. And the Gospels, while extolling heart religion, take good care to drive home the lesson by warnings against Rabbinic formalism. The rite of the *tephillin* is a conspicuous example. The Founder of Christianity, in his famous invective against the Scribes and the Pharisees—his usual appellation for the Rabbins—is reported to have expressed himself as follows :—" All their works they do for to be seen of men ; for they make broad their phylacteries ; they love the chief seats in the synagogues and the salutations in the market-places, and to be called of men Rabbi." And he continues :—" Woe unto you, Scribes and Pharisees, hypocrites ; for ye are like unto whited sepulchres, which outwardly appear beautiful, but inwardly are full of dead men's bones, and of all uncleanness. Even so ye also outwardly appear righteous unto men, but inwardly ye are full of hypocrisy and iniquity."

Now in this alleged attack upon the Pharisees, Jesus was either guilty of great unfairness, or he has been grossly misrepresented. He knew well enough that while some of the Pharisees, as even the Talmud itself admits, were hypocritical formalists, using a punctilious observance of the ritual law as a means of gratifying a sordid ambition, or as the cloak for an ignoble life, many of them were as sincere in motive and as spiritual in character as he was himself. The Talmud indeed anticipates or echoes his indictment. It speaks of men who prostitute this very rite of the *tephillin* for unworthy ends, and applies to them the same epithet of hypocrites. Nevertheless there this Gospel invective stands without one particle of qualification, and it stands as a condemnation either of the good faith or sobriety of mind of the

Teacher who uttered it, or of that of his biographers. The Pharisee makes his phylacteries broad so that he may catch the eye of the crowd and be saluted as Rabbi; he is a whited sepulchre, fair and comely without, but within full of hypocrisy and iniquity. The Talmudic literature shows him, or the best specimens of him, to have been something quite different. The phylacteries —so the selfsame Pharisees declare—must be put to no ignoble purpose, or they are desecrated. Far from being flaunted in the faces of men, they must be deemed as warnings to the soul of him who wears them, as appeals to its native love of purity and rectitude. Far from being regarded as effective substitutes for true religion, they must be used as incentives to more, and yet more, religion. For to put on the *tephillin* and then to go and sin is to " bear the Name of the Lord in vain," impiously to steel oneself against its splendid inspiration.

Need I add that what the Rabbins said about the *tephillin* is typical. They said precisely the same thing about all ritual observances. The test of the efficacy of religious ceremonial was the depth it added to a man's spiritual life, the height to which it raised his moral stature. All observances must have, as their indispensable accompaniment, at the very least as their necessary consequence, greater purity and nobility of life, or they are worse than useless. "First," says the Talmud in a memorable passage, " first accept the yoke of the kingdom of Heaven, and then take upon thyself the yoke of the ritual commands." The thought of God, belief and trust in Him, must precede observance, to hallow it and make it fruitful. According to some of the Rabbins, indeed, a man must not venture to put on the *tephillin* until he has read the *Shemang*. He must prepare himself for the rite by confessing the existence and the sovereignty of the Supreme and the paramount duty of devoting himself heart and soul to loving service of Him.

So much by way of dispelling a common misconception and of vindicating a body of teaching too often maligned.

There remains something to be said from the broader point of view. Rightly or wrongly we have allowed the rite of the *tephillin* to fall into disuse, and with it has vanished the danger of our committing the precise error which the Rabbins denounced. If we do not wear the *tephillin*, they cannot betray us into bearing God's name in vain. That is so much to the good. But have we got rid of all the danger ? It is easy to avoid formalism by discarding forms. But religion remains, or ought to remain ; and we may sin against it no less culpably than did the degenerate Pharisee of old who made his phylacteries broad. When we have cast off the *tephillin* and many another ancient symbol as outworn and unmeaning we shall still not be secure against the sin of bearing God's Name in vain.

For we do bear that Name. Everyone bears it who remembers that he is a child of God, created in His image, possessor of an undying soul that links men to Him in spirit, depository of a law of righteousness whose realisation unites them to Him in being. Every time we are heedless of the appeal of our Heavenly lineage—every time we fail to give effect to our Divine sonship in conscious endeavour after the noblest life of which we are capable—we bear the Name of God in vain. It is as though we put on our spiritual phylacteries, and then went and sinned !

But if the old saying applies to us as men, it applies to us with redoubled force as Israelites. Who more truly bears the Name of the Lord than the Lord's people, " the kingdom of priests and the holy nation," chosen by the Supreme, self-dedicated to Him, from the far-off Sinaitic days ? " Thou are called by the Name of the

Lord "—so Moses admonishes the Israelites—and they are to justify that high privilege by righteousness, to justify it especially in the sight of the nations. By worthy living Israel is to prove to the world that he is indeed the Lord's people, that his talk about bearing the Divine Name is no empty vaunt.

And the admonition never loses its force. We hear much about the Israelite's mission, less about his election. We talk of our rights; we are all but silent about our duties. But rights imply duties. Would we fulfil our mission? Would we help forward the great cause of moral and spiritual progress? Would we help to uplift the world? Then let us look to ourselves, to our own lives, personal and corporate. We bear the Name of the Lord; let us see to it that we do not bear it in vain. A sublime religion has been assigned to us with the name of its Divine Giver—do we fully live in the light of it? Do we yield ourselves to its inspiration? Do we suffer it to lift us out of the depths where half mankind grovel—to lift us to God? Nay, do we find all the pride and the joy that we ought to feel in possessing it, in bearing God's Name, in being called by the name of Israel? Or do we lightly regard our high descent, grander far than the ancestry of a hundred Earls, or apologise for it as though it were something derogatory?

But to be conscious of noble descent, and yet to lead ignoble lives, is the most heinous of all sins. It is like the patrician who, retaining his illustrious title, glorying in it, boasting of it, drags himself down by degrading vice to the level of the lowest hind. He makes his phylacteries broad, and flaunts them in the faces of men; he indeed is the " whited scepulchre." *Noblesse oblige.* Would that this truth might sink into the consciousness of the Jew, and exert its potent effect upon his daily life! Then all reproach would be rolled away from his faith and his name. Nothing sordid would any more be identified with them. The action of the Jew of high degree who died this week, and who, it is said, cut himself off from the majority of his brethren because of the contempt brought upon the ancestral faith by the ignoble lives that some of them led, could not possibly happen. The Jews with one accord would live for this world certainly, but in the highest sense of the phrase; they would live in order to make it better by their example. Then there would be no more Jew-hatred, for the transcendent virtues of our people would kill such hatred by depriving it of every shred of pretext. Then the Jew would no longer bear the Lord's Name in vain, no longer be impervious to the call of his highest traditions, his sublimest ideals. His life would square with his pretensions; his old-world dream of a Kingdom of Priests and a Holy Nation would become a sober reality. With or without his phylacteries, he would carry with him that sense of consecration, that consciousness of the indwelling God in his own soul, which would keep him pure and upright under the mightiest temptations, make him a king among men, "a witness to the peoples, a leader and a commander to the nations."

ISRAEL'S ANCIENT VIRTUES

"And he urged him to take it; but he refused."—
2 KINGS, v., 16.

LEGENDARY as much of Elisha's story unquestionably is, the portrait of his character is real enough. His virtues represent the ethical ideal of the ancient Israelites at their best. Less mysterious, less distant, more human than Elijah, his master, he gets closer to the lives and probably the hearts of his people. He is ploughing when the Prophetic call comes to him; and his first thought is for the dear ones at home. "Let me," he cries, "kiss my father and my mother; and then I will follow thee." The incident of the bears and the mocking children is the one harsh note in his story; and it is instructive to find the Rabbis declaring that, for his part in the episode, Elisha had to suffer his punishment. But otherwise he is gentleness itself. He restrains the King of Israel, who would slay the enemies that are at his mercy. "Smite them not; set bread and water before them, and let them go." The Shunammite woman, her son dead or dying, flees to the Prophet for help. Gehazi, his servant, would thrust her away; but he rebukes him. "Let her alone," he says; "for her soul is vexed within her." But he is strong as well as tender. Naaman, the famous soldier, comes to him with horses and chariots, asking to be cured of his leprosy. But, unmoved by the great man's magnificence, the Prophet lets him stay at his door, and sends out his prescription to him by another hand. His dignity, as the messenger of the Lord of Hosts, far surpasses that of this mighty man of valour; and the proud Syrian must be made to feel it, to recognise his insignificance as compared with the representative of Almighty God. And, in like manner, when Naaman is healed, and gratefully presses a gift upon him, Elisha sternly puts the offer aside. "As the Lord liveth, before whom I stand, I will take nothing. And he urged him to take it; but he refused." Gehazi, the servant, has less scruple; and his punishment is that Naaman's leprosy shall cling to him for ever.

Incidents such as these help us to understand, as perhaps no formal maxims could, what Character meant for the Israelites of olden days. Sturdy independence, the hatred of being beholden to any man for gifts or worldly boons of any kind, contempt for material goods when measured against serenity of mind and inward dignity—these were the virtues that our ancestors honoured most. Abraham, refusing to accept from the King of Sodom aught of the spoil that he himself had recovered, the Shunammite woman just mentioned who, in response to Elisha's offer to speak for her to the King or the Captain of the Host, declines all return for her kindness to him, protesting with simple dignity "I dwell among my own people"—these are instances of the same fine temper. It is because of the many examples of it that occur in the Hebrew Bible that our Scriptures have come to be known and to be praised for their robust ethic. If little or no stress is laid upon the beauty of this type of character in the Gospels, it is, let us hope, because the lesson, having already been well learnt, insistence upon it had become superfluous. But, on the other hand, I am bound to point out that the Talmud, at once contemporary with, and later than, the New Testament, still deems such insistence desirable. "Flay a carcase in the street for a pittance"—so it exhorts us—" and be beholden to no man." And, reciting the old form of the Grace after Meals, the Jew to this day asks to be delivered from the necessity of having to rely upon " the gifts of flesh and blood." " Upon *Thy* bounty alone," he prays, " let us, O Lord, be cast, so that we may never be put to shame." For in the eyes of the pious Israelite of old there was no greater degradation than that of having to take, or to sue for, the favours of others, no greater nobility than that of independence. Significantly does Maimonides close his chapters on " Benevolence " by affirming that it is the duty of every man to avoid charity ; and, he adds, the Rabbis of old intentionally pursued their sacred calling without fee or reward. " They were hewers of wood and drawers of water, builder's labourers, ironworkers and smiths ; they asked nothing of their congregations, and would take nothing if aught was offered to them."

We of these days live in different conditions, and have necessarily had to shift our point of view somewhat in dealing with such matters, though I often think that it would be better for both pastor and congregant, better for Religion, if the ministry were still a purely honorary vocation, as it once was. But the general lesson taught by these old-time facts and utterances for ever holds good. Certainly this is not an age marked by love of what the poet calls " the glorious privilege of being independent." The gentler virtues still get their full meed of recognition ; the sturdier ones, which meant so much for our forefathers, get less attention, and enjoy only a diminished vogue. Despite the levelling tendencies of the times, wealth paradoxically commands not a declining, but an increasing deference, and its possession has become more than ever the symbol of power and the criterion of well-being. The Elishas, who keep Naaman waiting at their humble door, and send out their message to him by a servant, are few and far between; and equally rare is their refusal of the gifts that the big man presses upon them. It is a pity; for this lowering of the old ideal has far-reaching consequences for Character. To bow down before wealth is to get our moral values wrong almost throughout the whole scale. We take over the rich man's conception of rectitude, faulty though it may be; we forgo our opinion for his; we are obsequious, and servile, and immorally humble. We part with our one source of dignity—the only true source of dignity that any man has, and which the most ignorant and the poorest share with the most gifted and the richest—the righteousness, the fineness of soul, which makes us sons of God, created in His image. We imperil likewise our chance of real happiness. For nothing but wretchedness lies in an undue exaltation of the value of money and the worth of its possessors. It is a trite reflection, and I am not going to enlarge upon it. The example of Spinoza will serve my purpose better than any abstract doctrine. Spinoza deliberately chooses philosophy as the surest avenue to peace and well being. "Men, as a rule," he says, "set their hopes on wealth, or fame, or pleasure—in a word, on fleeting things; and with them pass the chances of happiness that are based upon them. I will choose that which is imperishable, and my happiness will be imperishable too." There speaks the truly wise man. In spite of his poverty and his merely two score years of existence, Spinoza got more out of life than thousands of his contemporaries. Well, we cannot all cultivate philosophy; but we can all choose the right objects on which to fasten our hopes of well being. The clear conscience, the "clean hands and the pure heart" lauded by the Psalmist, service of our fellowmen according to our several opportunities and capacities—these are within the grasp of everyone. And because they are the things that endure, the happiness they yield is also enduring, and therefore real.

It was a distinct type of character, then, which our ancient teachings tended to form. You may call it Spartan or Stoic if you like, and I admit that it found honour among other ancient races besides our own. But, while acknowledging that it is not exclusively Jewish, let us understand that it *is* Jewish, that it did distinguish our race in olden times, and ought still to distinguish them. If we have lost or obscured some of its elements under stress of age-long persecution, if no little of the historic *Juden-schmerz*, no little of the tragedy of Israel, springs from the decline under suffering of his ancient virtues, it is time that we made an effort to recover or to revive them. For healthy self-reliance did not make the whole of the moral type so dear to our ancestors. It included also that filial reverence of which Elisha's farewell kiss to his father and mother was the eloquent expression. This, too, with its attendant virtues, needs re-kindling in an age which is fast loosening the ties that bind child to parent. I say its attendant virtues, for with filial reverence there is intimately connected the old Jewish view which exalted the home into a sanctuary, which made it the abode of love indeed, but the nursery, too, of virtue, which saw in the inviolability of the Family the one guarantee of individual rectitude and of the stability of the State. With it there is also closely bound up that reverence for personal purity, male no less than female, which is an equally characteristic Jewish ideal. These conceptions are being assailed with increasing violence and with proportionate success in our day. All the more strenuously must these tendencies be resisted, and resisted especially by us Jews, whose traditional teachings they directly contravene.

And then, finally, there is the old-fashioned virtue of tenacity, of faithfulness to principle, to opinions and ideas hitherto held sacred, with which we need to renew our covenant. Elisha, refusing sordid gifts in the conviction that he is dedicated to the highest service—Elisha, declining to compromise his position as Prophet of God by paying court even to one of the highest personages in the social hierarchy—is the everlasting type of this unflinching loyalty. Again and again is the conflict in which he was victorious forced upon us. Shall we forget the higher summons in weak deference to the lower? Shall it be self and the world, or God and Heaven? Shall it be fusion with our non-Jewish surroundings, with ease and comfort for its reward, or separateness, and independence, and resulting hardship? Shall it be an alien religion perhaps, irreligion more probably, or Judaism? That is the eternal issue for us Jews. Elisha, the high-souled, solved a like problem in one way, Gehazi in another. With whom will we side? With the Prophet, or with the slave?

HAVE THE JEWS A MISSION?

> "I the Lord have called thee in righteousness, and will give thee for a covenant of the peoples, for a light of the Gentiles."—
> ISAIAH xlii., 6.

IF there is one characteristic axiom of Jewish theology, it is that which affirms the missionary character of Israel. Israel, it declares, has been divinely chosen not only to promote his own moral and spiritual ennoblement, but to spread right conceptions of religion among the families of men. This is a fundamental dogma of Judaism. So, at least, we have always been taught to think. But of late years our ideas on the subject have been rudely shaken—shaken, moreover, by hands which, we should have thought, would have been the last to disturb them. We turn to Zionist doctrine as preached even by its most spiritual-minded expounders, and we find that they deliberately go out of their way to deny a conception which we have always regarded as being of the essence of the faith. Thus the gifted essayist who writes under the name of "Achad Ha-am," explicitly affirms that the Jew has no mission, that he never had one, and that the notion is a myth, born, within the last hundred years, of the struggle for Jewish emancipation. It is an amazing assertion—all the more amazing because it comes from the most unexpected source, and from the wing of the Zionist party which rightly prides itself upon its idealism. And yet it is not difficult to explain its origin. The Zionist pins his faith to Palestine—and to Palestine only. Outside the boundaries of the Holy Land he can discern no real or lasting good, past or future, for Israel. All the well-being of his people, all the finest manifestations of its spirit, he declares, with very questionable historic accuracy, have been achieved within those confines, and within them exclusively will its highest potencies be realized in the coming time. Elsewhere the Jew is a stranger; he is in *Goluth*, in exile. If he is truly to find himself, he must return home. But the Zionist may be gently reminded that in spite of exile, the Jew may still flourish even in the higher and spiritual sense. He may remain where he is, and, by the very fact of so remaining, may realize a world-wide purpose, accomplish a sacred mission Providentially assigned to him. The whole earth may be his real home, and his true destiny may lie in cultivating that ample domain. It is an apt, a formidable rejoinder. And there is only one way for the Zionist to meet it; and he takes it. "A mission for the Jew!" he cries; "there is no such thing. It is a chimera."

A bold assertion; let us see whether it will bear the test of historical investigation.

A missionary Israel, says the Zionist, is a new notion, not more than a century old. In saying so he forgets his Rabbinic teachers, whom he especially might be expected to remember. They lived not one century, but some nineteen centuries, ago, and they had a very definite belief in a Jewish mission. "I will sow them among the peoples"—so God is pictured by the Prophet Zechariah as saying of Israel. A Talmudic Rabbi interprets the promise; Israel, he explains, has been designedly scattered among the nations in order the better to realize the high purpose of the Supreme for the well-being of mankind. Like seed sown broadcast over the earth, Israel is to yield a rich harvest of souls won for the true God. That is perhaps one of the finest utterances on the subject left us by the Fathers of the Synagogue; but it is typical of many similar sayings. That the Jew has been chosen for even a larger aim than his own personal uplifting, that he holds his spiritual wealth in trust for humanity, whom it is eventually to enrich and bless—this is a cardinal doctrine of the Rabbinic religion. And so we find it obtaining expression in the ancient Prayer Book. Israel is to re-possess his own domain in God's good time—yes; but, side by side with this conviction, is the belief in a yet finer, because more spiritual empire extending over all the earth, which the Jew is to help to establish. "The kingdom of God" —so it is styled. Every service in the synagogue, held according to the ancient rite, closes, even to-day, with the prayer of *Alenu*, which, in its second paragraph, voices the devout Jew's belief in the great day of the Lord, when all peoples shall bend the knee to Him with one accord, accept the yoke of His rule, and acknowledge His unity. The world is to be perfected under the sovereignty of the Almighty: the God of Israel is to triumph. What does this mean but that He is to triumph *through* Israel, that Israel is to share in the triumph—share in it as the recompense of his age-long labours for its consummation?

Listen again to this magnificent prayer, one of two of similar tenor, that meets us in the Service for the New Year Festival:—"Our God and God of our fathers, reign Thou in Thy glory over all the universe and be exalted above all the earth in Thy splendour, and shine forth in Thy august might upon all the inhabitants of this terrestial world, Thy domain, so that every living being may know that Thou hast made it, and every created thing may understand that Thou hast created it, and whatsoever hath breath in its nostrils may say,

The Lord God of Israel is King, and His rule extendeth over all."

Earlier still are the Apocrypha. Ben Sira, in Ecclesiasticus, from whom these prayers are probably derived, asks God to put His fear upon all the nations :—" Let them know Thee as we also have known Thee. Give testimony unto those that were Thy creatures at the beginning, so that all they that people the earth may know that Thou art the Lord, the eternal God." Even more explicitly does the author of Tobit set forth the idea of the Mission :—" Give thanks unto God before the Gentiles," he cries, " ye children of Israel ; for He hath scattered us among them. *There* declare His greatness, and extol Him before all the living." *There* declare His greatness !—let the Zionist, who can discern no future for Israel, save on Judean soil, ponder the phrase !

But what of the Bible ? Are we dreaming, or is it a sober fact that the one conviction that chiefly inspired and upheld the Seers and the Psalmists, revived their faith in God, and comforted their hearts under national tribulation, was that of a regenerated world won for the higher life by the efforts and the example of Israel ? " O Lord, my strength and my stronghold, my refuge in the day of affliction, unto Thee shall the nations come from the ends of the earth, and shall say, Our fathers have inherited nought but lies, even vanity and things wherein there is no profit "—so cries Jeremiah. And our own Prophet, in his turn, declares to his people in the Divine Name " Ye are my witnesses." To what are they to testify, if not to the divine truth and to the supremacy of righteousness ? The witness, it is true, may be, in a sense, only passive. The mere existence of a consecrated people, with its apostolic title of " a kingdom of priests and a holy nation," its very endeavour after faithfulness to its historic trust, is testimony enough.

Nothing can surpass it for power. No compassing of heaven and earth to make proselytes is needed; the people itself, with its heaven-born heritage, its splendid aspirations, its sanctified life, is the all-sufficient witness. A good Jew is God's missioner, though he raise not a finger to admonish, speaks never a word of exhortation. The chosen Servant, of whom our Prophet speaks elsewhere, the Servant upon whom God has put His spirit, does not cause his voice to be heard in the street; he does not break the bruised reed, nor quench the smoking flax, and yet he "brings forth judgment in truth." Shall I be told that his mission is only to his own, that he is sent exclusively to Israel? Our text is before us to refute the idea:—" I the Lord have called thee in righteousness, and will give thee for a covenant of the *peoples*, for a light of the *Gentiles*." Still more sharply is the truth emphasized:—" It is too small a thing," God is pictured as saying, " that thou shouldest be My servant to raise up the tribes of Jacob; I will also give thee for a light to the Gentiles, that thou mayest be My salvation unto the ends of the earth."

No less clear is the doctrine when it is taught by implication. All the poets of the Bible call to the nations to come and praise God for His mercies and His wonders. What does that suggest but the consciousness of a mission? How can these great souls invite men to pray with them to the common Father unless they themselves believe that they have been Divinely chosen to offer the invitation? And the same conviction animates the Seers of a sterner school—the Elijahs and the Elishas. Their story would teach only half its message but for the hint of a world-wide vocation that underlies it. Elisha heals Naaman of his leprosy, and the miracle extorts from the great soldier a confession of faith in the wonder-working God:—" Now I know that there is no God in all the earth but in Israel." And so of Elijah in his turn. He saves a widow woman and her son from death by hunger. But who is she—an Israelite? No; a stranger, a Phoenician. It is she who is the chosen recipient of the wondrous salvation, to the end that she may know and acclaim the true God. "Thus saith the Lord, the God of Israel, the barrel of meal shall not waste, neither shall the cruse of oil fail, until the Lord sendeth rain upon the earth." Homage to the God of Israel won from them that know Him not, a proclamation of His power, and truth, and pity to the heathen world—this is the main purpose of the episode. To accomplish it is the aim with which the Prophet takes his long journey. He has a mission to others besides his own people—to those who live outside the sacred land of Palestine—and, in performing it, and in the story of its performance, the consciousness of a like charge and vocation is deepened in the hearts of Israel.

Elsewhere the same evidence meets us. The missionary idea is bound up with the very beginnings of Israel. Why does the Supreme interpose to redeem the Hebrews from Egypt? To right a grievous wrong, to break the intolerable fetters of the slave—yes; but also, as the Rabbins themselves point out, to vindicate eternal justice and the supremacy of the moral law, to proclaim God's sovereignty, to humble the besotted hearts that deny Him. "The Egyptians shall know that I am the Lord, and My name shall be published through all the earth"—such is the clearly-stated purpose of the wondrous intervention; and it is realized when Pharaoh, who has dared to measure himself against the Almighty, confesses, in the hour of his defeat, "the Lord is righteous, and I and my people are wicked." But that high purpose was not locked up in the Divine Mind; it was imparted to Moses, and by him announced in turn to

Pharaoh. It was, equally with the longing to deliver his people from the misery of the slave, his overmastering thought when he gave himself to God as His instrument. It was, beyond question, the animating conviction of the writer who penned the sacred story. The missionary consciousness filled his soul, and the souls, too, of those who conned the impressive epic in every generation.

And the same truth is brought home to us when we pass from Egypt to Sinai. The people are led to the flaming mount, there to receive the " law of fire " which is to burn itself into their consciousness for all time. They are to be God's own people, set apart from all nations unto Him who can say " all the earth is Mine." Why ? First, for their own moral and spiritual uplifting, but also for the uplifting of mankind. By the consecrated life to which they are pledged they are to bear everlasting witness to God, to be His missionaries among the peoples, and so, in the fullness of time, to win them for Him and His service. They are to be " a kingdom of priests and a holy nation " ; but " a priest pre-supposes a congregation, and a kingdom of priests a world to minister to." A chosen people would be unmeaning if the truth, whose possession makes it the chosen, were shut up within its confines, if it were not to overflow those boundaries and bless the whole world with its fruitful waters. An elect people must, in the very nature of things, be a missionary people—a people witnessing to the God who has chosen it. The Father of mankind—and this God is even in the Pentateuchal teaching—must needs care for all mankind and desire for them too the blessings of the saving truth He has entrusted to His elect.

More ancient still is the idea. Abraham learns to know the true God. But the attainment of that knowledge does not suffice ; he is to go forth into the wide world, bearing the Divine doctrine so that he may impregnate with it the hearts of men. Not without justification does ancient tradition describe him as intentionally winning converts for the true God. The idea is not only implicit in the story, but clearly set forth. Wheresoever he pitches his tent the Patriarch sets up an altar beside it as a testimony to his faith, and a call to the world to share it with him. Notable it is that Abraham is a missionary in the full sense of the word; he performs his appointed task in, and by, wandering. He is homeless—Providentially made so, it would seem, in order the better to bear his witness. He must see men and cities so that, by direct contact with them, he may the more effectually make known to them the saving truth. Let the Zionist and the territorialist who hold that, denied a land of his own and the advantages of a commonwealth, the Jew is a blunted instrument in the hands of God, ponder the fact.

The Mission, then, is an idea deeply rooted in the Hebrew consciousness. Instead of being a hundred, it is some thousands of years old. The facts of history are an additional proof. The Gospels reproach the Pharisees—the Rabbinical party of their day—with excessive missionary zeal; they "compass sea and land to make one proselyte." And the reproach is repeated by the historians of the early Roman Empire, who tell of the numerous converts made by Judaism even among the leaders of pagan society, so that, as Seneca phrases it, "the vanquished give laws to the conquerors." This was surely no automatic process. So signal a success could only have been achieved by men fired with proselytising ardour, for whom the Mission was a reality, who deemed themselves enrolled to be "a light of the Gentiles."

A distinguished Jewish writer, in the last number of

HAVE THE JEWS A MISSION? 49

an important monthly Review, criticises his brethren of these times for lack of this missionary zeal. "Did Israel," he says, "stand out staunchly for his mission the evils due to the absence of a territory would cease to count. The nation of martyrs would then wear persecution as a crown, and welcome death as a privilege. Unfortunately I have not detected in any of the preachers of the Jewish Mission the faintest attempt to convert their concept into a working reality. By a mission they seem to mean a passive expectation of a Providential millennium. There may be occasions when 'they also serve who only stand and wait'; but that this is the sole variety of service open to a great historic people is a superstition more contemptible than the lowest gospel of race-Zionism." Reading these words, one seems to hear the echo of an old controversy, with which the name of the late Professor Max Müller was closely associated. Is it really impossible to work for a mission by passive means? What of the ideal Servant of the Lord, of whom I have already spoken, who "does not cry or lift up his voice in the street," and yet fulfills his divinely-assigned errand by "bringing forth judgment in truth?" The writer of the article from which I have quoted summons the Jew to active effort in fulfilment of his historic vocation; but what would he have us do? Are we to stand at street corners and shout invitations to the passers-by to come and embrace the truth? Are we to go out of our way to court contumely and suffering, to "give our backs to the smiters and our faces to shame and spitting?" Martyrdom?—well, the Jewish life always is martyrdom, more or less pronounced. It is almost as hard to live for Judaism as it is to die for it. Even to-day, and in this free England of ours, it means painful struggle and an almost equally painful patience—struggle with the temptation to take the easy path of disloyalty, patience under suspicion, and distrust, and calumny. And is not this a species of martyrdom, a true because a faithful witness to God, for whose sake we endure, and suffer, and deny ourselves? And what of the silent witness of the Jewish life, and of the men who, pen in hand, have both expounded and inspired it? Is not every faithful Jew who finds in his religion an impulse to whole-hearted service of God and man—is not every Jewish book that explains and defends Judaism to the multitude—a fulfilment of the Mission? And is it seemly, is it fair, to describe these things as the outcome of a contemptible superstition?

That there are Jews who know nothing of a divine vocation, or ignore the responsibilities it lays upon them, is unhappily only too true. And sometimes we are tempted, when thinking of them, to deride in our inmost hearts the very idea of a Mission. What a hopeless gulf, we say, lies between these sordid lives and the kingdom of priests! But then we remember that the mere possession of an ideal is the promise and potency of better things, and we take courage. Despite these ignoble specimens, despite, moreover, the smallness of our numbers, we are not fairly chargeable with arrogance in believing that we have a message for the world, which it has begun to heed, and will heed more fully still in God's good time. Every religionist holds a like faith; he can consistently do no otherwise. If we Jews are arrogant in believing in our mission, in believing in ourselves, then we sin in company with many millions of the world's best spirits.

Let us, then, hold fast to the old missionary idea. Our mandate will never be exhausted while the kingdom of God is smaller than the whole earth, or human brotherhood than mankind. It is our one justification for our existence. If there is no spiritual triumph in store for

HAVE THE JEWS A MISSION?

Israel, if all his pathetic story is to lead nowhere, then Judaism is vain. Let us ring down the curtain and put out the lights. The historic tragedy is already played out, and its miserable futility, its heart-breaking anti-climax is its crowning element of tragedy. Why continue the age-long self-sacrifice, if it is to yield nothing but tears? But a mission explains and justifies everything.

And the inspiration of it! There is a harvest in store, and we willingly give ourselves as labourers for it, though our eyes will never behold the full ingathering, Mankind won for God and righteousness through us—who would not work for the consummation? From time to time the little congregants at our Children's Service are asked to sing these lines:—

Let Israel trust in God alone, and in His power confide;
For He is faithful to His word, if we in Him abide.
His counsels must for ever stand, all nations bow to His command.

Let Israel strive for truth alone, in love to bless mankind,
And in the bonds of brotherhood all nations soon to bind.
So that they all, with one accord, acknowledge and obey the Lord.

Shall these tiny worshippers be told to sing these words no more, with all their pictures of the splendour of Judaism, with all their incitements to the noble life? I cannot believe it.

LEADERSHIP

" And it came to pass that the man whom I shall choose, his rod shall bud."—NUMBERS xvii., 5.

THUS was the authority of Israel's great leaders to be vindicated against the murmurs of Korah and his fellow rebels. The man whose staff should miraculously bud should be by that fact declared the Divinely-chosen leader. But the very form of the miracle told its tale. Why was just the blossoming staff used as the sign, if not to suggest the qualities for which Aaron and his yet greater brother had been made the chosen? Their selection was no arbitrary one. It was based upon the attributes needed for all leadership:—the consciousness of a mission, profound reverence for it, self-denying ardour, an unquenchable idealism. These men, moreover, were no saints, no demi-gods, but ordinary human beings—their daily lives were lived amid the familiar scenes of this workaday world—and yet they could aspire heavenward, and they knew how to make this earthly life bloom with a Divine beauty. Aptly, then, did the dry staff blossom, while the rival rods, whose possessors lacked the potencies of leadership, remained dead to the stimulus of the Sanctuary. It was an emblem of the gracious life of those great souls—a life which constituted their real vindication, the true source of their authority. The miracle merely confirmed their leadership—set upon it the Divine seal, so that the most doubting hearts might believe in it for ever.

And to-day, when the age of miracles has long since passed, the ancient wonder still retains its significance.

Its lesson is for every age. The struggle for the headship of men is still going on, and will never cease even though the new order that fills the dreams of the socialist become one day a sober reality. Some master-minds there must be in every phase of human society, to whom the sceptre falls. What shall constitute their indefeasible title to the power they claim? How shall the false leader be distinguished from the true? Shall it not be by the capacity of the seemingly dry staff to bud and blossom? Let the would-be leaders of men have the gift of transfiguring their work by high endeavour; let them toil for ideals nobler even than those they seem to pursue; let faith in the justice of their cause, faith in themselves, faith in their divine right, uplift them; let them know what they would do, and do it with their might—and they will prove themselves the chosen ones—secure for their claims the highest of all sanctions.

Is not the truth worth remembering? This is the day of many shams. Superficiality too often does duty for depth, pretence for sincerity, in the domain of thought and of action alike, in literature, in science, in statesmanship, in philanthropy. Men come to the front by sheer cleverness and dexterity, by simply *affirming* that they deserve a front place, or by pushing their way to it. These are the dry rods that remain dry to the end. Their owners scheme, and clamour, and cause their voice to be heard in the street. But their success is transient. Not for them will history keep a place in its list of leaders. They are the Korahs, who are forgotten, or remembered only to be scorned. It is only the true leaders, with aspiring, self-sacrificing souls, who truly lead, not only in their own day, but for all time.

The lesson of the blossoming staff has many applications. Leadership is the coveted prize, not only for individuals, but for peoples. England is one of those peoples. Thus far she has made good her title to headship. Her leader's staff wears many a flower; she has formed a lofty conception of empire, and faithfully striven to fulfil it. Let her take heed that she keeps these qualifications, if she would keep her leadership. Let you and me take heed that we so discharge our duties as citizens that nothing we do, nothing we suffer to be done, shall ever tend to lower England's traditional ideal—ever blight the blossoming staff and make it barren.

And to us, as Jews, the lesson comes home. Leadership is of the very essence of our historic calling. "Behold I have given him for a witness to the nations, a leader and commander to the peoples." We Israelites live only in order that we may pioneer our fellowmen along the path of righteousness and truth. It is a mighty task. Have we the necessary equipment for it? Is ours the blossoming or the sterile staff—responsive or dead to the inspiration of the holy environment created by a great ideal? For leadership there is needed the very consciousness of a call, pride in it, the resolve to forgo everything for its realisation; and for spiritual leadership there is needed a love of the spiritual, continuous traffic with it, a certain scorn of the world, the exaltation to the chief place of the things of religion. Do we possess these attributes? If we do, then our leadership is confirmed from on high, and will prosper; if we do not, it is a sham and a mockery, and the very shadow of it will pass away. "Only that organisation," say the Rabbins, "will endure which works in the name of Heaven."

To me, as a Jew, this question is the one absorbing matter of interest which transcends all others. Upon it hinges the destiny, the existence of Israel. Last week a Service of Thanksgiving at St. Paul's celebrated the meeting of the Pan-Anglican Congress, assuredly a tremendous event in the history of the English church. To the vast congregation then assembled the Archbishop of Canterbury spoke these words :—" When and how shall the kingdoms of this world become the kingdom of our Lord ? " And he answered, " When common, prosaic men and women in the church of God shake off the paralysis of faint hearts and believe in the grandeur of their Christian calling, their royal priesthood." Thus Christendom has the same problems, the same preoccupations, as Jewry. Like Israel, the Church deems itself called to the spiritual empire of the world ; but it doubts its strength and its capacity, as Israel may well doubt his. But the admonition of the Primate, his appeal to his communion to rise to the height of its great vocation, is just that which we ourselves need most seriously to ponder. His words might appropriately have been addressed to a Jewish audience. If we would win the world for the God of Israel, we must be penetrated with a sense of the glory of the task ; if we would fulfil our mission, we must have faith in it, and in ourselves. The men and women of the Church are to shake off the paralysis of faint hearts and believe in the grandeur of their calling, of their royal priesthood. Who needs courage in these days more than the Jew ? And whose calling is so grand as that of Israel, with his spiritual consecration more than thirty centuries old ? Yes, and who can boast of a priesthood more royal than that of a people whose title of " a kingdom of priests " was acclaimed by the thunders of Sinai ?

If we could only realise the dignity, historic and intrinsic, of our vocation as missioners to men, as spiritual rulers of men, then indeed the staff would blossom and our leadership be a fact. But how painfully distant is such a consummation! What is his sacred mission to the average Jew but an empty phrase, to which he listens impatiently or without understanding? What is leadership to him save worldly hegemony, social or financial? We—a people without a constitution save the Bible, without collective traditions save those that are eloquent of God—we are daily doubting, rejecting, the materials on which our State is based, tearing up the very foundations of our own existence. There is nothing we believe in less than the greatness, the saving power, the Divinity, of our Judaism. As a keen observer has well said, the Jewish soul is not working. We have the apparatus of religion, but it is perishing of disuse, of dry rot. Our synagogues are not merely empty, but misused, discredited even by those who should chiefly champion them. Most of them are regarded as financial machines, at best as devices for maintaining a merely mechanical bond between the Jew and his community, rather than as instruments for sanctifying the lives of those attached to them. "Judaism," I said lately to a prominent representative of a powerful orthodox synagogue, "Judaism must surely prove an ennobling factor in the Jewish life; we may confidently trust it to redeem the Jewish character." He smiled; "There is no such virtue in it," he said. And yet he devotes his life to the upholding of the synagogue! It is a grim paradox. "Faith unfaithful keeps us falsely true." It is a canker that is eating out the heart of English Judaism!

Nor let us think that orthodoxy alone is involved. To us Reformers the admonition is addressed. We aspire after leadership; we would show the way and set the tone of Jewish truth and practice. Do these pretensions imply no responsibilities? Or shall the ancient rule be exceptionally broken in our case, and the barren staff proclaim the chosen ? On very many of us Reform sits far too lightly. It is a licence rather than a bond, a justification of laxity and indifference instead of a summons to especially strenuous endeavour after the religious life. If Judaism is not to go down after its age-long struggle, Reformer and Traditionalist alike must mend their ways. There must be a revival of the old consciousness of a mission, a greater desire for it, a deeper reverence for it.

Which of the existing religions is to constitute the ultimate religion of the world is an alluring subject of speculation. But of this let us be sure that it will be the religion whose adherents have the strongest consciousness of its dignity and the firmest conviction of its ultimate triumph. Will Judaism be that religion, or at least its inspiration ? I believe that it will. " Sooner shall this staff blossom than regeneration be thine "— so cries the Pope, in the legend, to penitent Tannhäuser. But the wonder is wrought none the less. And so will it be with us. The seemingly dry staff will bloom as of yore. "The new heavens and the new earth," of which the Prophet of old spoke so rapturously, will be a reality in the coming time, and a new generation will spring up who, by its very faith in its election, will prove itself the chosen, " the blessed of the Lord."

ISRAEL A NATION

> "Fear not to go down into Egypt; for I will there make of thee a great nation."—GENESIS xlvi., 3.

So speaks the Divine voice to Jacob when he was about to depart for the sojourn in Egypt which was to have such tremendous consequences for the life story of his descendants. " I will there make of thee a great nation " —this promise, already made to the earlier Patriarchs, was given anew to the last of them. It was a promise which was to reward their faithfulness to their great religious trust, to keep them in good heart throughout their arduous battle in its behalf. Not they, but their descendants, were to be blessed. When they had long since left this earthly scene their spiritual heirs would reap the fruits of their ancestors' heroic steadfastness in the proud consciousness of nationality.

" I will there make of thee a great nation "—was the promise redeemed ? Has Israel ever been a great nation ? In a sense he has not. Compared with the power and the magnificence of Egypt, of Assyria, of Rome, of twentieth-century Britain, he was, even at the period of his greatest prosperity, puny and insignificant. But in another sense the promise has been amply fulfilled; Israel has been a great nation. He is a great nation still, though a whole chorus of voices may shriek against the heresy. "Some nations," says a recent writer, " attain to unity, and express themselves as units, much more emphatically than others. These are the great nations. They are nations with a soul, and so with a higher kind of life than that of more loosely knit communities. Their unity usually means power, but it means something far more important than power; and when it means to them only power, their very nationality is threatened." It is finely said. The greatness of a nation depends not upon its size, nor upon the extent of its territory, nor upon its martial prowess—it may have these, and glory in them, and by the very glorying in them compromise its greatness—but upon the quality of its soul, upon the vividness and the strength and the loftiness of its ideals. Let a noble spirit inform it, a sublime aim inspire it—let it nourish a sense of election, of responsibility, the consciousness of a high mission assigned to it by the Hand that shapes the world's destinies, and, though it be few in number, and boast not an inch of territory, it is a nation, and a great nation.

If this be true, then Israel is a nation even to-day; and so long as it is true to itself it may justly claim to be a great nation. The finest ideals it has; a sense of election and of responsibility to the highest it has. Next in importance to the belief in the Divine unity, and logically flowing out of it, there is the conviction that the Jewish people has been appointed to spread among men the most exalted conceptions of religious faith and duty. This conviction is Israel's unifying bond; defying the mighty forces which make for fusion and extinction, it keeps him apart—a nation among the nations. And not a nation merely, but a great nation; for what consciousness can be finer than that of consecration, what ideal can be more sublime than the winning of the world for righteousness and God? If a great nation is a nation with a soul, a nation that expresses itself emphatically, then Israel is assuredly a great nation. At any rate, a nation he is. The very word Israel proves it. No mere sect or religious community could appropriately bear such a name. It implies not a race only, not a spiritual ideal only, but the two combined—a race animated by a spiritual ideal. And the phrase expressed the conditions that go to make a nation.

This theory will meet with objections. Israel, I shall be told, lost his national character more than eighteen hundred years ago, when Jerusalem fell before the battering rams of the Romans. Ever since that time, it will be said, the Jews have taken their nationality from the people who have given them shelter. But, if so, the writer whom I quoted just now is altogether wrong, and let me say that I was quoting from a leading article which appeared in the *Times* newspaper five years ago. A nation, the *Times* confessed, is indefinable; but you can see it. Some instinct makes you recognise it. Well, Israel is recognised as a nation by those who see it; no one can possibly mistake it for a mere sect. To deny Jewish nationality you must deny the existence of the Jew.

It will be further objected that to speak of Israel as a nation is absurd inasmuch as it is impossible for a person to belong to two nationalities at one and the same time. We English Jews are Englishmen, it will be said. Our life is bound up with the life of our country. Our interests, and hopes, and ideals are the interests, and hopes, and ideals of Englishmen at large. We cannot regard ourselves as belonging both to the British nation and to the Israelitish nation without being false to one or the other. There must needs be a conflict at times between the two sets of interests, the two sets of duties. The contention may perhaps have some force if we understand Jewish nationality in the sense in which it is understood by the political Zionist, though I pronounce no opinion upon the matter. But, as we have seen, nationality does not necessarily postulate a political consciousness. A nation can exist even though it has lost its independence and all desire for it. The essentials of national spirit go down far deeper, are drawn from more vital things. I am not speaking at random. The leading article in our great English newspaper, to which I have just referred, was suggested by a meeting of an influential society which aims at fostering among the Welsh an enthusiasm for their ancient culture. The keynote of the speeches delivered at that meeting was the conception of the Welsh as a nation—as a nation, and not as a mere section of the kingdom or the empire. The speakers enlarged on the glory and the duty of keeping alive the language and the literature and the traditions of the principality. "I am an immense believer," said one of them, "in these separate nationalities"; and he spoke approvingly of "the romantic movement" which gives to those who take part in it " a deep and passionate interest in the past, and to which they owe their interest in folk-songs, in folk-lore, in the old literature, in the old laws." Such a movement, he added, tends to make every inhabitant of this island "remember his origin, the origin and history of the particular part of this island in which he lives, and yet feel in full consciousness that all this leads up to a greater and fuller national life." The man who spoke these words was not a Welshman, nor was he an obscure person. He was Mr. Arthur James Balfour, now Lord Balfour, once Prime Minister of this country. With the clearness of vision which marks the true statesman, he could see not only the possibility of a double nationality, but the advantages that may redound from it for the State. He could see that the preservation by the Welsh of their separate identity, of their historic culture, is something which not only honours and ennobles those who give themselves to the task, but enriches the larger nation of which they are a part. "It leads up to a greater and fuller national life."

The Welsh do not stand alone in this reverence for their past, this passion for keeping alive their old national spirit. They are joined by the Irish and the Scots. Are we Jews wrong if we follow their example? Again I say that this matter is not a political one. We can sufficiently maintain our national consciousness by preserving our old culture—by keeping alive the study of our ancient language and history and the great ideals, intellectual, moral, spiritual, to which they give expression. It is the Zion which Israel carries with him in his own breast to which we must renew our allegiance again and again. But that allegiance will be poor if it have not a national consciousness to replenish it. What is needed is a revival of the Jewish spirit—a deeper reverence for our ancient heritage, a greater pride in the name and the past of Israel—above all an end to the illusion that such feelings are anything but honourable to the Jew or loyal to the nations among whom he lives. On the contrary, to give ourselves more earnestly to Jewish culture, to add its fruits to the common treasury of Englishmen, is *to enrich England, to show ourselves capable of the very highest patriotism*. It is, as Lord Balfour said, to help in creating a greater and fuller national life.

Those words are an encouragement, but also a rebuke. Some time ago I attended a lecture on the Poetry of the Old Testament, delivered by one of the foremost scholars in the kingdom. With extraordinary fervour the speaker, a Christian minister, declaimed some passages in Hebrew from the Hebrew Bible, which were followed with rapt attention by his hearers. The profound impression created by the recital was unmistakeable. The audience numbered many hundreds, but the Jews among them could have been counted on the fingers of both hands. What is the secret of this painful contrast? Why do we leave to others an enthusiasm for our own great possessions? Why do we labour for every interest, strain after every prize, try to savour every joy, but those which, in the truest sense, belong to our own domain? Why is the fine soul which alone makes the great nation slowly perishing within us for lack of sustenance? It is a hard question to answer. But, unless this spiritual decline is arrested, Israel's nationality must perish and, with it, Israel too.

PALESTINE'S FUTURE

" And I will remember the land."—LEVITICUS xxvi., 42.

"I will remember the land "—it is a striking utterance. Exiled Israel, turning in penitence to the Heavenly Father, will be mercifully received. For God will remember His covenant with the patriarchs of ancient days, the covenant by which He bound Himself to take and keep their descendants for His people. But He will remember something else ; He will remember the land, enjoying its Sabbaths indeed, but the Sabbaths of desolation ; He will remember the land, idle, solitary, bereaved. It is a beautiful thought. The very soil is as a mother mourning for the children torn from her embrace, and God is mercifully mindful of her as He is of the contrite exiles and of their fathers " that sleep in the dust." The Rabbins put a similar interpretation upon the text and clothe it in a charming parable. It is like a king, they say, with beloved children, whom he gives into the charge of a handmaid. When he sends to inquire after the children he graciously bethinks himself of the handmaid, and inquires after her likewise. The land is dear to God, for has it not nourished His sons ? And when it mourns the loss of them He sorrows with it.

" I will remember the land "—an apt text for a present-day sermon. For the promise it breathes seems to be on the way to fulfilment. God seems to be remembering Palestine now ; " the time to have pity upon her, yea, the set time is surely come." We, at any rate, are thinking of her more intently than ever, asking ourselves what the approaching days have in store for her and for her exiled people. And men generally are asking it too. At this moment British soldiers are fighting their way into the Holy Land, and the end of the war may see it under a just and clement rule. Every humane heart must long for the benign change if only a fraction of recent reports about Turkish barbarity proves to be true. Hence the folly of the extremists in Russia, with their cry of "no annexation" as a condition of the coming peace. If the end of the war is to bring no territorial adjustments, no freedom for oppressed nationalities, then the old misgovernment of Palestine will begin anew, and the regeneration of the homeland of our race will be deferred again for many a weary decade. Humanity and justice alike protest against this abortive outcome of the fiercest of world struggles. If there is one section of the inhabitants of Palestine that especially deserves to dwell in peace and security it is the Jews, its historic owners, who "take pleasure in her stones, and have pity upon her dust."

The civilised world joins in the thought. But men are not casually thinking of Palestine now; they are planning its future, and in that future the Jews are to play a prominent part. What are we English Jews doing in regard to this question? Surely we shall not be content to remain idle in a matter of vital concern to us when the world at large is actively busying itself with it. What is to be done with Palestine when the war is over? If it is offered to us, ought we to accept it? And if we ought, to what extent? If an organised Jewish settlement on a large scale in the Holy Land is desirable, what shape ought it to take? Some attempt must be made to crystallise Jewish opinion on the question, or it will be solved without us, and possibly in a manner detrimental to the true interests of Jewry.

I assume that, even for us Reform Jews, Palestine is still a holy land, one fraught for us with sacred memories, dearer to us than any other country save the land of our birth. We still retain some of the old love for it which moved the Psalmists to "prefer Jerusalem above their chief joy," and impelled their spiritual child Jehudah Halevi to express his soul and, as the story tells, to breathe out his life, in a song of yearning for Zion. We still pray for the peace of Jerusalem. We do more than this. "Lead us, O God," we have asked this very morning, "lead us securely to our land." Lead *us* to *our* land—think of it, ye Englishmen of the Jewish persuasion! If these prayers are meaningless, let us be honest and strike them out of our liturgy. But we have deliberately retained them. What is this but a confession that in Palestine there centre for us not only memories, but hopes, and that, in dreaming of the future of our race, we keep a place in the vision for the land of our fathers given back to its natural owners and blessed once more by their renewed possession of it.

What destiny, then, do we desire for it? Many schemes for fashioning that destiny are fermenting in the minds of men, both Jew and Gentile—from the extreme Zionist programme, with its dream of a re-established Jewish State, to the far humbler idea of a greatly extended Jewish colonisation. If I am to express my own personal view, I would say that the less political the new Jewish order in Palestine proves to be the nearer it will approach the ideal one. If we except the age of Solomon, it would, I think, be true to say that never has Israel been politically great among the nations. His greatness was to be of another kind; it was to be the unique greatness achieved by a people living for the God-idea and striving to enthrone it in the hearts of mankind at large. A nation we may still be; but we are a nation, as the great Rabbi Saadyah said, in virtue of our religious ideals only. It is a paradox, but upon it is based the cardinal theory of Israel's election and mission. "Ye shall be unto Me a kingdom of priests and a holy nation"—the words come aptly now when we are in sight of Pentecost, with its reminder of the great Sinaitic charter. A later voice echoed the impressive truth: "This people which I have formed for Myself shall set forth My praise." Israel was to be the one nation that had God for its King, and the divine doctrine for its constitution. To ask for a human sovereign was a sin; to live under the divine rule alone, and so to demonstrate the possibility of such a life to the world, was the specific task of the elect people. Other nations might pursue aims of empire and aggrandisement; God had chosen Israel *for Himself*, as the living witness to His existence and to the everlasting supremacy of the spiritual ideal.

This fundamental thought must, it seems to me, determine, as that choice spirit, "Achad Ha'am," maintains, the character of the new order in Palestine. It must be essentially a spiritual order, and in the spiritual the intellectual is necessarily contained. This does not mean that the practical life should be ignored. The new Palestinian community must be duly organised and enjoy a certain measure of autonomy. The arts of peace must be diligently cultivated. Industries must be encouraged, the countryside made to smile again. The land must have her children given back to her. But all this must be only the means to an end, the necessary condition of the growth of that spiritual power, the exercise of which is Israel's life-task and the one justification of his continued survival.

In a word, Palestine must become more Jewish—more

worthily Jewish—than it has been hitherto, with its mere handful of colonists and its larger company of less desirable indwellers. There must be more Jews in it, enjoying a better social status, speaking their ancient language as their everyday tongue, and finding their highest purpose in the development and the dissemination of those characteristic ideas which, taking their rise in the Bible, and informing the later literature, have come to be included in the term "Jewish Culture." Israel is still able to teach the world doctrine which it greatly needs to learn, and he may teach that doctrine most effectively from a spiritual centre such as Palestine may afford. "From Zion the law will go forth, and the word of the Lord from Jerusalem." It will go forth to the world, but to the Jew also. Such a spiritual centre would help to quicken the Jewish consciousness in the soul of the Jew all the world over.

It is no easy project, and at least one serious objection may be urged against it. To make Palestine truly Jewish, it may be argued, might conceivably imperil the position of the Jew elsewhere. With a land of his own, he might come more plausibly than ever to be regarded as an alien in the land of his birth. A few days ago some English people, sitting together in a public place, began to speak about the Jewish question. "I hear," said one of them, "that there is a talk of the Jews going back to Palestine after the war." "I shall be delighted," said another, "to join in a subscription to pay their fares." These people were obviously well educated and of good social standing. There is no doubt that anti-Jewish prejudice does linger on in the most civilised countries, and it is possible that the realisation of the cry of "Palestine for the Jews" will strengthen it. "These Jews," it may be said, "have got their own land now, let them go back to it." But we must face this danger, as we have braved many worse ones in the course of our troubled corporate life, hoping that a new era may bring in new and juster ideas. Against it we may set the blessings that will accrue both to mankind and to the Jew from a spiritual revival on Palestinian soil. From the hilltop of Zion, as from an uplifted beacon, the light of religious truth and of noble thought will shed its radiance far and wide. All the sublime teachings and aspirations of our finest souls, uttered at intervals through the centuries, will be focussed and vivified; all their yearnings after the higher life, more articulate and more impressive than of yore, will challenge the attention of men. And besides this there will be an ideal community to teach its silent lesson by the powerful influence of example. It will be a community marked by exalted strivings, held together by sacred interests, seeking peace and pursuing it. It will be an object lesson in the practicability of the ideal, applied to the lower life both of the individual and the State, a witness to the eternal truth of the prophetic words, " Not by power, nor by might, but by My Spirit, saith the Lord." What greater benefit could we confer upon the world than that which would flow from the establishment of such a community? What greater service could we render to Israel? Rooted in Palestine, he would see his scions flourishing more mightily than ever in other lands. The Jew of the Diaspora would gain a new dignity, a greater worth, a larger esteem, in virtue of the nobility of the parent Israel. Palestine would inspire and uplift Western Jewry. Reversing Canning's famous programme, we should call in the old world— the old world of the romantic age of the Bible—to redress the balance of the new! Is it an idle dream? It need not be if Western Jewry will but remember the land— its present state, its pathetic call, its splendid potencies —and, remembering—act.

THE HEBREW UNIVERSITY

"And they shall call them the holy people, the redeemed of the Lord."—ISAIAH lxii., 12.

THE seven Sabbaths between the Fast of Ab, which commemorates the fall of Jerusalem, and the New Year Festival, are known as the " Seven Sabbaths of Consolation." On each of them the Prophetic reading is taken from the last chapters of the Book of Isaiah, which are mainly a promise of future restoration for Zion, of ultimate rehabilitation for Israel. In conformity with this ancient practice we have read one of these utterances this morning, and the text forms part of it. Israel, hitherto deemed forsaken, smitten of God, shall in the coming time be taken back to the Divine arms, and be called " the holy people, the redeemed of the Lord."

Every faithful Jew cherishes the vision ; but the interpretation of it varies with the soul that cherishes it. Some postpone its fulfilment to a remote future ; others look for its speedy coming, even declaring that it is already in sight. But, however much Zionist and non-Zionist may differ, they agree on one point : both hold that the hoped-for regeneration of Israel can be no automatic process, irrespective of any merit in the Jew himself. If Zion is to be uplifted out of her low estate, it must be by the force of her own righteousness. Israel will be redeemed only because he deserves to be redeemed—deserves it in virtue of the high ideals and strivings that sanctify his corporate life. The old Rabbis seem to have taken this view. " I the Lord will hasten it in its time "—so the prophet pictures God as speaking of the promised redemption; "a self-contradiction," remark the Rabbis, "for if God hastens the glorious day it cannot be said to come in its time, and if He brings it in its time where is the hastening?" But they solve their own difficulty. "If Israel," they explain, "is worthy of deliverance, God will hasten it; if not, it will come in its appointed time"—slowly and tardily, the fruit of the gathered influences of the years and the centuries, the stored-up effects of hope, and patience, and quiet effort. But even in the latter case the great consummation will be brought about, under Providence, by Israel himself; his own deserts will have justified it and achieved it. Our Prophet teaches the lesson in clearest language: "They shall call them the holy people, the redeemed of the Lord"—not merely a people, but a holy one, lifting its head again under the impulse of a sense of consecration, not merely the redeemed, but the redeemed of the Lord, saved by faith in God and in itself, saved to uphold that faith for the ennoblement of men. This is the Prophetic ideal. The most modern of latter-day expositors so understands the Prophet's words: "The holy people"—it means, he says, "the priesthood of humanity." When Israel, inspired by his religion, consciously gives himself to the service of mankind, then his redemption will have begun.

A few weeks ago, in the presence of the representatives of Great Britain, the liberator, and her allies, and of the world's three great religions, the foundations of a Jewish university were laid on Mount Scopus, in Jerusalem. It was truly a symbolic event. It betokened the freedom of the sacred soil from the tread of the oppressor, and it foreshadowed that respect for men's holiest convictions, that sense of human brotherhood, which is to distinguish the policy and the aims of the new Jewish order in Palestine. More than this, it proclaimed the essential character of that order. The first public act of the nascent community now in course of organisation under the ægis of Britain, it declared that the new Israel will be such as our Prophet dreamed of—a spiritual Israel, seeking the source of its power, not in worldly greatness, in widespread empire, in military or economic supremacy, but in the things of the mind and the soul. It was thus an historic act in more than one sense of the phrase. It will live as a landmark in the annals of the world; it closely harmonised with the story of Israel himself. For that story is a spiritual one throughout, marked by continuous martyrdom for a sublime idea, made glorious by a passionate love for learning, by single-hearted search after truth. The hands which laid those foundations were labouring in the spirit of a Moses, who made the religious idea the base and the crown of the State he framed, of an Ezra, who built up the Jewish polity anew upon reverence for Divine law; of a Ben Zaccai, who replaced the fallen Temple and the ruined Nationality by the seminary and the schoolhouse. Thus the requirement of our ancient teachers seems in course of fulfilment. The high aims of the new order vindicate it; they contain the potency and the promise of ultimate success. Israel will live again, more vigorously and more nobly than hitherto, because he deserves so to live.

But in spite of this happy prospect, misgivings are not wanting. This event, so significant and so moving, has evoked criticism, though it has come, characteristically, almost solely from the Jews themselves. For when did they ever fully appreciate their own good fortune? " Why a Jewish University ? " some of them are asking. " Surely knowledge can be imparted anywhere and by anyone, nor can there be such a thing as a specifically Jewish presentation of knowledge without disloyalty to truth." A recent Jewish writer, no friend, certainly, of

THE HEBREW UNIVERSITY 73

Jewish nationalism, has, without intending it, just answered the question. " We need," he says, " we need men who will create for us a philosophy of the present, a philosophy of religion which shall preserve for Judaism her wisest Jews, and shall expound Judaism to the wise that are without." The paramount aim of a Jewish University could not be more effectively set forth. Besides fostering a love of knowledge, and proclaiming the intimate association which subsists between that love and Israel, it is to interpret Judaism to the world as the one necessary step towards winning the world's homage for it, and further to interpret Judaism to the Jew himself, to justify it to his conscience, to convince him that it is worthy of his continued adherence. Is this not a desirable, a necessary task ? And where can it be attempted with better prospects of success than in the City that is reverenced by Jew and Gentile alike, the City whose sacred associations will quicken the ardour of teacher and student, and give a peculiarly powerful sanction and authority to the doctrine that goes forth from it ?

Nor is this all. A Jewish University will set the hall-mark of the spirit upon Jewish life, both in Palestine and elsewhere. It will be a rebuke to sordid aims, a call to the plain-living and high-thinking which beseems not only the scholar and the devotee, but every Jew who would be worthy of his high charge and calling. It will do more even than this. The Jew has a culture all his own, a sacred lore, a distinctive view of life, which go to make his historic and inalienable heritage. He has not only a literature, but a language. Are these not worth preserving ? There are Jews who complain that no one among us fully reveals the spiritual riches of our people, that the attempt is left to the inapt or not too sympathetic hands of the Gentile. The Jewish University will remove the reproach. It is a task well worth doing if only as an act of self-vindication. For if we are not a nation in the ordinary sense of the term, we are, at least, a people. Can we think of ourselves otherwise ? Can we class ourselves with the sects—with the Baptists, and the Methodists, and the rest—and say we are nothing more than they ? We have only to envisage the thought in order to recognise its absurdity. We are possibly no longer a nation, but *we have been*—that is the great determining fact. It is impossible to put one's finger on any point in Jewish history—upon the Babylonian captivity, upon the fall of Jerusalem before the Romans, for example--and say, " here our national life ceased for good and all." You cannot do so, for the past never dies. Moses, and the Prophets, and the Psalmists live in our blood ; their consciousness, their outlook fashion ours. We are a people, then ; and what people can contemn its literature or its language without injuring its own soul, without losing its soul ? Ask Welshmen, ask Scotsmen, ask French Canadians what they think about it.

The Hebrew University will help us to save our literature and our language ; it will do more ; it will help us to save ourselves. It will be a centre, rallying the minds and the hearts of our people all over the world, deepening their Jewish consciousness, strengthening their self-respect, their sense of dignity. It will draw to it, and to them, the equally widespread respect of their fellow-men of all religions. It will set the seal of consecration upon the new community in Palestine, dedicating it to the service of God and men, offering it as the much-needed mediator among mankind that may help to establish peace and love more firmly in the earth. It will help to realise the Prophet's dream : " And it shall come to pass in the latter days that the mountain of the Lord's house shall be established in the top of the mountains, and shall be exalted above the hills : and all nations shall flow unto it. And many peoples shall go and say, Come ye, and let us go up to the mountain of the Lord, to the house of the God of Jacob ; and He will teach us of His ways and we will walk in His paths ; for out of Zion shall go forth the law, and the word of the Lord from Jerusalem. And He shall judge between the nations and shall reprove many peoples ; and they shall beat their swords into ploughshares, and their spears into pruning hooks : nation shall not lift up sword against nation, neither shall they learn war any more." The new University, set high above Jerusalem, will uplift the mind and life of Israel ; it will play a part in the ennoblement of the world.

THE PSALMS IN JEWISH LIFE

I

A BOOK full of interest and charm has recently appeared from the pen of Mr. Rowland Prothero. It is entitled "The Psalms in Human Life," and it is designed to illustrate the part played by the Psalter in the spiritual experience of great souls throughout the ages. Starting from early Christian times, and coming down to our own day, the author cites some of the chief men that have lived during that long period, and indicates the solace, the strength and inspiration which they have drawn from Israel's great manual of devotion. All who would realise the blessing which the Psalter has been to humanity should study this modern appreciation of it. It cannot fail both to deepen their veneration for the Psalms and to increase their sense of the world's debt to Israel.

The author has written primarily for Christian readers and therefore it is not surprising that the Jewish aspect of his subject should not have secured his attention. And yet that aspect is of extreme importance. The Psalter is, in the fullest sense of the word, a Jewish work. It was written by Jews and, in the first instance, for Jews. In it Israel has expressed his soul—his soul at its best. If we would know what the finest spirits of our race thought and felt and hoped and longed for in Bible times, if we would measure the high-water mark touched by Israel's spiritual life, it is to the Psalms we must go. That they have outgrown their original

THE PSALMS IN JEWISH LIFE 77

purpose, that from being the utterances of a few Jewish singers, telling of their own and their people's spiritual feelings, they have become the medium through which the heart of civilised humanity loves to express itself, is only a proof of the remarkable insight with which those more or less unknown poets realised the primal emotions of mankind. But there is something more to be said. If it is possible to speak of the Psalms in human life, it is also possible and proper to say something about the Psalms in Jewish life. If the Psalter has ever been the valued possession of the Christian world, it has been cherished with at least equal affection by the people from whose inner experience it sprang. It has helped the Gentile to live and die nobly ; but what a strong rock has it been to the Jew in life and in death ! To use its own phrase, its words " have been his songs in the house of his pilgrimage " ; they have been his " rod and staff " in his passage " through the valley of the shadow."

And so one could wish that some Jewish hand would take up the task where the author of the book of which I am speaking has left it, and tell us the story of what the Psalms have done and been for the Israelite in various ages. This present discourse, with the one which I hope will follow it, besides introducing this new work to such of you as do not know it already, is intended to show that a Jewish supplement to it is possible and would be both interesting and useful. It certainly seems an anomaly that while there should be a book about the influence of the Psalter upon Christian life, there should be none about its influence upon the life of the Jew. Let me help to remove the smallest fragment of that reproach.

And first a word as to the purpose which the Psalms were originally intended to subserve. It would be a mistake to suppose that they were written solely or even mainly for the Temple. Just as we have now accustomed ourselves to believe that David wrote few if any of them, but that they represent the contribution of more than one poet and more than one period, so we are beginning to see that they were composed for even larger congregations than those which thronged the courts of the Sanctuary in Jerusalem. As Duhm tells us, the greater part of the Psalms were probably never heard in the Temple. Many were used for private devotions—devotions often carried on in the nighttime; others were introduced into the synagogues. The Psalter, Duhm concludes, was chiefly intended to be a people's book—a devotional book, and a book that should enkindle the ordinary man's ardour for the study and the fulfilment of the religious law.

Thus the 141st Psalm opens with the following words, which are clearly the outpourings of a soul worshipping alone :—" Lord, I have called upon Thee ; make haste unto me. Let my prayer be set forth as incense before Thee, the lifting up of my hands as the evening sacrifice." The suppliant is evidently praying in private, and he asks that his prayer shall be accepted as an efficient substitute for the more formal and more ornate rites of the Temple. And as to prayer in the night season, we are reminded of the 119th Psalm, with its cry, " At midnight I will rise to give thanks unto Thee because of Thy righteous judgments." But perhaps no passage shows so conclusively the essentially personal and individualistic spirit in which many of the Psalms were written than the first section of the 102nd Psalm, with its heading : "A prayer for the afflicted when he is overwhelmed, and poureth out his complaint before the Lord." Here we have the outcry of a troubled heart, taking its pathetic story straight to the Father in

Heaven—the plaint of "the alone to the Alone." And the personal note thus struck makes the music of the supplication itself :—" Hear my prayer, O Lord, and let my cry come unto Thee. Hide not Thy face from me in the day of my distress ; answer me speedily. I watch and am become like a sparrow that is alone upon the housetop. I have eaten ashes like bread, and mingled my drink with weeping. My days are like a shadow, and I am withered like grass." It is passages like these which have made the Psalter the devotional text-book of mankind, seeing that, to use Mr. Prothero's metaphor, they " are a mirror in which each man sees the motions of his own soul." And perhaps the old Jewish legend which declares that David wrote Psalms even before he saw the light of this world, is an anticipation of this idea. For the songs with which tradition has linked his name voice those elementary yearnings which are common to the human race at every stage of its history.

But though the Psalter was written with this larger— I had almost said this universalistic—aim, there is no doubt that parts of it were used in the Temple Service, and were even destined for it. There is a tradition preserved by the Talmud, which affirms that in the Temple a special Psalm was sung on each day of the week— the 24th :—" The earth is the Lord's and the fulness thereof " on Sunday ; the 48th :—" Great is the Lord and exceedingly to be praised " on Monday, and so on until we come to the seventh day, when the 92nd Psalm, " A Psalm, a Song for the Sabbath Day," was sung. Each of these Psalms, according to the Talmud, was selected because of some correspondence between its contents and the special act of Creation associated with the day in the first chapter of Genesis. But the 92nd Psalm, the Sabbath Psalm, the Talmud beautifully interprets as a hymn in honour not only of the Sabbath itself, but of Immortality. It is, in the Talmudic words, " a Psalm and Song for the endless Sabbath, for the repose of the life everlasting." The tradition is unquestionably ancient, and is still kept alive. Each day of the week has its Psalm assigned to it in the Prayer Book, and the arrangement, so far as orthodox practice is concerned, is identical with that which was adopted in the Temple.

But I need hardly remind you that the place occupied by the Psalter in Jewish public worship was not limited to the recital of one Psalm daily. In the Temple probably, and in the Synagogue certainly, the collection was more largely drawn upon for the purposes of the Service. As to the Synagogue, though the primitive Service, was originally very brief and simple, it was supplemented by the recital of Psalms by the individual worshipper. And when in later times a fixed liturgy came into existence the Psalms acquired a prominent place in it. If we would know how important that place was, we have only to imagine our own Sabbath Service shorn of some of its earlier passages.

It is interesting, however, to note that even when a selection from the Psalter became definitely incorporated into the Prayer Book the old practice of using the Psalms to supplement the liturgy was still kept up. Pious members of the congregation would assemble before the Service began and prepare their hearts for worship by readings from the Psalms. This custom was either the cause or the consequence of the division of the Psalter into groups of Psalms in such fashion as admitted of its being read through in its entirety either once a month or even once a week. Nor was this pious usage confined to the Synagogue. It found its way into private devotions. Whenever a Jew, under the stress of some personal crisis, felt himself impelled to a special

THE PSALMS IN JEWISH LIFE

act of worship, if some joy or trouble had come to break up the fountains of the mighty deep within him, he would turn to his Psalter for aids to meditation or prayer, for grateful utterance or for comfort. Nay, more, the pious men of the Psalmists' days would, as we have seen, call upon God in the night watches. Their spiritual descendants were wont to do the same, and the Psalms were their favourite devotional medium. They would keep awake on specially solemn occasions—on the Day of Atonement for example—the entire night, and, with the Psalter, they beguiled the long hours in prayerful exercises.

There were saintly men who went further and sanctified in this manner some part at least of every night. Literally imitating the Psalmists, they would arise at midnight and offer their tribute of worship. They had a twofold aim. They wished to pour out their lament for Zion, ruined and desolate; and they also desired to bring themselves into that close communion with God for which the night-season offered a peculiarly favourable opportunity. The old Prayer Books provide a special form of service for the purpose, and Psalms have naturally a place for it. There is, on the one hand, the 137th Psalm:—" By the rivers of Babylon there we sat down, yea, we wept when we remembered Zion," and the 79th:—" O God, the heathen are come into Thy inheritance; Thy holy Temple they have defiled." And there is also the 42nd Psalm, with its passionate yearning for the Divine fellowship:—" As the hart panteth after the water-brooks so panteth my soul after Thee, O God "; the 43rd, with its exquisite cry for the Divine illumination:—" O send out Thy light and Thy truth; let them lead me "; and finally the 51st:—" Create in me a new heart and renew within me a stedfast spirit; cast me not out from Thy presence, and take not Thy holy spirit from me." If the existence of such sublime utterances bears witness to the profound spirituality of the Israelite of ancient times, the use of them in subsequent ages demonstrates that the endowment was a heritage transmitted to far later generations.

I have just mentioned the 137th Psalm :—" By the rivers of Babylon." It has served another purpose in Jewish life besides supplying some of the materials for midnight worship. It has formed the prelude to the daily Grace after Meals. The old-fashioned Jew, with greater leisure, and perhaps greater patience, than we moderns possess, did not mind making a long Grace longer still by prefixing a Psalm to it. It shed a sanctity upon it in advance. And so he sang this Psalm, feeling that in the satisfaction born of gratified appetite it was but seemly to give a regretful thought to Zion, the widowed. But on the Sabbath, the day whose gladness might not be alloyed, he attuned his mind to wholly joyous thoughts. The 137th Psalm was replaced by the 126th, which sings of Jerusalem indeed, but of Jerusalem redeemed :—" When the Lord turned again the captivity of Zion we were like unto them that dream. Then was our mouth filled with laughter. They that sow in tears shall reap in joy ; they go forth weeping, but come back bearing their sheaves."

II

Another Psalm associated with meal-time is the 23rd : —" The Lord is my shepherd." But this was also the children's Psalm, which they were taught to repeat every day at morning-prayer. It was a happy selection. The Psalm is short, and therefore well-adapted for little people ; but it also accustoms them to think of God

THE PSALMS IN JEWISH LIFE 83

as the Good Shepherd, upon whom they depend for all they have, and who, if they obey His voice, will lead them by green pastures, and make them lie down beside the still waters.

But it was the old as well as the young that were exhorted to make the Psalter their medium in their daily approaches to God. Introductions to old Prayer-books prescribe eight verses of the 119th Psalm for recital by the pious Israelite on setting out for the Synagogue at early morning :—" Teach me, O Lord, the way of Thy statutes, and I shall keep it unto the end "—an appropriate verse for one to repeat who walks abroad for the first time in the day. And the passage ends :—
" Behold I have longed after Thy precepts ; quicken me in Thy righteousness." And as the day begins so it closes. At night, before retiring to rest, the devout Jew recites the 91st Psalm, which promises the faithful soul in sleep the shelter of the Most High and the protection of guardian angels, the 3rd Psalm, with its confident exclamation, " I lie down and sleep ; I shall awake, for the Lord will uphold me," and lastly the solemn verse from the 4th Psalm, " Stand in awe and sin not ; commune with your own heart upon your bed, and be still."

From worship I pass to history. Here, too, the Psalms have played no insignificant part. The stronghold of the individual soul in the hour of trouble, they have served to hearten the multitude in times of national crisis. Especially have they stood the Jewish warrior in good stead. They have furnished him again and again with his battle-cry. The wars of the Maccabees supply some signal examples. Like the Puritans under Cromwell many centuries later, the Maccabean heroes would go into the fight with a Psalm on their lips. " The high praises of God were in their mouth, the while a two-edged sword was in their hands." Gathering his slender band together for their encounter with the Greeks, Judas Maccabeus addresses to them a few eloquent words of encouragement. "The enemy," he says, "trust to arms, and withal to deeds of daring; but we trust in the Almighty God, for He is able at a beck to cast down them that are coming against us, nay, even the whole world." The words are a distinct reminiscence of the 20th Psalm, with its cry, at once martial and religious, "These trust in chariots, and these in horses; but we will make mention of the name of the Lord our God. They are bowed down and fallen; but we are risen and stand upright." And, we read, having given as the watchword "The Help of God," Judas throws himself upon the foe. Later on, at Modin, his battle-cry is "Victory is God's," a phrase taken from the concluding words of the 3rd Psalm.

Yet another historical illustration I may cite, borrowed this time from the story of far later ages. The time is the fifteenth century, and the scene is Spain. The Inquisition is doing its hideous work. The Jews, already despoiled of their worldly goods, are offered the choice between apostasy and death. Torquemada, through his monks, preaches Christianity to the devoted Jews. The Rabbis, on the other hand, urge their flock to stand fast by the ancestral faith. But their exhortattions are not needed. The people themselves admonish and encourage each other. "Let us be strong," they cry, "steadfast to our religion in the presence of the enemy. If they suffer us to live, we will live; if they slay us, we will die. We will not defile the covenant of our God. Our hearts shall not grow faint; we will walk in the name of our God." The words are reported by a contemporary historian, and again they reproduce both the spirit and the language of the Psalms. What

THE PSALMS IN JEWISH LIFE 85

support the utterances of Israel's sweet singers were to the Jews in their anguish will never be accurately known. But that it was great indeed, that it inspired the martyrs to play their heroic part is certain. Words that have passed into a people's literature and history must needs have taken deep root in its soul and be the seed of its noblest achievements.

The Psalms in Human Life, the book that has suggested these two discourses, contains a pathetic story. Some 60 years ago two Englishmen were thrown into a noisome dungeon in Bokhara. They were kept there two years, and then executed. Later on a Prayer-book belonging to one of the prisoners was discovered; on the leaves of it he had kept a record of his captivity. "Thank God," he writes in one place, "that this book was left to me. We did not fully know before our affliction what was in the Psalms." What the Psalms were to these hapless prisoners they must needs have been to countless Jews in the time of the Inquisition and earlier in the no less tragic period of the Crusades. Again and again did the Psalmist's cry, bitter, but exulting, go up, "For Thy sake are we slain all the day long; we are counted as sheep for the slaughter." There is a legend in the Talmud which tells how once some Jewish maidens fell into the hands of a brutal enemy, and dishonour seemed to be their inevitable fate. They took counsel together. "If we slay ourselves," they argued, "to escape this threatened shame, shall we still inherit eternal life?" The question is answered by the eldest among them. She quotes the 68th Psalm:—"The Lord said, I will bring back from the depths of the sea." "What," she asks, "do these words mean but that God will take unto Himself in Heaven those who go down in the waters?" And thus reassured, the maidens throw themselves into the sea straightway. The story is a legend, but it is historic none the less. It has been enacted countless times in the age-long period of Jewish agony. Many and many a time has the Israelite preferred death to faithlessness; nay, many a time has he sought it; and the Psalms have been his warrant and his death-cry. Themselves often the songs of martyrs, they have both foreshadowed and fashioned the words and the deeds of martyrs equally noble. Closely connected in the Talmud with the story I have just quoted is that of the famous mother and her seven sons. The tyrant would urge the children by guile or bribes into apostasy. It is the mother herself who bids them be staunch, though she knows she is sending them to their death. She prevails, and as the last and youngest child perishes a voice is heard in Heaven acclaiming her in the words of the Hallel, "A joyous mother of children." Here is legend again; but it proves the temper of those who preserved the tale and the degree in which that temper was fostered by the Psalms.

Between literature and history there is an intimate union. If a people's literature is an expression of its life, it is also one of the makers of it. What we are and what we do are largely determined by what we read. Therefore he who would trace the impress of the Psalter upon Jewish life must necessarily set forth its influence upon Jewish literature. A volume would be needed to treat adequately of this single phase of the subject. It would show how largely the Psalms have been pressed into the service of theology. They have formed a veritable treasury of religious truth. Think, for example, of what a verse like that in the 102nd Psalm:—"A people which shall be created shall praise the Lord" came to mean in the hands of the Talmudic teachers. The people to be created are the penitent. It is they who are born anew—become a new creation; and they it is who may

THE PSALMS IN JEWISH LIFE 87

justly praise God for the power to rise into a better life.

Think, too, of that sturdy Rabbinic saying which declares that greater than the God-fearing man is the man that labours and eats of the fruits of his toil. It is a saying suggested by the opening words of the 123rd Psalm:—"Blessed is every God-fearing man who walketh in His ways. When thou eatest of the labour of thy hands happy shalt thou be and it shall be well with thee." The God-fearing man is simply blessed; but the labouring man is twice blessed; he is happy and it is well with him.

Again what wondrous music is wrung from the 5th verse of the 50th Psalm:—" " Gather my saints together unto Me: those that have made a covenant with Me by sacrifice." According to the Rabbis the words mean a covenant for self-sacrifice, and thus they become a glorification of the saintly men who, in virtue of their compact with God, have yielded up their very lives for duty's sake, claiming no reward for their service save the very joy of serving.

Finally there is the 16th Psalm, with its cry, "Shew me the path of life." It is the elementary prayer of every devout heart that desires to know in what the true life consists. See what the old teachers make of it! "Shew me the path of life"—so David prays. "Woulds't thou," asks the Almighty, "have life, then hope for tribulation"; for through tribulation it is that the eyes of the spirit are opened, and the soul is raised above the deceptive delights of this world into life with God. The verse, as you know, continues as follows:—
"Abundant joys are in Thy presence." The Hebrew word for *joys* is *Semachot*, and the Rabbis have borrowed it and used it, strange to say, as the title of a Talmudic treatise on the laws to be observed by mourners. The title is more than a mere euphemism, more than a device

for veiling a sombre theme under a cheerful name ; it is the embodiment of a profound religious truth. For the partings and the sorrows brought about by death, like all the other troubles of life, have their consoling, their joyous side if we will but search for it ; they are always blessings, seeing that they come from the beneficent Hand that does all things well. There is a " soul of good in things evil "—good to be won in this life, a yet greater good which only the life to come will make possible. And thus it is to the Rabbins we owe the interpretation of this Psalmist's words which has made them some of the most precious in the Psalter. " Thou wilt show me the path of life ; abundant joys are in Thy presence ; at Thy right Hand is everlasting beatitude." Here, under the guidance of our great teachers, we discern the promise of immortality—that promise which, more powerfully than any other promise in God's Book, has helped to instil comfort and hope into the sorrowing heart of humanity.

Here I close. Utterly inadequate, as a treatment of the subject, though these discourses have been, they will at least have given you some idea of the important place which the Psalter has filled in Jewish life. Is it too much to hope that they may also have served to stimulate you to read and ponder more diligently, and so to love more deeply, this unique devotional collection, and that the Psalms may be, in some measure, the well-spring of solace and religious inspiration to the Israelite of to-day that it was to his forerunners of past ages ?

HOPE
(Passover)

"So He bringeth them unto the haven of their desire."—
PSALM cvii., 30.

THE 107th Psalm, the special Psalm for this Festival, is essentially a Psalm of hope. These and these wondrous things God has done in bygone days; He will assuredly do them in the days to come. Again and again has He satisfied the hungry soul; therefore let every longing soul take courage. Those who have sat "in darkness and in the shadow of death" He has led forth into light; therefore let all who suffer now, or at any time, be comforted. Those who go down to the sea in ships He has wondrously rescued from the raging tempest; therefore let all who are beaten and broken by life's storms hope in Him, since for them, too, the waves shall be stilled, and they shall be brought unto the haven of their desire. Thankfulness to God for His past mercies to all sorts and conditions of men, but trust in His coming mercies to the individual soul—this is the lesson of the Psalm.

Hope—the Bible is steeped in it; it is the everlasting theme of its exhortations, the implicit burthen of all its story. And no wonder. For the Bible is Religion's book, and Religion is hope incarnate—hope in God, in a wise and loving government of the world, in the final victory of righteousness, in the ultimate conquest of pain and sorrow by perpetual joy. Hope—it is the message of this Spring-time, with its promise of coming splendour, whispered in the opening leaf, in the re-awakened song of the bird. Hope—it is the lesson of this great Festival, with its story of a people going forth from bondage, their hearts alight with the radiant dreams of the free. Nay, it is the meeting-point of the season and the Feast, the theme of their united doctrine. For the final and the most glorious hope of all is the hope of immortality, the vision of a better and an ampler life which is to crown and complete this earthly life of ours. And of that blissful existence we have the promise and the presage in the wondrous resuscitation of Israel, his spirit slain by slavery, and in the yearly magic that bids the earth rise out of the death of winter into the abounding life of the spring.

Hope is the most precious of God's gifts to men. By hope we live; bereft of it we die. Rightly the old Greek fable tells how, when all else had escaped from Pandora's box, Hope still clung to it. For it is the last possession that remains with the living man. While there is life, we say, there is hope; but it is also true that while there is hope there is life. To each of us God has given the gift of prophecy. We look into the future, and fashion its story out of our hearts' desires. God teaches us to do this in order that we may have the energy to live; since every beat of our hearts is inspired by hope. But not for that alone—else would the boon be of dubious value. God has given us hope so that we may have the energy not merely to live, but to achieve. Did we not dream of success we should fail; did we not believe that happiness awaits us it would elude us. Just because we hope we attain; the hope gives us the needful strength. Our dreams come true because they have the power of fulfilling themselves. But, whether they do or not, at least we have had the joy of hope, the rapture of dreaming. What would life be without that rapture, without those havens of our desire that gleam upon our sight as we peer through the mists of life's storms? It would be dark and wintry indeed. But, instead of this, it is glorious. The beggar becomes a king; the weary are in paradise; the care-laden are lapped in infinite peace. When all else has fled hope abides. Like God Himself, it seeks out the lonely that it may dwell with them—the forsaken that it may befriend them. We all know how one of the greatest English painters has pictured it. A figure, bowed and sightless, plays on a broken harp—on its one remaining string. So persistent, so indomitable, is Hope. Do you say that Hope is oft defeated? So it is; but it is never destroyed. It renews itself, like the Springtime, again and again—"creates from its own wreck the thing it contemplates." And what if we never see the fulfilment of our dearest hopes, can we say with certainty that their disappointment has not been better for us than their realisation? Does not God know what is best for us more surely than we do?

Let us open our hearts to the lesson thus taught us. And first let us thank God for His gift of Hope. Many a time has it kept us alive in the bygone days—kept us alive to sing our song of praise for it on this glad Festival. But let us take the lesson with us into the future; let us hope—hope in the right way, and for the right things. "Be strong, and let thy heart take courage; yea, wait thou on the Lord"—so the Psalmist cries. Yes, on the Lord—that is the secret of all right hoping. From God comes our power to hope—to Him let us consecrate it. Let Him be the inspiration of our best dreams, the centre about which they revolve. Hope, I have said, is life—its impulse, its mainspring; but the full life, the truly living life, is impossible that is cut off from the Divine source of all life. Life is energy, achievement, with all their attendant joys; but you cannot have those things in full measure unless you take God for your help, unless your hope is touched with a heavenly gleam, and transformed into faith. You may try to live your lives alone, to do your work alone, and you will succeed—up to a point. But for complete success, for real joy, you want something infinitely greater than yourselves—some support, some driving power, stronger than you can get from your own unaided souls. You want to be reasonably sure that all is for the best in this world, that life is not a hopeless tangle, that the Universe is on the side of goodness, that death will be swallowed up in victory; you want this to nerve your arm, to ease your heart, to give you gladness far transcending that of the worldings, "when their corn and their wine are increased"—and that you can get only by setting your hope in God. Ah, that phrase!—it recalls the teaching of the Psalmist who describes the true end of all training; it is, he says, that the children "may set their hope in God." It is a notable saying. For what blessing can you confer upon your boys and girls comparable with that hope? Knit their hearts to their Father in Heaven, and you will help them to live; you ensure them a fortitude, a tranquillity, a happiness, which will last as long as they do.

Hope, then, in God if you would be brought to the haven of your desire. You who suffer in any way—in body or in mind, from ill-health or anxiety, from disappointment, or worldly reverse, or the wounds of stricken love—be strong and of good courage. These afflictions will end; you may end them yourselves by looking at them straight in the face, by seeing in them the instrument of your own ennoblement, by regarding them as parts of an infinite and a gracious ordinance planned by the loving Father. Just as your hearts thrill to that mystic touch of the Spring which makes the humblest blade of grass quiver with new life, so let the thought of God pour into your souls at this season of revival, and flood them with the gracious tide of Hope.

But there are larger interests than our own personal happiness. We think of Israel our people, of Judaism our religion--think of them especially at this Paschal season, fraught with historic memories and sacred obligations. To-day we are exhorted to renew our hopes as Jews, to share in a spiritual resuscitation of which the redemption of our enslaved Fathers was the type. For we are apt at times to distrust the future. We look about us and note how materialism, on the one hand, and grinding oppression, on the other, seem to be eating away the very soul of Jewry. And we ask "what hope is there for Israel and for his Mission ? Can these dry bones live ? " But, again, let us look up to God, and believe that He will bring us to the haven of our desire. The momentous work that was begun on that fateful night in Egypt, when our ancestors marched forth to freedom, may seem to languish ; but perish it never will. It is ever being carried on. It cannot fail to be carried on if only we—we of the doubting heart, casting aside our misgivings, will take part in it. Let there be but one faithful soul left to cherish the old tradition and to work for it, and it must survive. Let there be but one heart left to dream of Israel's triumph, of the conquest of a pure and exalted Judaism over the minds of men, and that dream will ultimately come true. Like every vigorous and worthy hope, it will fulfil itself.

And, finally, there is the larger hope of which I have already spoken. Poor, sorely tried mortals as we are, living forever " in darkness and in the shadow of death," in sight of life's eternal tragedy, " our joys three parts pain," our laughter fringed with tears, to us Hope still calls with its cheering note. It bids us set our hearts on God, who of old has delivered His children from their woes, and will assuredly deliver them once more, but with a yet greater and more enduring redemption. "He hath broken the gates of brass, and cut in sunder the bars of iron"—all the seemingly invincible barriers that stand between men and their ideal happiness, between the slave and liberty, between the sinner and forgiveness, between the starving soul and satisfaction, between the storm-tossed pilgrim and the haven of his desire. His Hand has not waxed short. What He has done He will do again, and yet again—till the end of time, in Eternity itself. The shadow of death shall be chased away—swallowed up in everlasting radiance; the slave shall be free from his master, and the weary be at rest; the hungering spirit "shall be satisfied, when it awakes, with the likeness of God."

THE GARDEN OF THE SOUL

(Pentecost)

"Also in the day of the first fruits, when ye offer a new gift unto the Lord."—Numbers xxviii., 6.
"I went down into the garden . . . to see whether the vine budded and the pomegranates were in flower."—
Song of Solomon vi., 11.

The message and the symbolism of Pentecost are both made up of contrasts. Hard upon the thunders of Sinai follows " the still, small voice." " I am the Lord thy God; thou shalt do no murder; thou shalt not steal "—the listening people hear the dread words and tremble; but at once follows the tranquillising promise: " Every place where I cause my name to be remembered I will come unto thee and bless thee." In like manner the stern Commandments have been recited to us this morning in a synagogue decked with flowers, one of Nature's most gracious gifts to men. For Pentecost, the Feast of the great Manifestation, vouchsafed from riven heavens to a quaking earth, is also the Day of First-fruits, the day which carries to the heart the glad promise of summer, and exhorts it to offer, in gratitude for His repeated bounty, " a new gift unto the Lord."

The gentler appeal of the Feast is as mighty as its severer one. This week I was speaking about it to some hundreds of Jewish children whose homes are in the slums. I told them how, in olden times, the Jewish husbandmen, going into his orchard or garden at this season of the year, would come upon some early ripened fruit and, instead of taking the coveted product for himself, would dedicate it to the Divine Giver in a delightful spirit of gratitude and renunciation. As I was speaking I was disturbed by the thought that I was saying something very remote from the children's personal experiences. They lived, I remembered, in mean streets, and seldom saw a garden; certainly they had no gardens of their own. It seemed to me that I was perhaps speaking to them in an unknown tongue. But immediately came an idea which enabled me to bring home this old-world ordinance of the First Fruits to the consciousness of my small hearers, and to make it a living command even for them. "The houses in which you live," I said, "have no gardens; but you have, each of you, a garden within yourselves, the garden of the soul. *That* you may diligently cultivate, and make truly beautiful. You may dedicate it to God as the Israelites devoted their first fruits to Him in ancient days." And the children showed by their answers that they understood, and had taken the lesson to heart. I was speaking in a great school, itself standing in a slum, but upon what, as I happened to know, was once a garden. That old garden, to my mind, seemed still to exist, but transfigured. It was living again in those children's souls, and the holy doctrine taught to them in that school from day to day, was the seed of the precious fruitage that would come later on to ennoble and bless their lives. That spiritual garden is far finer even than the garden of trees and flowers which it has replaced. The ideal lives on mightily when material things have perished.

Well, I carried my thought away with me, and I offer it to you, my present hearers, to-day. We have all of us, old as well as young, a garden within us, which we are asked to tend and to keep for God's sake; and the ideal for ever triumphs over the actual. We keep our

THE GARDEN OF THE SOUL 97

peaceful Pentecost undeterred by the thunders of war ;[1] we desert the noisy world for a moment to listen to the message from the romantic world that passed into the silence ages ago. But—and this is my chief point— we have all a garden in the soul, a potentially rich heritage given to the poorest.

How often a garden meets us in our religious lore ! The paradise of our first parents was a garden ; and a garden will be the universal Paradise hereafter. " The Garden of Eden "—that is the Jewish name for the Heaven that is to be, and the mystics picture it as filled with beautiful trees and fragrant with the breath of a thousand flowers. The love-drama in the Bible, called the Song of Solomon, has for its chief scene a garden, into which the lovers go down hand in hand to see whether the vine is budded and the pomegranates are in flower. For the Prophets, too, a garden is the type of the most exquisite delights. Zion, comforted in her sorrow, is to be " the garden of the Lord," and the joyous heart of the penitent, taken back by the Father, is a garden cleansed and refreshed by the vivifying rain. " God," cries the Seer, " shall satisfy thy soul in dry places, and thou shalt be like a watered garden." And here he almost seems to anticipate the modern idea, and to find a garden in the soul.

But the tendance of the soul as man's chief treasure is a thought which our ancestors clearly voiced. One of our most cherished prayers gives expression to it. " My God, the soul which Thou hast given me is pure. Thou hast breathed it into me, and wilt one day take it from me, to give it back to me thereafter. As long as the soul is within me I will do homage to Thee, O Master of all things, Lord of all souls." This prayer we recite in the course of the Morning Service, but our fathers of olden

[1]Preached in 1917.

times were accustomed to repeat it as soon as they awoke each day. It pledged them to keep the spirit, taken from them in sleep, and given back in their waking hour, pure and undefiled by the world, to hold it for God until He should take it once more in the final sleep. And so urgent was this duty that, translating " homage " by penitence, they closed their prayer with a humble confession of their sins, so that the day might begin with a clean record.

Let us imitate their piety. Let us cultivate the garden of the soul, bringing from it every day a new gift for God in the loving service with which we fill each day's story. For the ordinance of the First-fruits is an ordinance for ever; it is given " for all our generations and all our dwelling places." Our homes may lie far away from Palestine; we may not own an inch of land; but the ancient command stands fast always, for it is addressed to the undying, changeless spirit which is in every man; it is concerned with the fundamental things of life. " How can I give back my soul to God in the state in which He gave it to me? "—that, says an old Jewish teacher, is the one supreme question that the good man will be always asking, and trying to solve. In one sense it cannot be so given back. The soul enters the world unspotted by the world; it knows no thought of sin, knows not the meaning of it. But as the years multiply its innocence fades. And yet has it necessarily deteriorated? Is it necessarily defiled? No. It knows good and evil; but with the knowledge comes conscience, and its ennobling sense of responsibility. Temptation has scorched and seared it; but the scars may be honourable, tokens of battles bravely and gloriously fought. So we may give back the soul to God pure as He gave it to us, but with a positive purity rather than the negative one with which it came to us, splendid with a beauty plucked from the ugliness of sin, filled with a music wrung from the discords of the world. God gives us the soul as a garden ; He plants it, as He did the primitive Eden, with all manner of beautiful trees. It is for us so to tend our divine domain that it shall yield fruit worthy of the Master's acceptance. This—and this only —is what life essentially is and means.

What shall that fruit be ? The Israelite of old was enjoined to bring "a new gift" to the sanctuary on Pentecost. What shall the new gift be that we ourselves offer to God with every new day ? The ancient ordinance itself tells us. Recognition of God as the source of all one's blessings, gratitude, humility submission—these duties the command to lay his Firstfruits on the altar taught the Israelite in ancient days ; and these it may teach us in our turn. The duty of sharing, too—of sharing our blessings with those unblest, of denying ourselves some precious thing so that impoverished lives may be made less poor. For the Firstfruits did not belong to their so-called possessor ; he gave them up so that they might deck the sanctuary and gladden other hearts.

But to us, as Jews, and not as men and women only, the lesson comes home with its strong appeal. Under the beautiful symbolism of the Rabbins our second text is made to yield a new meaning—the lover in the Song of Solomon is God. He it is that goes down into the garden to see the green plants of the valley, to see whether the vine has budded, and the pomegranates are in flower. He goes down into the garden of the great world, to see how Israel is faring—Israel, the " scion of his planting "— to see whether His people are putting forth the fair blossoms of goodness ; He goes down into the synagogues to see whether they are filled with worshippers, whether they are made fragrant with the incense of prayer, even as the vine is laden with the budding grape, and is sweet with perfume; He goes down into the schoolhouses to see whether they are thronged with children, beautiful as the pomegranate-flower. So the Rabbins. Does not the allegory touch our own consciences? To-day God has come down among us, as He came down of old on Mount Sinai—not to make a covenant, however, but to ask about its fulfilment. How shall we answer that question? What of Israel, God's chosen, impervious to the grandeur of its mission? What of His House, visited by a few week by week, while the many pass by on their worldly quest? What of the children who, graced with the higher knowledge and its resulting virtues, should make the home fair as the garden of the Lord, but are taught instead to put their faith in worldly prizes rather than to set their hope in God and in the spiritual triumph of their people? No; not to make a covenant has God come down, but to ask about its fulfilment, and to exhort us to renew it. For on every Pentecost the day of Sinai comes round again. It offers us once more the old compact, reiterates the old commands, affords the old glimpses of the Divine. Shall we reject the gracious chance—be heedless of the inspiring Voice—and write ourselves down as degenerate?

No; we will be true to our high calling—worthy of it. It shall not be said of us among the Gentiles that while we have diligently laboured in earthly fields, sometimes, indeed, for the world's great good, we have failed to "tend our own vineyard." We will give God our faith, our trust, our service, in return for His choice of us, His trust in us.

Well, these are simple things to fill our garden with—simple materials out of which to fashion our lives; but they are the best. They are the best because God loves them best: " I dwell with him that is of a humble and lowly spirit "—so cries " the High and Lofty One that inhabiteth eternity." They are the best because they are expressed in the one word " love "—love to God and man ; and love, the gentlest of all virtues, is likewise the mightiest of them all. After the thunder the " still, small voice," with its promise of blessing—that it is which heartened the terrified people at Sinai in olden days, and that it is which tranquillises and comforts men in every age and in every place. Love—it is the one choice fruit with which to deck and scent the garden of the soul.

A HAPPY NEW YEAR

(Rosh Hashanah)

"Grant us a happy new year."

A quaint ceremony marked the advent of this solemn Festival last evening in those Jewish homes in which old-time observances are still cherished. Immediately after the Kiddush, or Prayer of Sanctification, the master of the house, dipping some sweet fruit into honey, distributed it to the various members of the family, who, before partaking of it, offered up the prayer, "May it be Thy will, O Lord, to grant us a happy, a honey-sweet year!" The act expressed in picturesque form the desire which inevitably dominates the heart confronted with the unknown changes and chances of a new year. So potent is that desire that it finds frequent utterance in the liturgy, notably in the sentence from the impressive prayer of the *Abinu Malkenu*, recited this morning, which I have taken as my text:—" O, our Father, our King, grant us a happy new year."

It is a very natural petition. Happiness is the desire of every living creature, certainly of every human creature. And that boon we long for most intensely, ask for most earnestly, at a time like this, when the old year, with its troubles and disappointments, still casts its shadow upon us, and the new year, with its uncertainties, fills us with misgiving, if not with anxiety. And even if the old year is leaving not sombre, but pleasant memories with us, even if it is sinking from sight, not in shadows, but in a roseate glow, our longing,

A HAPPY NEW YEAR

our prayer, is still the same. The happiness we have, we would keep ; we would carry with us the joys which the passing year has brought us to the very last day of the year just begun.

Yes ; it is all very natural. I would not have this cry for happiness struck out of our Festival Service, though it may seem to be a somewhat sordid utterance with which to greet a sacred period—a period which is to give the soul its great opportunity. For happiness is not only the chief desire of men ; it is what the Father of all men desires for them. It is by happiness that they live, and by happy living that they serve. "The dead cannot praise God," cries the Psalmist ; no, nor can the miserable, whom misery inevitably stunts and maims. They cannot praise Him, or work for Him. Joy—we need it for our own sakes, for God's sake. That is the characteristic and the consistent doctrine of Judaism.

Happiness, then ; let us go on praying for it. And yet not for happiness unqualified. We must interpret our terms, and interpret them rightly. The lower happiness, provided it hurts neither ourselves nor anyone else in the getting or the keeping of it—this we may not improperly ask for. A happy new year—even if we understand the word "happy" thus, we may go on framing the wish both for ourselves and those we love. But let us beware of too narrow an interpretation of our terms, of clinging to the lower interpretation to the exclusion of the higher. Here is the danger. It lies not in asking for earthly boons, for the full purse, for the pleasures of the senses, for the realisation of worldly hopes and ambitions, but in asking for them only. When we speak of a happy new year, and make it the object of our most passionate supplications, we mean—too many of us—a good year, in the familiar and conventional sense of the expression ; a good year, in the moral sense, we do not mean. And yet that should form part, and the chief part, of the purport of our request, if this holy season is to do its work, and if we are not to put ourselves out of court for petitioning the high tribunal of Heaven in a selfish spirit. We do not need a New Year's Day or a penitential period in order to set our hearts longing for worldly boons; they will do that of their own accord. We want it for something that we may easily miss without the help and inspiration of these solemn days. We want it to inflame our yearning for the real joys of life, to help us to see that they *are* real—joys which it is worth all our prayers, all our souls' energies, to win and retain.

A happy new year—let us give the phrase a higher meaning, then, and, by happiness, mean blessedness—the blessedness that lies in the consciousness of self-fulfilment, of having played our part on our little stage worthily—the consciousness of having lived. A happy new year—let us mean by it a prosperous year indeed, a year in which our work for God has thriven—that Heavenly work which, finding its materials chiefly in our daily work and its scene amid the commonplace incidents of the daily life, we have been set on this earth to do.

And then as to the sources of happiness. There are people who live on the sunny side of life, and who ask little more of the coming year than that it shall be as bright as the dying one. But there are others, with experiences far otherwise, whose one hope is that the new year may help them to forget the old. Will their hope be realised? Who shall say? But certain it is that if it is to be realised, they must go forth into the new year with a sane outlook and a high courage. They would be happy; do they always remember that the springs of happiness are not outside us, but within us?

We long for better days, forgetting that to-day may be one of them if we will only make it so; if instead of pining for what is not we take what we have and distil peace and joy from it. Happiness, someone has said, is always the possession of other people. Is it not true? Other lives, which we see only on the surface, and whose joyousness may be deceptive, become our standards of well-being. How foolish we are! We may have far more reasons for gladness than those have whom we envy; but we will not see them—we will not look for them. And our punishment comes in the hour when the sources from which we might have drawn happiness perish. Health, love, intellectual delights, the very power to enjoy—these we only learn to value when they have been taken from us. So let us be wise. We ask God to give us new things; let us rather ask Him to let us keep the things we have and help us to cherish them better than we have done.

A happy new year—we want the coming year to be not only happy, but new. Even the most fortunate would like it to be better than the old year, good as it may have been. We would all like it to make us richer, to end our troubles, to give us ease instead of pain, "a garland," in the Prophetic words, "for ashes, the oil of joy for mourning." We would have life make a new start for us. Again a natural desire. But let us not reserve all our fervour for it. Instead of only asking God to banish our troubles let us ask Him for help to bear them, for insight to recognise them as part of a righteous, a beneficent dispensation. Some of us have to struggle with adverse worldly circumstance, with poverty, with disappointment, with failure; others have to suffer in body or in mind; others again, more stricken still, have to witness the suffering of those they love better than themselves. What is the right prayer for them to offer? Is it not a prayer that they may be delivered from these afflictions in the sense of being saved from their destructive influences, from the shipwreck of faith and courage—a prayer that the new year may be new in the sense of bringing the afflicted a new power to turn his woes to good account, to accept them with submission, to make them the materials out of which to build a braver and nobler life? For who of us can see what is best for him? Only God can. What we call misfortunes He may intend as blessings. "A new year," say the Rabbins, "should be the starting-point of a new life." To all, to sorrowing and joyous alike, the admonition is addressed. The dawning year must be better than the old—morally better—if we are to vindicate our right to it. It must find us with a quickened conscience, with higher ideals of service, with stronger determination to fight God's battle with our own wayward hearts.

A happy new year—both happy and new, it will, we hope, be a *year*, a full year. We would see it end as we have seen it begin. Let no one quarrel with the desire. For by the very craving for life we live. Let life cease to be desirable, and we slowly perish—the founts that feed our vitality dry up, and God is robbed of His instruments. But can that be a full year that is only full of days? Is not something else needed to complete it—the wish, the resolve, namely, of those who live through it to be God's instruments, to make every day of the 350 or 60 yield its precious, its rightful harvest? And if we form that resolution, then our petition will assuredly be granted. The year will be given to us; it will be given to us because we give it to God and man. It will be a full, because a fruitful and a blessed, year— a year of high endeavour even for the lowliest, a year of glorious service even for the greatest. And this it will be whatever its actual duration. For whom it will run its course to the end, for whom, on the contrary, its career will be cut short, we know not. Our times are in God's hands. But this we do know that complete it will be, seeing that its days have been consecrated days —consecrated to the best conception of life that we can form. And so let us pray as of old, " Grant us, O Lord, a happy new year." For the prayer only needs to be nobly interpreted in order to find the best of all answers.

ONCE IN THE YEAR

(Kol Nidre)

" And this shall be an everlasting statute unto you, to make atonement for the children of Israel for all their sins once in the year."—Leviticus xvi., 34.

Speaking on the recent Day of Memorial, I asked my hearers to consider what they were going to do with the new year just begun. Now, standing as we do, on the threshold of this most solemn of days, I put a like question to you, " What are you going to do with it ? " It is in the hope of helping you to answer that question aright that I preach this sermon.

" Once in the year "—are we, then, to think that this holy day, wondrous as is its power, alone brings absolution to the sinner, that the solemn period, of which it is the climax, alone finds the Supreme seated on His high throne and dispensing justice to His human subjects ? Our ancient teachers, though they emphasise the high importance of the penitential season, take care to warn us against so erroneous a notion. " Man," they say, " is judged every day, every hour." For every deed of ours is automatically registered in the everlasting books ; it weaves itself into the fabric of our lives, and helps to fashion our destinies for good or for evil. And on the other hand, the power of moral recovery is given to every human soul, not at this season or that, but at all times, as the inalienable attribute of its humanity. Weak under temptation, it is yet strong enough to rise out of its moral wreck. Nor is any term

ONCE IN THE YEAR

set to the exercise of that power. " As long as the soul is within its earthly frame"—so run the familiar words of our Atonement liturgy—"God waits for man's repentance."

Why, then, this " Once in the year " ? The answer is that there is a magic in this time of grace after all, an efficacy in the Day of Atonement which no other day can be said to possess. True, there are occasions in life—crises in experience, of which the date cannot be calculated beforehand—which have at least an equal might. Some overwhelming sorrow may turn the heedless or rebellious soul to God, even as it has been known to whiten the head in a single night. The earliest cry of his firstborn may recall a man to himself, and redeem him. Or from the shadow of death, wonderfully put back on the dial, there may emerge the light of a new and a nobler life. But these are rare incidents, upon which we cannot count. This sacred day, on the contrary, comes every year with unfailing regularity, bringing the same message, making the same appeal, proffering the same opportunities. And just because it comes so regularly, just because it is a consecrated day, set apart for one holy purpose and that alone, it has this almost miraculous power. Now, if ever, we are judged, because now, if ever, we judge ourselves ; now, if ever, we shall atone, for the Day, with its sacred character, its impressive rites, its moving associations, summons us to repentance with voice unique in its eloquence.

" To make atonement once in the year "—does this necessarily mean that atonement is sure ? Does it mean that the influences of Kippur are automatic, irresistible, that no one can go from its observance unmoved, unshriven ? Would that we might think so ! But we know that, while to some the Day brings healing and peace, to others it may come in vain. A few hours spent in God's house, a few prayers repeated, or listened to, with more or less devotion—and that is all. A ripple on the surface of experience, but the low-lying depths, which hold the springs of the spiritual life, unstirred, untouched. Such is the story of too many of us from year to year! But let us not be too pessimistic. It is something to get men and women to break for once the round of the worldly life—something to bring them near to God for an hour, or even a moment or two. Who knows what blessing even this brief experience may not leave behind it, what gracious seed it may not sow in hearts all unconscious of the gift, to germinate and to ripen in the after years? Let us welcome here to-night "him that is far off as well as him that is near," the penitent and the devout who long to grasp the hem of God's robe as He passes by, but those, too, with un-awakened soul, who will not come here again till another Day of Atonement brings them. Who knows? Another and a humbler day may dawn for some of them, when it will be seen that something of the Divine has crept into their hearts, and been kept and nourished there after all.

But may we not hope for more than this? May we not hope that some of those who have never yet adequately responded to the Day's message may be receptive to it now? This is the point to which I would direct your thoughts. Even if Kippur has done little for you in former years, it may still do much for you this year if you will only put it to right use. Once more, then, I ask, what are you going to do with it? And do not be deterred from considering this question by the difficulty that meets you on the very threshold. Do not say, "What can one short day avail to retrieve a life, to change its whole direction and character?" It may do much. It may stir the will-power that alone is needed to plant your feet on the higher way. "One poor day!

Remember whose, and not how short it is. It is God's day. A lavish day! One day, with life and heart, is more than time enough to find a world." So the poet makes Columbus speak on the eve of his great discovery. May we not echo the cry? One day " with life and heart," with hope and courage and energy, will lead us also to our new world—the new world of nobler ideals and finer strivings.

And the first step towards this realisation of the Day's purpose is prayer—prayer which, born of hope and courage, gives them back to us strengthened and increased—casts us down at God's feet as before the Lord of our lives—those lives which are ours only that we may make them His. If there are any here to-night who have never really prayed since that time, long past, when they stood as children at their mother's knee, I entreat them to begin to do so now. It is no hard thing to ask for. Our Atonement service includes petitions and meditations which must needs find their way to every heart, so sublime are they, so human. Quite recently I had to minister to one of our congregants as he lay on his deathbed. He indicated to me some passages in a book which he desired me to read to him. He had evidently read them to himself many times before in his sore sickness. " How beautiful they are! " he said when I had finished. The book was the one you have before you now—the Prayer Book for this Atonement Day. If those prayers are suited to the needs of the dying, they are equally suited to the needs of the living, for those, happily, still in the full flush of health and vigour. For we are all—even the strongest of us— dying men and women, and it is by getting ready for death that we live best. Therefore, I say, try to pray, even though you are out of practice, even though you do not feel prayerful, yes, even though you hardly feel that you have anyone to pray to. Perhaps while you are musing the fire will kindle ; prayer may beget prayerfulness ; some secret fount within you will be unlocked ; some sight of God be granted to you. Wrestle with your own hearts, your apathy, your feebleness of will. In the words of the rough mariners to Jonah, as he lay asleep during the storm in the sides of the heaving ship, I say to each slumbering soul, " Up, call upon thy God."

But prayer is only the first step. Suppose you do not succeed in your effort after prayerfulness, still the fortunes of the Day are very far from hopeless. For repentance is essentially an affair of the character— " a fierce inner warfare," as an old Jewish teacher phrases it. It is a fight, in which communion with God will powerfully help us, but which the soul must wage for itself with all its resources. Nor is there any discharge in that war. You may have no definite religion, but still you must take your part in the battle. For, in the last resort, you owe that duty to your outraged selves, your sullied manhood or womanhood ; you owe it likewise to your fellow men, whose conscience you have offended, or whom you may have incited by your example to sin against the august law of righteousness, written on the fleshly tablets of the human heart. With God every transgressor who truly believes in Him must be consciously reconciled. His forgiveness must be asked for—forgiveness for revolt against Him, for the dishonour which every offence offers to His holy presence. But for everyone of us, whether profound believer or not, the moral law is a sacred thing—sacred by our own admission, overt or silent ; and we must expiate our violation of it in humility and sorrow if we would be at peace with ourselves, if we would be reconciled with the God in our own souls.

But—and here we reach the supreme task to which

we should dedicate this day—in order to effect this expiation we must recognise our shortcomings—come to close grips with our moral selves. This is the crucial point. The great reason why the Day of Atonement so often misses its purpose is that we do not see that we have anything to atone for. Our own characters are those which we understand least. We gloze over our failings, refusing to believe—honestly refusing no doubt—that they are serious, or even that they are failings at all. Or we make excuses for them, pleading the strength of temptation or the force of circumstances. Or we cite our good qualities as a sufficient set-off to our shortcomings. What a multitude of sins charity, for example, and not a particularly lavish charity either, is expected to cover with its ample robe! " I don't pretend to be a saint "—so runs the familiar formula— " I have led a man's life, it is true, but at any rate I am not guilty of the transgressions that many men commit." Or our extenuating plea is general usage. " What everybody does is good enough for me; why should I be better than my neighbour? "—so we argue. As though the truth were not the very reverse. " Where there is no man," our old teachers exhort us, " strive to be a man "; the cause of righteousness needs you— needs you all the more urgently because there are so few to uphold it. General laxity of practice or opinion, far from lulling us into acquiescence, ought to sting us into protest. If the world condones certain deviations from the path of old-fashioned rectitude, if it has left off condemning dubious business methods, detraction and backbiting, loose living, the unhealthy play, the unclean novel, then it is for us to say " I will clear myself of all complicity in such abominations, though in doing so I stand alone, and I have to pay the price in derision and worldly loss."

This is the temper which we must strive to arouse in ourselves now as the essential condition of atonement. On a memorable occasion a few years ago our King, jealous for the maintenance of the high position of his people among the nations, uttered the stirring cry "Wake up, England." To us all, as we stand under the sacred shadow of Kippur, a like call is addressed, "Wake up, Conscience." It is the most vital of all appeals. It concerns not our merely material interests, but our spiritual, our eternal well-being; it touches the things with which is intimately bound up the success or the failure of our lives. It is the most royal of all calls, for it comes from our *Divine* Sovereign, God. Hear it, my brethren, I beseech you. Awake—awake to a recognition of realities, to a sense of your true moral position, to an adequate appreciation of the solemnity of conduct, to a juster discrimination between rectitude and transgression. Awake to self-understanding. Pray to God with all your hearts; seek His pardon for the past, strength to do better in the future. But pray, too, that He may open your eyes, so that you may realise the need of pardon and amendment, that you may see yourselves as you really are, in all your weakness and strength, careless of the destiny of your immortal souls, but endowed with the unquenchable potencies of moral recovery, of repentance and redemption. So shall this day accomplish its glorious work. This year, and this once in the year, shall you make true and full atonement before the Lord your God.

PLANNING THE NEW LIFE

(NEILAH)

"He hath shewn thee, O man, what is good; and what doth the Lord require of thee, but to do justly, and to love mercy, and to walk humbly with thy God."—MICAH vi., 8.

THE planning of the new life is the essential task brought to us by the Atonement Day. With all its moving associations and its impressive worship, Kippur will do little for us if it has not impelled us to this momentous enterprise. The new life! What it ought to be must obviously depend upon what the old life has been. And that varies with the individual. No preacher can hope to make his practical counsel exactly fit the needs of each separate soul. The heart, moreover, knows its own bitterness, its own penitent regrets, its own shortcomings. Nor can anyone say what is amiss with a life, in what it requires to be changed and amended, save the man or the woman that is living it.

And yet practical suggestions of some kind must be offered if the exhortations of the pulpit at so solemn a juncture are to attain their maximum effectiveness. There are defects of character and conduct which, though many happily escape them, are sufficiently common to be made the basis of the preacher's appeal. He knows enough about human nature to discern those defects; and, discerning them, he is bound to take them into account in his call to the new and the better life. Many miss the great opportunity that Kippur brings them because they do not know how to begin. A practical word might help them. Surely it is a duty to say that word.

The new life—if we have not planned it already, it is time that we began the task. The shades of evening are beginning to close in upon us; the Day is nearing its end. Soon, with all its unique possibilities, it will be a thing of the past. And then the world will claim us, and the old round of work and play, of striving and feeling, will begin over again. Is it to be quite the old round? Or something a little better and nobler? Are we satisfied to go on altogether as we have done hitherto? Or is there not something, here and there, that we would improve if we could? Are we quite satisfied with our moral story as it repeats itself from year to year? Or are we conscious of a certain distrust of it, a not inglorious discontent?

There must be some among you who know that feeling; and to these I speak, proferring in all earnestness and affection such guidance as I am capable of, trusting that even at this advanced stage of the Day's solemnities I may be privileged to aid their endeavour after the better way. And perhaps no passage in the whole range of Scripture can more effectively help me in the purpose I have set myself than the words of the text. The Bible contains many a summary of human duty, but none more comprehensive than this. "He hath shewn thee O man, what is good; and what doth the Lord require of thee, but to do justly, and to love mercy, and to walk humbly with thy God." The very form of this memorable utterance is striking. The Prophet has been besieged with suggestions of specious methods of reconciliation with God by those who, with more or less dubious sincerity, profess a desire to atone. But he brushes them all aside. "Away," he cries, "with such far-fetched expedients. The means of reconciliation are not far off: they are within you. God has shewn thee, O man, what is good—written the message in thy conscience and thy soul. And what doth He require of thee? Only that rectitude of purpose, that loving kindness, that lowly attitude towards Him, which are enjoined by the elementary dictates of every heart. Here and nowhere else, lies the path which thou must tread if thou wouldst go back to God. It is the old path made new by the new spirit. The new life is the old life, lived, it may be, on the lower heights and amid the familiar scenes, but transformed and transfigured in the light of a nobler purpose.

To us, in our turn, the ancient formula is offered. It has lost none of its force and application after five-and-twenty centuries. If we would rebuild the edifice of the moral life, we cannot do better than take the Prophet's scheme for our guidance. To do justly— the English is inadequate; righteous living, stern self-conquest, the subjugation of ignoble impulse—this is what the words imply. Here is a whole continent of duty presenting itself to those who seek after amendment. Justice to our fellowmen, justice also to ourselves. To our fellowmen, honest and equitable treatment in every relation of life; for ourselves that cleanness in thought and deed which reverences the divinity, the manhood, in our own souls. Justice to ourselves—to every part of ourselves—the effort after self-realization, not by the lower methods only, but by the higher ones too— for this we are asked. We are not required to shun worldly delights, but to purify them. We are asked, not to starve any side of our manifold nature, but while heeding the claims of the flesh so to satisfy them that they may minister to the higher life, the life that beseems us as sons of God. Here surely is something for us to think about, for those especially whose lot is cast in the busy, sordid world, for men with their special temptations to overstep the line of rectitude and purity. I know those temptations; I know, too, how many of you daily, almost hourly, fight and vanquish them with heroic persistence. I do not ignore that heroism, but honour it, when I say, Let it grow; let it find the widest imitation.

But to men and women both the appeal is made. There is room for a stronger resistance to unworthy instincts—to ill-temper, to envy and jealousy, to harsh words and yet harsher judgments. There is room for a more strenuous effort to be just to those about us— to spare those with whom we come into daily contact as employers or servants, as acquaintances or friends. There is room for justice, for forbearance, for self-abnegation in our attitude towards the hearts we love best—hearts living under our roof-tree, sharing our very lives. Along this way, too, lies the new life, fashioned out of commonplace materials, but the sane and the sweet and the heavenly life nevertheless.

To do justly, but to love mercy too. This is the second item in the gracious programme. Can we say that it has lost its meaning to-day? I think not. It is an age of humanity, of a quicker compassion, perhaps, than that of olden times. But is that compassion quite as profound, as real, as it seems? Men hate to hear of cruelty and suffering; would that the feeling found expression in a more self-sacrificing effort to cure those ills! The way of improvement for not a few of us lies in the direction of a truer altruism, of a greater willingness to forgo in order that others may have, to suffer in order that others may suffer less. Our hearts are sensitive enough to the great human tragedy; what is needed is not so much the self-pity that comes of that sensitiveness, as the commiseration for the victims which makes it impossible for us to be still under the thought of their anguish, which compels us to do our utmost, at whatever cost of personal loss or inconvenience or pain, to relieve it. This, it seems to me, is one of the most crying needs of our day, one of the most obvious forms that our penitent efforts should take. The Prophet, whose words we read this morning, felt the want keenly in regard to his own times. He is speaking of the acceptable fast, the acceptable atonement. "Would you fast to good purpose," he says, "then feed the hungry; would you truly afflict your souls, then take the afflicted souls among your fellowmen —those who have gone down, or have always been kept down, in the world's great struggle—and satisfy their dire need. Ah, my friends, is the exhortation superfluous even to-day ? Can we truthfully say that we are doing our duty by these hapless fellow creatures of ours ? Is not the gulf between their sorrow and our joy, their want and our abundance, their distress and our well-being, wider than it need be ? Do we truly *love* mercy, as the text tells us that we ought—love the very virtue so as to give up all else for it—or do we not love ourselves better ?

And then there is the third requirement of the Prophet —to walk humbly with our God. Again humility; it is an essential of all the Prophetic ideals of goodness. None of us can successfully plan the new life who has not that saving quality in his heart. On the Day of Atonement in ancient times the High Priest, discarding his golden vestments, ministered in the inmost shrine of the Temple in simple robes of white, symbol of the lowly, child-like temper that must go with penitence. The lesson is eternal. We must be humble in the sight of God, conscious of our weakness, full of trust in His help, submissive to His decrees, if the future is to be brighter than the past. Prosperity and adversity alike shall find us staunch. For "out of the mouth of the Most High cometh there not evil for good?" But the Prophet's words are assuredly susceptible of a larger interpretation. The lowly life includes the simple life—a phrase often used to justify many a grotesque experiment, and the favourite mark for cheap and vulgar ridicule. Divested of all extravagant meaning, it still retains its potent appeal. There is room for simpler living in our new scheme. We live—many of us—too luxuriously in these days, to the detriment of the physical, to the still graver detriment of the moral, life. Is it not time that we began to practise a greater self-denial? The new man and the new woman that amendment is to create must be braced up in character; and if this be true, where shall we look for means more effectual than the curtailment of the excessive self-indulgence which is the bane of the age? To have but few desires ungratified, to have the power of self-denial atrophied by disuse, is to be morally unstrung, to be unregenerate even though every other infirmity seem removed. The self-indulgent life is unsound at its very roots.

But the text, you will observe, asks for the lowly temper as a special attitude towards the Almighty. "To walk humbly with thy God"—so the Prophet phrases it. What he prescribes is, in effect, the religious spirit, the religious life. Justice, mercy, humility—yes; but these virtues inspired and dominated by a consciousness of the Unseen. Here, again, and to its last word, the Prophetic formula holds good for our day. Righteousness—that undoubtedly is the final end and aim of existence; but we are also told, that, while that end is attainable without religion, it is most surely and most completely attainable with it. The man who would live the good life will have the best chance of realising his desire if he lives that life in the Divine company, and under its potent inspiration.

And the details of that life? Well, the Prophet warns us that they do not consist necessarily or entirely in outward observance. Not sacrifices, he cries, but sacrifice; not calves of a year old, but the dedication of the heart and the spirit. I would like to see more observance than actually obtains; for, soberly and rightly used, it is a religious safeguard. The old Rabbins did not talk at random when they praised the excellence of making a fence to the Law. But let that be. A minimum of conformity, for such as cannot render more. Only let it be sincere and fervent. Let us try by some settled practice to get into constant touch with higher and deeper realities than those that go to the making of the ordinary daily experience. A simple prayer in the morning, asking for help in the day's battle, another at night, atoning for the day's defeats—this, at least, let us insist upon for ourselves. We are all able to offer that recognition of the needs of our souls, that homage to the King of kings.

And yet something more. There is need of a strengthening of the religious life in other directions. There are the children; might not more be done for their spiritual well being? Devoted parents you all are, brimful of love for your boys and girls, ready to make any sacrifice to ensure their happiness. Might you not attach a higher meaning to that happiness, and assign a larger place among the factors of it to religious training? Connected with this Synagogue there are several means to this end—weekly Religion Classes, Sabbath Services for the young, the Confirmation rite, with all its vast and solemn significance for character and conduct. Might not these salutary aids to the religious life be more largely used ? Instead of neglecting, ought we not to cultivate more diligently every opportunity of providing a corrective to the worldliness and the materialism of the age ? And can we confer a greater boon upon the children we love so dearly, or establish a stronger claim to their affectionate recollection of us when we have passed beyond these voices than by training them to that humble walking with God which will keep their hearts pure and true, their courage high, their souls serene, amid all the changes and chances of the after-years ?

But if this happy fate is to be theirs, we must first ensure it for ourselves. If the children are to walk with God, the parents must live in fellowship with Him. The good life—this is what you are asked to plan and to found here and now, as the supreme and indispensable task of this holy Day ; the life that is good, not because it aims at an impossible saintliness, an extreme self-renunciation, but simply because it is better than the old has been. The good life, which you may all try to live, seeing that it is to be fashioned out of the homely materials that strew your daily path ; the life built up out of rectitude and loving kindness and lowly submission to your Divine Maker. Oh, my friends, even now, at this closing hour of the Day, you may achieve the Day's great purpose, if you will only realise its solemnity, and, casting yourselves upon God's merciful help, pray for strength to perform it. May that mercy and that strength be vouchsafed to you ! **Amen.**

THE SUCCAH
(TABERNACLES)

" And there shall be a tabernacle for shade in the day-time from the heat, and for a refuge and for a covert from storm and from rain."—ISAIAH iv., 6.

ONE of the distinctive emblems of the present Festival is the leaf-crowned hut which is raised and decked in honour of the Holyday. What purpose is the Tabernacle intended to subserve? The Pentateuch never explicitly sets it forth. The reason for the ordinance it gives, but not the moral or religious lessons it was to teach. The Tabernacle, it says, is to recall the huts in which God caused the Israelites to dwell when they were wandering in the desert. But it says no more. When the command had been obeyed, when the Tabernacle had been built and dwelt in, and the wandering life of the liberated tribes duly remembered—what then? What had religion—what had righteousness—gained by the ceremony and the reminiscence? Scripture does not directly answer the question. And so, as in the case of other Biblical enactments, we are thrown back upon inference and conjecture. Nor need we travel far in order to find the explanation of which we are in search.

It is a twofold explanation. In the very first place his festal booth was meant to remind the Israelite that he had sprung from humble beginnings—a wholesome reminder indeed! He had gained the Promised Land; he was a free man living under his own laws; he had built goodly houses and dwelt therein. Might his heart be lifted up at the thought of his good fortune? No.

He had not always been prosperous or free or at peace. He was once a slave, a landless, homeless wanderer. This hut, in which he was commanded to dwell for a space, was, so to speak, a relic of that dark period in his life throughout which he had been upheld, and from which he had been ultimately delivered by the gracious mercy of God. And so it became for him, in the Prophet's words, " a tabernacle for shade in the daytime from the heat." In the fierce sunshine of prosperity, gratitude and humility laid their cooling touch upon his heart, and kept it pure and sweet.

That this is no fanciful interpretation of the Scriptural precept we may see from analogy. Again and again the Israelite is exhorted to keep in mind his former low estate. " Thou shalt remember that thou wast a slave in Egypt "—it is a reason used to point more than one great commandment :—the hallowing of the Sabbath and the observance of the Passover, but also the exercise of compassion towards the poor and the orphan and the friendless stranger. *Because* he had been a slave, ill-used and sad-eyed, whereas now he was free and glad-hearted, the Israelite was to be lowly always— lowly towards God and his fellow-men. Of the one he was to be a bond-man ; to the other he was to give his heart's best service. The past must never fade from his thoughts, if the present was to be duly sanctified. Never must " he scorn the base degrees by which he did ascend." He must think of them from time to time, and let the thought consecrate and transfigure his prosperity.

This was the message of the Tabernacle to the Israelite of old. Has it not a like significance for us ? Does it not exhort us, first of all, to keep alive the memory of Israel's ancient past, great though the gulf is by which both Time and circumstance have separated it from the present ? Is it because we " walk at liberty," physical and mental, because our religious thoughts are not, in every case, our remote ancestors' thoughts, nor our life-conditions theirs, that we are entitled to forget the old days or the old faith ? Shall we fail to remember that God is the God of our fathers—fail to thank Him for His old-time mercies to our race ?

Shall we not infuse humility, too, as well as gratitude into our religious life ? For we think we can make a new Judaism for ourselves, which, devoid of connexion with the historic past, shall yet be Judaism. It is a mistake. Every religion must grow if it is to live. But like the plant which the gardener's care and skill wonderfully brings to new developments and to greater perfection, it must preserve the broad characteristics of its original stock. Development—yes ; but it must be along Jewish lines, or we shall have a Judaism changed beyond recognition, with all its distinctive elements, all its vitality, refined away.

Nay, the Tabernacle pleads for itself and its kind. It asks us to keep the gracious symbols which, for many an age, and for myriads of souls, have preserved, as in a sheltering husk, the precious kernel of religious truth and idealism. For we are prone to think these old-world emblems out of date. They savour, we say, of the East, whereas our home is in Western lands. But is the contention sound ? The quaint Tabernacle, the citron and the palm, redolent as they are of the Orient, types of a life remote in more even than in time from our own, are, on that very account, justified. It is just by these startling anachronisms, these alluring incongruities, that Judaism lives. Omit them from its constituents, and you strike out much that differentiates it from other modern religions, and challenges the wonder and respect of the onlooker. When the Gentile inquirer comes to a Jewish place of worship to-day what is it that most powerfully impresses him with a sense not only of the charm, but of the vitality of Judaism? Is it not such symbols as the palm-branch and the Tabernacle, the manuscript of the Law, the Hebrew of the Service? These things make the past live for him over again. They are proofs for him of the imperishableness of the Jew's religion, of the imperishableness of Religion. Shall they be less mighty, less reverend, for the Jew himself, their hereditary possessor. Therefore, I say, let us be humble in the presence of our old-world Tabernacle and its companion symbols. "Let not the ordinance of the Succah," say the Rabbins, "be trivial in thy sight." We cannot afford to forget ancient times or ancient rites, lest we come to forget ourselves—our faith and our obedience, our humility and our gratitude, all that helps to make our best selves.

But the appeal of the Tabernacle is personal, as well as general. It has its significance for the individual soul. The Israelite was admonished to remember his former servitude, so that it might keep him chastened in spirit. May we not take the admonition to ourselves? Would it not be well if we—those of us, I mean, who have risen in the world from small beginnings—were to look back now and again, and let the retrospect chasten us? Are we not too much given to cover up the past as though it were shameful, when it has only been humble, to hide our early obscurity as though it were a crime? There are those who are distant to the kinsfolk who have not kept pace with them in the worldly march, who turn to the wall the portraits of the parents whose homely mien or garb tells of a sphere of life from which they themselves have long since emerged. It is a temper as harmful as it is despicable. How inevitably pride of this sort corrodes the character! There was once an excellent man, much respected in the community, who, by patient toil, had won his way to affluence from a condition of poverty. He began life as a hawker, and his rounds often led him through a London square, where there happened to be a block of stone, and upon this he was in the habit of resting when he was tired. In after-life, when he had prospered, he begged for that stone, and had it placed in his garden, so that he might have something to remind him of his early struggles. It was a fine act. We may well emulate the spirit that prompted it. Let the Succah be to us what that stone was for the good man of whom I have been speaking— a voice urging us to remember the past, the rock from which we have been hewn, and to make its very humbleness our strength, an inspiration to gratitude, to sympathy, to loving service of those who have never risen, or, worse still, have fallen never to rise again.

But, finally, our text speaks of "a refuge from the storm" as well as of "a shade from the heat." Here a further explanation of the Tabernacle meets us. Those huts in which the Hebrews sheltered in the desert— surely they were a welcome refuge from the physical discomfort incidental to their wandering life, a witness, moreover, to the saving protection of Almighty God. And is that protection less real in these latter days? Can the lapse of centuries—of thousands of years— diminish our need of the supporting Hand? Despite our progress and our accumulated knowledge we are no less human, no less weak and dependent, than our ancient fathers were. We are all, in the last resort, cast upon the Divine help and mercy. With that help we may do anything; without it we can do nothing.

The difficulty is to accustom ourselves to this thought —to make it a permanent part of our consciousness. All the circumstances of the age—its sharpened struggle for bare subsistence, its growing materialism, its increasing self-indulgence—are against it. The personal, the lower life looms ever larger on our horizon, God ever less. There is a Psalm—the twenty-seventh—in which the poet speaks with rapture of God hiding him in His tabernacle, where he is safe and at rest amid the troubles of this weary world, secure when a host encamps against him, protected, befriended when even his father and mother have forsaken him. That is how we, too, must feel if we are to be at peace amid life's turmoil, safe amid its perils, glad amid its sorrows. There is One to whom we can always turn for help and solace; there is a pavilion, made by no human hands, which will be "a refuge and a covert from storm and from rain." The Tabernacle which we deck in honour of this Festival is the visible symbol of that spiritual pavilion. In proportion to the strength of our belief in the all-sufficiency of the heavenly refuge, in the vanity of earthly strength and help, in the reality and the omnipotence of the Everlasting Arms, will be the tranquillity and the joy that come to bless our lives.

ON RAIN

(TABERNACLES)

> "And it shall come to pass that every one that is left of all the nations which came against Jerusalem shall go up from year to year to worship the King, the Lord of hosts, and to keep the Feast of Tabernacles. And it shall be that whoso goeth not up to worship upon them there shall be no rain."—
> ZECHARIAH xiv., 16, 17.

THE distinctive feature of the old liturgy for the present Festival is the prayer for rain. On the Great Hosana, as the seventh day is called, passionate petitions for rain impart a peculiar fervour to the Service, and they are followed by supplications of a like tenor on the eighth day of the Feast. To us, in these Northern lands, to pray for rain seems a strange thing; we should rather be inclined to pray that we may be spared it. We usually have a sufficiency of moisture for the needs of the country, more than a sufficiency for the comfort of the town. At least so it seems to us. But the prayer for rain on Tabernacles is a remnant, or a reminiscence, of the petitions which our fathers were wont to offer up when they had a land of their own. It is, moreover, a prayer for the present needs of Palestine—needs which may rightly have a place in the thoughts of our modern hearts side by side with the necessities of England. Nay, it is not a bad thing to be reminded that our supplications, for worldly boons at any rate, should be as unselfish as possible, that they should ask for the well being of others rather than for our own. This prayer for rain, as I have said, is a legacy from the past; it is as redolent of the East and the ancient life of the East as is the Succah by the side of the Synagogue which has been so charmingly decorated in honour of the

Festival, or as are the palm-branch and the citron which have lent a touch of old-world beauty to our Service this morning. Rain, at this Autumn-tide, is a dearly-coveted thing in Oriental lands. If it comes in abundance, next year's harvest is practically assured; if it fails, dearth and poverty and suffering are the lot of the people. The libation of water which marked the old Temple ritual on this Festival expressed the confidence of the worshippers that God, who holds the keys of the Heavenly storehouse, would not withold the precious gift of rain in the Autumn season just begun. And we read in the Talmud of pious men whose good offices would be invoked for intercession in time of drought. Their fervent prayers, fortified by their saintly life, were believed again and again to have opened the floodgates of the skies when the devout efforts of ordinary men had proved ineffectual. In the East, then, rain is a blessing; for the Israelite of old it was the very symbol of blessing. Our Prophet dreams of the day when even the nations who have fought against Jerusalem shall come and celebrate the Feast of Tabernacles in the holy city in token of their submission to the true God. Those, he declares, who refuse to perform this act of homage shall not share in the coming of the rain which is to reward the devout observance of the Festival. And, as we saw last Sabbath, Moses prays in his swan-song that his doctrine may drop as the showers upon the grass —be as fruitful in blessing as is the rain in its due season.

Rain—it is the most familiar of natural phenomena; but, on that very account, we miss much of its wondrousness. Literally distilled drop by drop by the Divine chemist whose laboratory is the universe—distilled from sea and lake and river while we are wholly unconscious of the mighty process—it is stored up in the great

ON RAIN

treasure-house above against the time when it is to descend and do its beneficent work upon the earth. We—especially we townsfolk—with our limited or sluggish imagination, are inclined to resent the coming of the rain. It interferes with our comfort and convenience; it forbids the outdoor enjoyment we have plannned for ourselves; it spoils our holiday and our clothes; it makes things generally moist and grimy and disagreeable. We forget what rain means not only for the parched fields and for the husbandman who draws his living from them, but also for what lies beneath the fields—the springs and streams underground, which must be replenished if the water supply of the town itself is not to be jeopardised. We forget that rain is not only the great fertiliser, but the great sanitarian. It sweetens and purifies the tainted atmosphere of the city; it cleanses the streets with a thoroughness which the most effective of Borough Councils, with their latest appliances, can only envy.

> How beautiful is the rain!
> After the dust and heat
> In the broad and fiery street,
> In the narrow lane,
> How beautiful is the rain!
>
> The farmer sees his pastures,
> And his fields of grain
> As they bend their tops
> To the numberless beating drops
> Of the incessant rain.
> He counts it as no sin
> That he sees therein
> Only his own thrift and gain.
> These, and far more than these,
> The poet sees.
> For his thought that never stops,
> Follows the water drops
> Down through chasms and gulfs profound
> To the dreary fountain head
> Of lakes and rivers underground,
> And sees them, when the rain is done,
> On the bridge of colours seven
> Climbing up once more to Heaven,
> Opposite the setting sun.

So cries the poet—shall we not say the true Seer? But we, just because we measure everything in Heaven and earth by the standard of our own personal and immediate needs, too often vote the rain tiresome, and wish we could be without it. How selfish and how short-sighted! For rain is as truly a blessing for us as it was for our Eastern ancestors who prayed for it so passionately as the most desirable of earthly boons.

And so we reach the lesson of the rain. Good lies hidden behind all the troubles and disappointments of life. The rain that stops that pleasant jaunt in the country upon which we had been counting brings well-being to a multitude. What is our disappointment compared with the fulfilment of their vital hopes? And so when some scheme of ours goes wrong, instead of dwelling upon our failure, and impeaching eternal wisdom because of it, let us rather fix our thoughts upon the wondrous way in which the infinitely larger design of God for the happiness of mankind is slowly moving on to its accomplishment. We are not the whole of creation, only a very tiny, a very microscopic item in it. Is it not well that we should remember the fact? Is it not well that our self-love, our tendency to be absorbed in our own concerns, should be rebuked, that we should learn to deem our little worries and troubles of small account in comparison with the welfare of the world? No; we are not everybody—far from it. There is the whole of humanity to be thought of and striven for; and in so thinking and striving, and not in struggling for our personal ends, or in moaning and rebelling when we fail to attain them, lies the great work of life. In an age when, despite the apparent growth of the socialistic idea, individualism in the lower sense— narrow self-seeking—seems to flourish more strongly than ever, when men are more intent upon getting something out of the body politic than upon giving up something for it, the lesson especially needs to be taken to heart.

But in our very failures and disappointments, as in the rain which blesses us when we are reviling it, there is the seed of good even for ourselves. What are our daily troubles but moral exercises that go to brace up character? The rain spoils your day's pleasure; but you bear the trial patiently. What untold strength generally do you obtain from your patience! And this is only an example. All our power to fight temptation, to triumph over the lower self, we get just out of our worries and troubles—out of the fortitude they call into play. We should be poor creatures indeed " if life were slumber on a bed of down." We should not even be happy ones, for the discontented mind will always find reasons for discontent. The story of the Princess and the crumpled roseleaf is for ever true. But moral creatures we certainly should not be. Why we should have to struggle for every foothold we gain on the upward way, I do not know; nor does my ignorance trouble me. There was once a King of Spain who said that if he had been consulted at the Creation, the world would have been a better place than it is. We may congratulate ourselves that his Majesty was not admitted to the heavenly councils. At any rate, since he was not we must take life as it is, and believe that it is ordered wisely and well. And seeing that revolt and repining are useless, it is the part of mere wisdom to bear the ills of life bravely, and to turn them to account by making them the instruments of moral uplifting.

In short let us go back to the old-fashioned way and believe that everything is for the best, not for a merely partial good, but for the best, the very best. We are inclined to give Providence only a qualified testimonial.

It is the besetting fault of the age. I remember once, at a time of prolonged rain, condoling with a poor working-man whose avocations took him much out of doors. " Sir," he replied, " I always think that we have the weather that is best for us." It was an admirable reply—no less admirable because it told against myself—a wiser utterance even than that of the invincible optimist who said that he knew of only two kinds of weather—good weather and better weather. For all the ordinances of God are equally good. If we distinguish two kinds of weather it is only because we do not see that the seemingly different kinds are one in the beneficence of their purpose, and that the flood and the snow and the storm, though they cause inconvenience, and something worse, to a fragment of human kind, are fruitful in benefits for humanity as a whole, that if they are attended by temporary drawbacks, the benefits which follow in their train are lasting. And the truth holds good throughout the entire realm of experience. We are only purblind mortals, groping our way along this earthly road. How much can we see of the vast cosmic scheme? Less than a fly can see of the globe on which it crawls. What can we finite beings know of the infinite mind of God? Good we behold coming out of His plan here and there; when we lose all trace of it shall we say that it is because the good does not exist? Shall we not rather ascribe it to our want of power to see the good? To our limited vision there seem to be many loose ends in the Divine handiwork. But let us be sure that the Hand that has spun the wondrous threads themselves will know how to weave them securely and beneficently into the great fabric of creation.

ABOUT TOYS
(Chanukah)
For Children

"There is a time for everything."—Ecclesiastes iii., 1.

This is the season for presents, but especially presents for the children. At this time of the year the toy-shops look their best. They are never so gay as in the dark days. The dolls wear their smartest frocks; the guns and the soldiers, that are warranted not to kill anybody, look more real than ever; the latest thing is to be seen in model engines and railway-trains and motor-cars. So I am going to talk to you this afternoon about toys. "About toys!" you will say; "what have toys to do with Chanukah?" Well, wait a little, and you will see.

I am very fond of toys. Though I gave up playing with them long ago I can still remember a certain little tin sword which I proudly wore when I was a child, and a drum given to me by a kind friend, which I broke almost as soon as I had it. Even now I like to look in at the toy-shop windows, and feast my eyes upon their treasures. And if this be so, what a delight a toy must be to a child! One of the most touching sights to be seen in London just now is the crowd of poor children outside the toy-shops. They are looking at fairyland, at a realm as lovely as fairyland, but just as forbidden. They can only look, and long. Not for them any of these magnificent things. I often stand and watch these poor children, and wish I had plenty of money so that I might say to the crowd of longing and wondering little ones, " Now, children, come in, and choose whatever you like best." Would that be a good thing for them ? I wonder.

" There is a time for everything," says the Wise Man in the text, and in that word " everything " he would certainly have included toys if he had known of them, as very likely he did. Toys are excellent things. When a child is ill a toy will make the long hours pass more quickly, and even help the sufferer to forget his pain. When a child is well, it will keep him in good temper ; it will rest him when he 's tired ; it will help him to do his work better. Yes, amusement is a good thing ; none of us could get on without it. But it is also true that we can have too much of a good thing, even of amusement. " There is a time for everything," which means that everything must have its turn—now play and now work, now toys and now lesson-books. Neither toys nor lessons alone can make us happy ; the two together do. Each sets off the other, and gives it its real value. Pleasure is good for a change, but only for a change ; it is not a good thing to have always. If we had it always, it would be pleasure no longer ; we should get tired of it. You can see that for yourselves. Cakes and puddings are very nice in their way ; but if you were forced to live on cakes and puddings you would soon cry out for the good old bread-and-butter ; would you not ? Sometimes you are promised a visit to the theatre as a treat, and you count the days and the hours until it comes off. But it is only a treat because it is a change, because it is something different from what you do every day. If you had to go to the finest pantomime day after day for only a week, you would not be amused, but bored. There are people who have to go to the theatre every night ; it is their business. Their greatest treat is to stay away. And so, too, with these toys

ABOUT TOYS

which we love so much. If a fairy were to come suddenly —as fairies, I believe, are in the habit of doing—and were to tell you that you might have as many toys as you liked, on condition that you played with them always without stopping, you might agree; but you would soon be sorry for your bargain, and ask the fairy to let you off.

Well, then, amusement is all very well at its proper time. " All work and no play makes Jack a dull boy "; but all play and no work would make Jack a miserable boy—yes, and a bad boy, too—idle, slack, selfish; it would take all the backbone out of him—make him something like those indiarubber boys that you see in the toy shops—flabby boys—boys that can be pulled anyhow and all ways at once.

Now, have you found out yet why I have chosen this festival for a sermon about toys? Perhaps not quite; but I am sure you are getting warmer, as they say in " Hide-and-seek." This festival reminds us of the big fight that Judas Maccabæus fought more than 2,000 years ago. He fought for many things; but one of them was about the proper use of toys—or, to be quite plain, about the proper use of enjoyment. The bad Jews—and he fought against them quite as much as against the Greeks, their friends—the bad Jews wanted to enjoy themselves at all times, in season and out of season; the good Jews, under Judas Maccabæus, wanted to enjoy themselves only at the right time, when they had earned enjoyment by having done their duty. The bad Jews said that pleasure was the whole of life; the good Jews said that pleasure was only a small part of it. The bad Jews wanted to be always playing; the good Jews wanted to be serious and strenuous, not refusing the playthings altogether, but keeping them for odd moments, and using them as helps to higher things.

Now this fight, though it was fought so long ago, has

been going on ever since. It is going on to-day, and we must all take sides in it. Well, then, children, are you for duty or for pleasure, for toys all day long, or for toys now and then ? Commonsense will tell you how to answer that question. We have seen which is the more satisfying, as well as the nobler, life. We have seen that those who try to gorge themselves with pleasure come empty away. There is a Talmudic story which I should like you to hear. A starving fox comes one day to a vineyard, and longs to get at the grapes. But a big wall stops him. Round and round the vineyard he trots, but always that nasty wall stares him in the face. After a time, however, he discovers a small hole in the wall, through which, as he is very lean, he is able painfully to crawl. What joys await him on the other side ! How he feasts ! What a time he has ! But the finest banquet comes to an end at last; he has to give up eating because he can really eat no more. And so now he begins to think about going home to his wife and children ; for—cunning fellow !—he recollects that the farmer may come at any moment, and he may have a big stick ! So the fox slinks back to the friendly hole ; but, when he tries to squeeze himself through, he fails ; he has got too fat ! What is he to do ? There is nothing for it but to hide, and starve himself until he is thin enough. What, then, has he got by his feasting ? And what do *we* ever get by wrong self-indulgence ? Nothing. We are no better off than we were before. Better off ?—we are worse off ; for not only are we not satisfied and comfortable, but we are lower, morally, than we were, and we have the pain of knowing it. And it is just this that happened in the time of the Maccabees. The bad Jews actually lost by their badness ; for the Greeks, with whom they wanted to curry favour, despised them as poor creatures, as cowards. But the good Jews were respected by the Greeks, who could admire heroism even in a foe. And, above all, these good Jews had the joy of a good conscience. They knew that they had been brave for God's sake, not only on the battle-field, but in the harder struggle of the daily life, and the thought was a blessing. And they could go back to their pleasures with all the keener joy because those pleasures had been sanctified by self-denial.

Yes, self-denial—that is the great secret of happiness. It is not a good thing to have all that one wants. It is a good thing to learn to do without. It is what is called discipline, strengthening our character, making us brave and obedient, as discipline does in the case of the soldier. I told you about the drum I had when I was a child. I remember that my friend, when she was about to buy it, begged me to have another kind of toy instead—something, I suppose, that would have lasted longer. But I refused. I had set my heart on that drum, and I had it. In an hour or two, it was broken. But that was not the worst part of it. Not only was I unhappy because my toy was useless, but I had missed the chance of giving up.

And this giving up goes very far. It has a delight of its own, which nothing can equal. These toys which we are talking about—why are they such a pleasure? It is not an easy question to answer. They are something new and bright and gay, something as fresh as paint can make them—that is part of the secret, though not all of it; for does not every little girl love her oldest and shabbiest dollie best? Then there is the feeling that our toys are our own property, our very own. We like to show them to Charlie or Mollie, and while they are being admired remember that they are ours. Greater still is the delight of sharing the pleasure our toys give us with others, to let Charlie and Mollie play with them a little. For what is the good of happiness if we don't let other people have a taste of it ? But, finer than all, is the joy that lies in giving away our pleasures, in depriving ourselves of them in order that others may have them. It is nice to nurse a doll or play with a box of soldiers ; but it is a hundred times nicer to give away the doll or the box of soldiers, in spite of wanting it very much ourselves, to some poor child who has got no toys at all and never will have any but for us. Then our self-denial gives us a delight which the keeping of our treasures could never afford us. To give up so that others may have—what greater happiness can there be than this ? And there could not be a finer way of keeping Chanukah than by doing such an act of self-sacrifice. If you were to send some of your best-beloved toys to a hospital ; or, better still, ask that some of the money intended to be spent in buying you presents at this time of year shall be used to buy, say, warm clothes for poor children, you would truly honour this festival, and at the same time fill your hearts full of real delight. For this sort of delight it was that the brave men whom we are thinking of this afternoon valued most—the delight of those who listen to God's law of love, which commands us to think of our fellow-creatures, to feel for their need, to pity their suffering, to make up to them out of our own stock of blessings the happiness which has been denied them. It is this law of love that the Maccabees struck so hard and goodly a blow to defend, and it has rewarded them by keeping their memory fragrant through the centuries. May God help you, dear children, to a like obedience, to a like recompense ! Amen.

OLD TIMES AND OLD FOLKS

(CHANUKAH)

FOR CHILDREN

"Remember the days of old."—DEUTERONOMY xxxii., 7.

So Moses spoke to his people just before his death. It is a fine saying, and we Jews do not fail to bear it in mind. We are fond of remembering the days of old. We remember them on this Feast of Chanukah, this Feast of Dedication, which we are keeping in honour of the Maccabees, who bravely lived and died 2,100 years ago. Their gallant deeds lit up the world of their day; but we take care that they shall light up our hearts in our day, just as our festival lamps, which you will see burning merrily in a moment or two, light up this synagogue. For the memory of brave deeds must never be allowed to perish from our hearts if we would show ourselves faithful and good.

> Honour the brave and bold.
> Long shall the tale be told,
> Yea, when our babes are old . . .

so Tennyson says of the men who charged at Balaclava. The story of true courage—courage in the performance of duty—will always be told, and told again, with reverence and delight. What you and I have to see to is that we are among those who so honour it, that we keep our hearts open to its message, that we allow it to pour its summons to be strong for duty's sake into our souls. We must not say "Oh, the story is old; two thousand years is a long time ago ; let us have something new." For what does it matter that the heroes are long dead and gone, and their very graves unknown ? Their courage and their goodness live after them ; time does not diminish their beauty or their power to uplift us. We can learn as much from the heroism of the Maccabees as we can from the latest act of bravery that the newspapers are praising. We can learn more. For the Maccabees were Jews, and it is a fine thing to think that we Jews have produced such heroes. Nay, what their story teaches us is to be true and faithful, but especially to be true and faithful to our religion, to the God for whom the Maccabees laid down their lives.

That is why Moses, with his last breath, tells his people to remember the days of old. One would imagine that he would have been thinking of other things, that he would have been looking forward to his death, which was so near at hand. But he did not think of himself —he never did that ; he thought only of Israel—how he might help them to be good when he was gone ; and he could find no better way of helping them than by telling them to remember the days of old—to remember God's love for them in the past and how often they had shown themselves unworthy of it. For let us be sure that if we would learn to live our lives well, we cannot do better than take a lesson from olden times. After Religion there is no study that can help you so much to be good as the study of History. If History warns us against the faults which have ruined many a character, it also bids us copy the virtues which have made many a character beautiful. "Lives of great men all remind us we can ake our lives sublime." Ah, it is a wonderful thing—this power of goodness to live on when the good themselves are dust ! It is like the scent given out by a

OLD TIMES AND OLD FOLKS 143

bowl of rose-leaves. How sweet it is! Nothing seems to kill its sweetness. But the roses have been dead perhaps for many a year.

Goodness, then, never dies; it never gets old-fashioned, as last year's hat does, or last year's way of doing one's hair. Thank God for that! Thank God that there is always some heart to love and cherish a noble example—some life which, after the lapse even of centuries, is made the better and the sweeter for it, just as the room is scented by the dead roses. Think of that, Children, and let the thought be another inducement to you to strive with might and main to be brave in right-doing. You never know how mighty your goodness may be, how many it may help to be brave and good in their turn, how many may thank and love you for so helping them.

But let us go back to our text. " Remember the days of old "—it is a command which we ought to think about in these times, when it is not the old, but the new, that people run after so much. The newer a thing is the better they think it is—the latest invention or the latest amusement, the latest music, however ugly, the latest frock, however dowdy. Children have this idea, too. They love new things just because they *are* new. They love new toys when the old ones are quite good enough; they love new clothes when the old ones are still quite wearable. I knew a boy who, when his father told him they were going to move into a new house, almost jumped out of his skin for joy. There was nothing wrong with the old house, and the boy didn't know anything about the new one; but he was delighted all the same. He was delighted because moving was a change, because it was something new. Now, I am not going to say that this love of change is altogether bad. If people always kept in the same groove, the world would never move on. There would never have been any progress, any science, any discoveries, any increase in human happiness—any happiness at all—but for the love of change, the desire for something new. Nor, although I have been praising the great story of the past, am I going to say that *all* its story is great. " The good old days " were not good in every way. These days are in many ways much better. In olden days people were so ignorant that they could not write their own names ; no one could go a journey of fifty miles without fear of being attacked by highwaymen ; if a person got crazy, people tried to beat his silliness out of him with a stick ; if a fever broke out in a town it was allowed to kill hundreds and thousands, and only stopped when, like a fire, it had burnt itself out. No ; the new times are good in their way ; and change is good in its way. The mistake is to think that they are good in every way, that the old times were altogether bad, and the old things are only fit for the dustbin. I said just now that children like their new toys best, and so, as a rule, they do. But I have seen many a little girl affectionately hugging her shabbiest doll, in spite of her having newer and quite gorgeous dolls, with rosy cheeks and splendid hair and magnificent clothes. That shabby creature —perhaps it has only one arm, and is short of an eye— is her very own, her darling. Why ? Who knows ? Perhaps it is the first doll she ever had, or some dear friend gave it to her; or perhaps she is fond of it just because it *is* so shabby and battered—does not a mother pet her ailing child most ? But the fact remains that the little girl does love that doll best ; and very pretty and very touching her love is. Let us learn a lesson from it. Let us learn not to think lightly of old things merely because they are old, not to change just for the sake of change. There are holy things that are holy

OLD TIMES AND OLD FOLKS

just because of their age, because they remind us of those we love, because they tell us of days long gone by, whose memory helps to keep our hearts fresh and our lives pure.

I am thinking of the things of religion. Never let us be tempted to say " Judaism is old ; let us have something new." For, like goodness, Judaism is always new, old as it is. It has a meaning and a message for every generation, and its meaning and its message are all the mightier just because it is old, because a long line of brave men and women, of whom the Maccabees are only examples, have lived and died for it, and consecrated it by their lives and their deaths. And I am thinking of old persons as well as of old things. Is it needless to remind you of your duty in this respect ? " Despise not thy mother when she is old "—so the wise man cries in the Book of Proverbs. How strange a warning ! Who would despise one's mother in her old age ? Surely time cannot alter our love for her. There may be threads of grey in her hair, a line or two in her face ; but what of that ? She is always the same to us—the same dear, sweet mother. And yet the wise man is right to warn us. Love and honour are two different things ; and while we keep the one for our parents to the last, we are not always sure of keeping the other. Be on your guard, then. Be modest and humble. Do not think that because you are young and your parents —yes, and your elders—are old, therefore you are wiser. It is not mere book-knowledge that constitutes wisdom, but experience—a practical acquaintance with the difficulties of life and with the right way of meeting them. And this true wisdom only comes with time. The older one grows the nearer one gets to it.

It is not easy to make children understand this.

They fancy they know so much better than the old folks. Some of you, perhaps, remember the story of the little, silly mouse. There was once a mouse who lived with her mother in a nice snug hole. The mother was wise, and tried to make her daughter wise also. "Remember," she said, "that in the large room yonder there is a big cat who will eat you up if she catches you; therefore never venture out unless I am with you." But one day the little mouse began peeping out of the hole, and behold! the room was empty. There was not a sign of that horrid cat, with the staring green eyes. "Ah," she said, "now I can safely have a little run all by myself. I know mother will not approve; but she is so timid, so very old-fashioned." So out she went, and there, facing her, was a beautiful little cage, with quite fascinating bars and—greatest joy of all!— a splendid meal of cheese temptingly laid out inside it. "Come in; come in," it said as plainly as possible, "come in and eat me." She could not resist the invitation; she entered, and ate. But it was her last meal; the cage was a trap. How many little mice there are among children, who think that they know better than their parents! And how often do they have to pay for their folly! Be warned, then. Keep your reverence for the old people and the old things—for the parents, whom God is lovingly sparing so that they may guide and help and bless you, for the old, old stories of courage and goodness, which will continue to teach and inspire as long as there is a heart left to beat high at the thought of noble deeds.

THE FRAGRANT LIFE

" Take thou also unto thee the chief spices, pure myrrh . . . and sweet cinnamon . . . and cassia . . . and olive oil . . . And thou shalt anoint therewith the tent of meeting, and the ark of the testimony, and the table and all the vessels thereof . . . and thou shalt anoint Aaron and his sons, and sanctify them."—
EXODUS xxx., 23, 30.

THE Tabernacle in the Wilderness, Israel's earliest place of worship, was a thing of wonder. It stood in the very midst of the camp, with a pillar of cloud resting on it by day, and a pillar of fire by night. The hastily-built sanctuary of wandering tribes, made of planks and skins, it was nevertheless a beautiful fabric, on which all the artistic skill and the loving devotion of the people were freely lavished. It exhaled, moreover, a fragrant atmosphere, scenting the camp and lending sweetness to the desert air. The whole experience of the Israelites in the wilderness was wonderful, romantic, with God ever moving among them, with miracles repeating themselves day after day, with a Divine government the like of which mankind has never seen. But equally marvellous and eloquent was the sweet-smelling house of God, fragrant within and perfuming the workaday world outside it.

The ordinance preserved for us in the text has a many-sided significance. Worship is the fragrance of the soul. Not for naught did the burning incense, symbol of the devout ascending spirit, take the highest place in the old sacrificial system, with an altar of gold, standing within the Sanctuary, reserved for it. Not for naught does the Psalmist ask that his prayer may be " set forth as incense before God." For never is the human spirit more sublime than when it bows itself in praise, and adoration, and lowly homage at the feet of the Most High. It comes nearer then to its Divine source, nearer also to that perfect union with God which is its true and ultimate destiny. The old mystics speak of an " added soul " which is given to the devout Jew on the Sabbath. It comes to him on the Sabbath-eve straightway from Paradise, laden with the perfume of the Heavenly Garden ; and at the close of the holy day it departs, with all its exquisite delights, its inspiring hints and reminiscences. But does the Sabbath alone hold the secret of this magic ? Is it the only keeper of the added soul ? Let us hallow the week with prayer, however brief—let us try to lift ourselves for a moment at any time above this noisy world into the stillness where God is, and some of the Heavenly fragrance descends, to gladden the spirit and to make the daily life glorious.

But the scented atmosphere of the Tabernacle was not fast shut up within its walls, to be breathed only at prayer time. The oil, fragrant with the myrrh, and the cinnamon, and the cassia, clinging to the vessels and the furniture of the Holy place, sent forth its sweet breath and perfumed the entire camp. Twice every day, moreover, the cloud of incense rose from the altar, and was wafted into the outer air. It should be so always. If the house of prayer achieves its gracious task it sends some of its atmosphere with us to sweeten the world outside. Some of the high thoughts and resolves, some of the visions of God, that visit us here, we must take with us for incitements to faith, and courage, and self-renunciation ; or worship fails of its true purpose. " To labour," the old monks said, " is to pray " ; for to work for God, to bless men, is itself

THE FRAGRANT LIFE

homage to Him who made men and loves them as His children. But the converse is also true; to pray is to work. For prayer, properly understood, is the impulse to the godly life, the fragrant life—the life which transmutes the prayerful spirit into action, which crowns worship with service and devoutness with renunciation.

Again, the sweet-smelling ointment, for which the text gives the prescription, was meant to consecrate the things it touched—the Tabernacle itself, the ark, the candlestick, the altar, and the table—the priests, too, and even, according to tradition, the kings as they successively came to the throne. But it was intended to scent the things it touched as well as to consecrate them, else why was it compounded of sweet spices only? Thus we are taught that the godly life, which prayer inspires, must be beautiful, winning—made fragrant with those chief spices, lowliness, and forgiveness, and forbearance, and love. Not the austere life, not the merely correct life, not the life of severe integrity and justice only, but the loving life, which diffuses peacefulness and joy, and every sort of blessing, is the true ideal. Such seems to have been the thought of that old saintly writer on Jewish law and ethics who named his book the *Rokeach*, " the Apothecary," or " the Perfumer," borrowing the word from the very passage in which the text occurs. He chose this word as his title, he tells us, because the sum of its letters, regarded as numbers, corresponded with the sum of the letters of his name Elazar, so regarded. But he might have found a hundred other words that so corresponded with it. Clearly, he chose the word as his title for deeper reasons. His book, like that holy product of the ancient apothecary's art, the perfumed ointment, would, he hoped, help to lend enhanced sweetness to the life of him who read it—make it holier, but also more gracious—humbler, gentler, saturated with self-surrender. He was a mystic, and, like all the mystics, he preached not only self-absorption in God, but patience under tribulation and love to all men, even to enemies, as the crowning human duty. A kindred spirit of modern times taught the doctrine in characteristic fashion. The good man, he says, "learns to welcome misfortune—learns that adversity is the prosperity of the great. He learns the greatness of humility. He shall work in the dark, work against failure, pain and ill-will. If he is insulted, he can be insulted; all his affair is not to insult." And he emphasizes the missionary effect of such a life. "Fear God," he says, "and where you go men shall think they walk in hallowed cathedrals." You take, he means, your Sanctuary with you; you build it yourself, and men enter in at its doors of their own free will, allured by the beauty of it.

Shall we not heed the lesson? To win others for the good life by the goodness of our own, to create love by dispensing it, to heal the wounds which life has dealt to our fellow-men, to "be to other souls the cup of strength in some great agony"—this is our supreme task on earth, supreme because there is nothing higher or mightier, nothing more beautiful in itself or abler to evoke the beauty that sleeps in other natures. Those who essay to perform it lead the fragrant life, the life which helps to sweeten the world.

There is a legend which declares that the holy anointing oil which Moses made in the Wilderness lasted until the fall of the Temple, sufficing for the needs of many centuries without suffering the smallest diminution. It was then hidden away with the Ark, and the pot of manna and the magic rod of Aaron, and it will be found again in the blessed Messianic time. For the fragrant life is indestructible. When it ends it still goes on "beyond these voices "—goes on even on this earth. The perfume clings to the fragments of the shattered vase; the cherished dead speak to us as of old; their memory abides with us, a never-failing benediction. Our mutual love, with the inspiration that springs from it, suffers no diminution either in life or in death. It is imperishable. Someone to love, says the poet, God gives us; but one day he takes the beloved from our embrace, and love alone is left to us. But that love retains its power. It continues to help and to gladden and to bless us always. And the day will come, in the golden age in Heaven, when they who made life gracious for us will be found again, and restored to us, and the old beautiful fellowships, the old vanished joys, which we shared in common, will be renewed, never to cease again.

SPIRITUAL EXPERIENCE

"God of the spirits of all flesh."—NUMBERS xvi., 22.

TWICE these words occur in the Pentateuch—first, when the faithful leaders of the people would save them from the destruction in which the revolt of Korah had involved them, and again when Moses prays that a man may be appointed to succeed him in the arduous task of ruling Israel. God is invoked as the Reader of all hearts, who can unerringly distinguish between the rebel and the loyal, and discern the soul best fitted for leadership. But it is possible to see in this appellation of the Supreme a deeper meaning still. The Almighty is the God of the spirits of all flesh in the sense of being, not only the judge of the human spirit, but its Lord. He is the master-soul, of whom all human souls are the dependents. "In His hand," cries Job, "is the soul of every living thing and the spirit of all mankind." The destiny of that soul, here and hereafter, is utterly in His hands; but, more than this, He is the master-light of which it is the pale reflection. The human spirit is close linked in nature to the Universal Spirit. Children of clay, men have in them divine potencies. In life they can lift themselves to God, just as at death they go to Him to enter upon an ampler being. In other words, there is an unseen world about us even here, one with which we are brought into organic relation by every spiritual effort of ours, by every noble thought and act, by every prayerful aspiration.

This, or something like it, we may not unfairly see suggested in the beautiful phrase that forms the text. And if the interpretation is sound, then our ancient forefathers had attained to loftier heights of spiritual

SPIRITUAL EXPERIENCE

perception than we are wont to imagine. "The God of the spirits of all flesh"—how sharply the words contrast with the mechanical phraseology of the Mosaic ceremonial ordinances! And yet there the words are—as real, as sublime, as the Priestly Benediction which comes to break with impressive effect the monotony of long categories of merely ritual prescriptions.

But another topic here presents itself, which may well occupy our thoughts for a few moments. This mystic realm, of which the text seems to tell—is it real? This alleged ability of man to get into touch with it—is it trustworthy? Some time ago Mr. Voysey, the venerable Theistic Minister, preached a sermon in which the following remarkable passage occurred:—" I feel bound to tell you that God has answered my prayers, almost without an exception, ever since I was old enough to pray at all, that my life and health and strength to almost four-score years have been preserved by Him through many dangers, that my arduous work would have broken me down long ago unless I had received from Him ceaseless help and strength and capability for doing what I believed He wished me to do. . . . My prayer binds me closer to His bosom. My uplifted hand He lays hold of in the hour of difficulty and temptation; and He cheers my heart in the night of my sorrow. I can leave all I want or care for, all my beloved relatives and friends safe in His keeping; He bids me to trust Him and to leave all to Him." These words were spoken deliberately, and by one who is not only an octogenarian, but a liberal thinker, who has weighed religion in the balance, and shown the hollowness of some of its manifestations. To him, personally, God is all in all, and communion with Him his one stay and support. Moreover he has scarcely ever prayed to Him without being answered. Certainly, as the preacher pointed out in an earlier part of his sermon, he has been careful to ask only for what he deemed the right things, for spiritual, rather than for exclusively material boons, especially for boons the grant of which would do no harm to others. But the fact remains that this keen-sighted old man, after a lifetime of prayer, deliberately affirms his conviction of its efficacy. It has unlocked for him the invisible world with all its inestimable treasures.

There have been many before Mr. Voysey who have made the same assertion. From the Prophets and the Psalmists downwards there have been, in every generation, countless souls able to testify to the power of prayer and to the existence of a region transcending this physical universe. Those who would have examples drawn from sources outside the Bible cannot do better than study that notable book, Professor James's *Varieties of Religious Experience*. Are we at liberty to ignore these spiritual revelations, to brush them aside as the products of fancy, the phantoms of self-delusion? The tendency of thought, even in this scientific age, is to warn us against such a course. This firm persuasion of the Unseen—as deeply rooted to-day as it was in the world's childhood—is not, we are told, to be curtly dismissed as an hallucination; the experiences on which it is based are not necessarily the outcome of hysteria or a disordered imagination. Exaggerated, even grotesque, as are some of the forms in which it has uttered itself, there is still an essential verity underlying them all. The very persistence of the persuasion is evidence of its truth. The spiritual world, it is contended, must be real seeing that millions of men have entered it, and had their being in it, since time began. Mankind cannot have been nourishing itself upon a delusion, keeping itself alive, nourishing its finest aspirations, upon it all these thousands of years.

SPIRITUAL EXPERIENCE

Is there not much force in the argument? God is proved by human belief in Him. It may be urged that this spiritual experience is purely subjective, that men have made God for themselves, just as in idolatrous ages they made them gods. But is this true? False as the gods were, they may have been incarnations of the truth, distorted images of a great verity only dimly perceived by those who worshipped them. And if men have the power of apprehending Deity, does not the very fact witness to Him? Whence that power? How is it that mankind have been able to conceive of a Being infinitely mightier than themselves, one holding them and the whole universe in the hollow of His hand, one coming to them at their call, except that the power has proceeded from Him? We say that Conscience itself, men's universal preference of good to evil, the discernment of righteousness as the only authentic rule of life, is a proof of the majesty and the binding force of the moral law. Why, then, should we not say likewise that the existence of belief in God is itself a witness to Him, that the yearning after Him, the conviction that it has been satisfied, testify that both He and the spiritual realm are alike realities?

The whole matter hinges upon the efficacy of prayer; for if it achieves what a Voysey declares, then all else follows. And by prayer I mean not formal entreaty, nor even the utterance of any words at all, but the prayerful disposition. It is an old truism that you may make many prayers without praying, and that you may utter no word, yet call all Heaven about you. It is the prayerful temper, whether it find expression in speech or not, that opens the celestial gates. Then, in the words of an old Jewish mystic, "We see, yet not with the eye; we hear, yet not with the ear; we speak yet not with the tongue." The whole region of the Unseen, with all its blessedness, becomes accessible to mortal man.

In what does that blessedness consist? It consists chiefly in the gift of the spirit—a clearer vision of the Divine, a deeper faith, a firmer trust, so that trouble becomes dwarfed and duty magnified; care is forgotten, rectitude gains undivided sway. The power of submission increases too; in the light of our own insignificance and of God's grandeur we are more ready than before to say "Thy will, not mine, be done." And these higher boons bring the lesser ones in their train. I knew a saintly Jewess once who would come from the privacy of her room and say "I have been resting." She meant that she had been praying. Communion with the God of her life had yielded her peace of body as well as of mind and soul. So intimate is the solidarity of matter and spirit that prayer helps us to triumph over physical disabilities, over weakness and pain. The Psalmist spoke only the bare literal truth when, after converse with God, he exclaimed, "My heart is glad, and my soul rejoiceth, yea, even my flesh abideth in safety." But the chief tranquillity won by the praying soul is the inner tranquility that comes to those who see this lower life in its true perspective, and opens to them vistas of a higher existence possible even in this world. "Prayer," says a modern thinker, "is the spiritual balm, the precious condiment which restores to us peace and courage. It reminds us of pardon and duty. It says to us 'Thou art loved—love; thou hast received—give; thou must die—labour while thou canst; overcome anger by kindness; overcome evil with good.'" Truly inestimable boons! They are the gift of the God of the spirits to the human spirit; and, in giving them, He makes to us His clearest manifestation, offers us His most irrefragable proof.

THE UNSEEN WORLD

"And, behold, the mountain was full of horses and chariots of fire round about Elisha."—2 KINGS vi., 17.

ELISHA seems to be in mortal peril. His enemy, the King of Syria, has sent an armed force, with horses and chariots, to take him, and they surround the city, his abiding place. His servant, ignorant, lacking the truer insight, is in despair. "Alas, my master," he cries, "what shall we do?" "Fear not," answers the Prophet; "for they that be with us are more than they that be with them." And then he prays, "Lord, open his eyes that he may see." The prayer is answered. The young man sees, "and behold, the mountain was full of horses and chariots of fire round about Elisha." The earthly forces, malign and deadly, are matched, and outmatched, by the gracious host of Heaven. The spiritual powers that dominate man's life are stronger than the physical ones. The unseen realm, visible to the elect soul, is real—more real, because mightier, more enduring, than this tangible world perceptible by the senses.

We learn, first of all, that the spirit is greater than the flesh, that the men of vision, it is, who have ever done the work of the world, and brought mankind on its way. The men of faith, who persist in seeing the good that will eventually come out of the evil, the idealists, who believe the best about the future of the race, who believe the best about God, who keep to the last the heart of the child, simple, hopeful, trusting—these are the helpers and the saviours of humanity. "Not by strength doth man prevail." The thought encourages and sustains us in this time of war. Immediate victory in the conflict will go to the strong ; but the ultimate triumph will be won by the spiritual forces engaged, by righteousness and justice and love. " They that be with us are more than they that be with them."

But the wondrous incident itself, which the text records, is our chief theme. It belongs to old-world story, to the domain of the miraculous and the legendary. And yet, so changeless is the human spirit, it claims to have repeated itself in recent experience. You have all heard of the wonderful apparition at Mons. During the British retreat from that place last year some of our men stopped of a sudden, and held at bay the pursuing enemy. An angelic host had appeared to them, helped them, put new heart into them. From that moment the fortunes of the day, of the campaign, were changed ; the retreat ceased ; the foe was baffled. The ancient wonder was re-enacted. The celestial army proved mightier than the earthly legions.

This miracle of yesterday has been much discussed. Some dismiss it as sheer illusion ; others believe in it implicitly—plain, sturdy soldiers among them, who were eye-witnesses of the incident, and saw the heavenly helpers with their own eyes. How are we to regard these statements ? The fiery chariots surrounding the Prophet of old, the celestial host rallying a twentieth century army—what are we to say to such alleged phenomena ?

From the very beginning of the human story man has been conscious of a region transcending this lower world. In the earliest times of which we have records we find him holding communion with the dead ; the task of pleasing and conciliating them was part of his everyday life. This belief in a spirit-world in close contact with our own is the origin of many surviving

THE UNSEEN WORLD

rites of primitive religion; it is one of the origins of Religion itself. How strongly it has coloured the Scriptural story we know well enough. The Bible shows us angels moving commonly among men. The region of the shades meets us in many of its pages. There is Sheol, the underworld, the twilight of the ghosts; there is the spectre of Samuel the Prophet called back to earth by the witch of Endor; and the like. Still more significant is the survival in our own day of the belief of which I am speaking. It is not enough to say that the idea of Immortality is the stay and solace of countless living hearts oppressed by the tragedy of life or torn by cruel bereavement. For many of them the dead not only live, but live here. They speak to their beloved on earth. Nor are all those who cling to this conviction untutored, ill-balanced minds—minds surrendering themselves feebly to a pleasant belief merely because it is pleasant, without the will or the power to bring their intuitions to the test of reason. Many a distinguished man of science of our day shares their certitude. I recall one such man who, accustomed by his studies and his life-work to demand proofs for every statement or theory, has more than once publicly affirmed not only that the dead live on, but that he has held personal communication with them. That communication, I need hardly say, belongs to a high order of psychic experience, incomparably superior to the manifestations dealt in by the professional spiritualist. Everyone, says this distinguished man of science, may attain to the same experience by dint of thought and concentration and due discipline of soul. The Pentateuch intelligibly discourages such efforts. It addresses itself to plain men and women, whose energies cannot safely be diverted from the pressing tasks and duties of the daily life.

How, I ask again, are we to regard these alleged

wonders, at once old and new ? We cannot brush them aside, saying they are delusions, merely subjective phenomena. It is true that even a trained scientific mind may be self-deceived no less than prophets lifted into a state of ecstasy by long meditations in solitude, or soldiers high strung by the excitement of war, worn by the stress of battle and fatigue. The point, however, is not whether these abnormal experiences are true in themselves, but whether the persistent claim to them made in every age, and by various classes of men, does not testify to a larger truth of which they are the shadowy and imperfect revelations. May not this widespread longing for communion with the spirits of the dead, the consciousness of its possibility, the effort after its achievement, imply that there are spirits to commune with, a super-sensual world peopled with them ? The fiery chariots may be only a dream, the angelic host, re-establishing the broken line, restoring the failing courage of the beaten army, only a vision ; but the dream and the vision may still be trustworthy in the higher sense. They may be—surely they are—the images, blurred and distorted it may be, of sober facts—facts enshrined in the deepest recesses of the human soul, imprinted upon it, woven into its texture, as a cherished reminiscence from the far-off time of its birth in Heaven. The great intuitions of the human mind, in virtue of their continuous and powerful sway over the life of man, in virtue of their very existence, have an indefeasible claim to respect.

Some years ago the argument would have been scouted. Beliefs, we should have been told, cannot prove themselves ; they must be proved by appeal to reason, to experience above all. But to-day the drift of philosophy is otherwise, a James and a Bergson being witnesses. And as to experience, if experience is the criterion the

THE UNSEEN WORLD

case is proved. For all these alleged incidents have happened; each of them is a very real event in the history of a soul. The whole story of mysticism belongs to the same category. The mystic has felt God; he has seen Him; he has spoken to Him, "needing," in the words of our Kippur Prayer, "no outer light, hearing Him with the ear of the spirit when the ear of the flesh is dulled." It is the assumption, the postulate, of the Bible itself, with its prophetic visions and communications, its Moses, meeting the Supreme face to face, its Isaiah, beholding the Heavenly King on His throne while the sanctuary shakes to its foundations, its Ezekiel, gazing at the opened heavens and seeing visions of God. You cannot dismiss all this mass of testimony, all this body of experience, as hallucinations. The facts are too big, too uniform, too insistent. We trust the reports of the senses; why should we discredit the witness of the spirit? One man says: "I saw the king yesterday," and we accept his statement. Another says: "I have seen the Divine King; I have been up to Heaven for awhile, for forty days and forty nights; I have lived in another world, better and lovelier far than this." By what right do we doubt him? Because his experience is not ours? The experience of the man who has seen the human king may not be ours; we may never have been in the royal presence. And yet we believe him. To doubt these spiritual events is to doubt Religion itself; for what is belief in such events but an extension of the idea of God, the Unseen, but Omnipotent One, the God of the spirits of all flesh? And you and I believe in Him, though He is unseen; or we should not have come to the synagogue to-day. Whence that belief, which has exerted so tremendous an influence over human thought and destiny? It must have its roots in a great momentous truth.

I have led you along this line of thought because, speculative though it is, is has a very direct bearing on the workaday life—the life which will begin for us once more when this holy Sabbath is ended. For if the unseen world be real—more real, more potent, as the Seers testify, than this visible world of ours—it follows that we must revise our conception of life, reconsider the aims we consistently set before us, the ideals which are for ever dominating us. The materialistic interpretation of the world must give place to the idealistic, the religious. As things are, the lower values predominate with most of us. We live for the passing hour, striving to get the maximum of satisfaction out of it, not caring greatly about spiritual things, hardly thinking at all about the eternal future. "I must ask you to reflect," said a distinguished public man the other day, "whether the achievement of wealth and power, to the exclusion of higher aims, can lead to more than a superficial prosperity which passes away because it carries the virus of its own doom with it. Do we not find in the worship of national success the seed of the pernicious ambition which has maddened a nation and plunged Europe into war?" The speaker was the President of the British Association, the one business of which is the advancement of science. Yet he was constrained to utter this warning, a warning all the more impressive because of the source whence it came. We are always in danger of ignoring such admonitions, not only in our national, but in our personal life. We see things dimly, and pass by without recognition the most solemn of all truths. But let our eyes be opened, let us behold the horses and the fiery chariots, envisage their power, their reality, and then everything is changed. Then this transient life is put back into its right place in the perspective. It becomes only a fragment of experience,

THE UNSEEN WORLD

its business but a small part of our rightful pre-occupations. We are ready, as of old, to take our share of our worldly duties and pleasures; but we regard them now with new eyes and in a new spirit. We see them, in Spinoza's phrase, "under the aspect of Eternity," in the illuminating light which streams from the inspired page, from the experience of souls greater and holier than ours. We ask ourselves, "What am I living for? Am I living for objects that harmonize or clash with the solemnity of the unseen realm about me? Am I living in a manner worthy or unworthy of my higher self, my spiritual destiny?"

And then there are the beings that people the invisible world. If they do people it, if there is truth, whatever its precise degree or character, in the report that they have spoken to kindred souls in this life, what an immeasurable joy is ours! Our hearts' desire is given to us; our beloved still live, and they are near to us, though we ourselves see them not, nor hear them, even with the organs of the spirit. Our whole outlook on life is altered, irradiated with unspeakable happiness, transfigured by noble resolution; our instinctive loyalty is reinforced. We will so live as to be worthy of the fellowship into which we have been consciously admitted. The goodness of those we have lost and regained shall be ours, as far as we can make it ours; they shall live again on earth in us; their exalted will shall be our law; "thy commandment," we cry, "all alone shall live within the book and volume of my brain, unmixed with baser matter." They will inspire and help us as in former days—inspire and help us to fight our earthly battle bravely and well. And so the spiritual forces will prove their might to us, as to the Prophet of old and the believing soldier to-day.

One final thought. If the spirit-world be real, then

we ourselves shall enter it one day. Through the gates of death we shall pass into the ampler life. There we shall greet the blessed company of the glorious dead; there we shall see the Father's face. We would all desire that experience to be happy. We would be enrolled in that company—meet the Paternal eye in humility and reverence, but also without shame or dread. But if so, we must prepare ourselves here. And thus prepared, we shall fare forth to the heavenly realm with hope in our souls. Then the fiery chariots and the angelic host, the sight of which has kept us strong and brave and true in this world, will be our companions on our fateful journey, and save us in the great life hereafter.

THE POWER OF PRAYER

" And He said unto Moses, Come up unto the Lord, thou, and Aaron, Nadab and Abihu, and seventy of the elders of Israel, and worship ye afar off ; and Moses alone shall come near unto the Lord . . . then went up Moses, and Aaron, Nadab and Abihu, and seventy of the elders of Israel ; and they saw the God of Israel ; and there was under His feet as it were a paved work of sapphire stone, and as it were the very heaven for clearness . . . And they beheld God, and did eat and drink."—
EXODUS xxiv., 1, 10, 11.

THIS is one of the most difficult passages of the Bible ; it is the despair of the commentators. I shall not attempt to expound it. All I would do is to bring out one of the many thoughts it seems to suggest. The events it sets forth are the prelude to the forty-days' sojourn of Moses on Sinai, whence he afterwards returns with the tables of the Law in his hands. On this occasion he is told to ascend the mount, and worship. But he is not to go up alone ; Aaron and his two sons, together with seventy of the elders of the people, are to go up with him. But he alone is to draw near to God ; the others are to worship afar off. The command is obeyed. But a strange and a significant thing happens. Both to Moses and to his companions alike the same glorious experience is vouchsafed. All see the God of Israel—see as it were the pavement beneath His feet, blue as sapphires, resplendent as the very heavens. Prayer has not only bridged the distance between men and God, but obliterated the distinctions between variously-gifted souls. They are made one by a common worship—one in spirit and in potency.

The power of prayer—this is my subject ; its power rather than its efficacy. There was a time, not so very distant, when the preacher, with his ear on the heart-beat of the world, was impelled to vindicate the efficacy in preference to the power ; he had to show how men could still look up devoutly to God in an age steeped in the scientific spirit, dominated by the belief in the universal reign of law. He had to justify prayer philosophically. But those times, and the temper begotten of them, have passed. To-day men are ready to pray, moved by that sense of the reality of the Unseen, which War, with its catastrophic episodes, has not created, but sharpened.[1] The soul and its needs count for much more nowadays than they did a generation ago. God has become more real ; greater store is set by spiritual values. Though dogmas and symbols alike are receiving new interpretations—nay, just because they are receiving them— Religion is stronger than ever. And the older creeds, Judaism among them, are re-acting, as was inevitable, to the stimulus. A striking instance is furnished by the proceedings of last year's Conference of American Rabbis. They included a Presidential Address, a lecture, and a sermon, all delivered by different speakers ; and the note struck and emphasized by each of them was distinctly spiritual. And the Conference only echoed the voice of the Synagogue. Under the impact of new religious movements in the United States the old objective presentation of Judaism is being largely exchanged for a subjective one. Once the appeal was mainly to the intellect or to the ethical conscience ; now it is as often addressed to the soul.

This changed tendency is manifesting itself here as well as across the seas, and the place of prayer in men's minds and lives is an illustration of it. We have shifted

[1] Preached in 1918.

THE POWER OF PRAYER 167

our point of view on this ancient question. " More things are wrought by prayer than this world dreams of "—Tennyson's assertion is seen to be something more than a poetic flourish. There is a might of the human spirit which, even for the man of action and sober thinking, transcends all material forces, victorious when in conflict with them, successful when they are doomed to fail. And this revived belief in prayer is the result of a new way of looking at it. A few years ago, moved by the thought of the unchangeable nature of God, by a sense of His limitless fore-knowledge and power, we said that the essential function of prayer was to influence, not Him, but us. " Who rises from his worship a better man," we affirmed with George Meredith, " his prayer is answered." But now the pendulum has swung back again. Chastening, and uplifting, and purifying, as of old, prayer, as some of us are beginning to see, has also an external effect. It lifts the soul indeed to God, but it also brings down God to the soul. It makes men worthy of the boons they crave, but it also helps them to win those boons. The spiritual striving it evokes creates a holy atmosphere fit for the reception of the Divine Visitant, who comes with healing on His wings, His hands loaded with gifts. It is the old-world idea revived. Even the lower, the less richly-endowed souls are transfigured in prayer. They get vision and power. They worship afar off, humbly conscious of their ignorance and weakness, but worship cancels all their disabilities. They share the privileges of the elect. They see the God of Israel and His splendour. They get their hearts' desire. It is as if, like the Elders of old, they ate and drank ; for their spirit is filled and satisfied.

It is an ancient idea revived, I say. The Jewish mystics in every age have felt this power of prayer to throw a divine environment about the worshipper, and so to make him accessible to the Divine grace. At the bidding of the aspiring soul Heaven comes down, and glorifies earth with hallowing touch, scents it with its perfume. Prayer, cry the Cabalists, is a celestial garment, clad in which the devout spirit penetrates into Paradise. But the idea is not even theirs; it is Biblical. Notable is the reason given in the chapter of Exodus immediately following the text-passage for the command to build the Tabernacle. "Let them make Me a sanctuary," says God. For what purpose? That they may tell Him of their needs, confess their sins, voice their sorrows? No, but that He may dwell among them. They have caught some glimpses already of the Divine splendour; it is " like a devouring fire on the top of the Mount." Now, called down by prayer, that splendour, that glorious Presence, is to be near to them always, to abide among them, so that the camp, the daily life, may be sanctified, and every blessing which they rightly desire may be assured to them. The Sanctuary, the visible embodiment of a people's worship, is to achieve its supreme purpose, and with it the supreme purpose of worship itself, in filling earth with Heaven.

This aspect of the matter has more than a merely speculative or theoretical interest. It belongs to the sphere of the practical. The perception of it is helping to make the daily life-story of hundreds of ordinary people to-day. Oppressed and tortured by the most poignant of world-tragedies,[1] devout bands of men and women are meeting regularly in London and elsewhere in order to bring the power of a common worship to bear upon the existing course of events, so that haply humanity may be delivered quickly from all this present ruin and woe. The spiritual arm, they are convinced, will prove mightier than the arm of flesh; even the destructive

[1] Preached during the War.

THE POWER OF PRAYER

power and the madness of war may, they believe, be overcome by the prayerful endeavour of tranquil souls. Not only will they get strength to fight against War when peace returns, but they will hasten its return. They will make themselves worthier of its coming because lowlier and more loving ; but, by some wondrous telepathy, they will also impart their own lowly and loving temper to others ; they will help to create a divine atmosphere, with all its promise and potency of peace. This is what they believe. Some will call it a pathetic faith, seeing that all the forces of the world are arrayed against it. I prefer to call it a beautiful faith, beautiful not only because of its courage and sublimity, but because of its truth. For this visible world is not all ; there is a larger world transcending it, in point not only of magnitude, but of reality. The spiritual is mightier than the material, as all the Bible was written to teach, and who shall measure the power of God or limit the action of the human soul, His kin ? The peace which is the one desire of all our hearts, the righteous peace which is to root justice, and freedom, and brotherly love more firmly in the earth, may well speed its coming in response to the invocation of devout spirits.

> Be not afraid to pray, to pray is right.
> Pray, if thou canst, with hope, but ever pray,
> Though hope be weak or sick with long delay.
> Pray in the darkness if there be no light,
> Far is the time, remote from human sight,
> When war and discord on the earth shall cease ;
> Yet every prayer for universal peace
> Avails the blessed time to expedite.

And, as of old, those who achieve the gracious consummation may be of various spiritual categories, those that worship afar off as well as those who draw near.

This idea of a common devotional effort after peace

ought strongly to appeal to us Jews, heirs of the men who saw God at Sinai, of the aspiring Prophets and the singing Psalmists. Or shall it be said that Israel is degenerate, and that every body of believers has evinced the fullest faith in prayer save the race which first taught its power and its sublimity to the world? Surely not. Prayer, say the Rabbins, is Israel's one weapon. What can be finer than to use it in order to win for humanity at large one of its choicest blessings?

THE FIERY CHARIOTS

"And behold the mountain was full of horses and chariots of fire."—2 KINGS vi., 17.

THE incident occurs in the chapter immediately following our prophetical reading of this morning. The King of Syria, intent upon capturing Elisha, sends an armed host, with horses and chariots, to surround the city in which the Prophet is lodging. Elisha's servant, terrified and despairing, tells him of their danger. "Alas, my master," he cries, "what shall we do?" "Fear not," is the Prophet's reply, "for they that be with us are more than they that be with them." And then he prays, "Lord, I beseech Thee, open his eyes that he may see." The prayer is answered. "And the Lord opened the eyes of the young man, and he saw; and behold, the mountain was full of horses and chariots of fire round about Elisha."

The story is cast in legendary form; but in all that is essential it is everlastingly true. Mankind has always been divided into two categories—the Elishas and the servants, the open-eyed, with their clear sight of a realm transcending this world of sense, and those, with dulled gaze and coarsened souls, who see it not. For the one, the horses and chariots of fire, the Heavenly host which proclaims the Divine King and his all-saving power; for the other, only the forces of this world, sinister, destructive, seemingly invincible. The latter are the common herd, the former the elect spirits, whom we variously call Prophets, Seers, Mystics. Sometimes, as in the incident before us, one of the first category passes over into the ranks of the other. Under the Prophet's influence the sealed eyes are unclosed, and get a faint glimpse of the splendid and comforting vision. The Seer fulfils his higher mission, and enriches another soul with the peace and joy that floods his own. Then mysticism, so often distrusted and derided, because so often misunderstood, is justified. So often misunderstood, I say; for all religion must needs have its element of mysticism—of mysticism, which is the actual *experience* of God, as contrasted with mere belief in Him, the sight of the fiery chariots and horses, not simply the picturing of them by the imagination.

All the old prophets were mystics, and the whole Bible is a mystical book. For Ezekiel in captivity by the river Chebar the heavens are opened, and he sees marvellous visions—flaming angels, the sapphire throne, the very glory of the Almighty; but Moses, the first of the Prophets, though no such detailed experiences are reported of him, is no less a mystic. As the fruit of long self-communion in the desert-silences and on the solitary mountain-tops, he sees God face to face. For him the realm of glorious being thus revealed was, we may be sure, far more real than was the wilderness, vocal with the cries of the grovelling multitude, lusting after the flesh-pots of Egypt. So that when, in these Books of Kings, we read of apparitions and miracles breaking the monotony of a prosaic and sometimes sordid story, of raisings of the dead alternating with famine and bloodshed and political intrigue, of the clash of the fiery chariots of Heaven with the iron chariots of mortal strife and sin, we are on firmer ground than most of us believe. For who shall set bounds to the experiences of the spirit? Who shall say of another "his visions are hallucinations?" Shall the blind man pass judg-

THE FIERY CHARIOTS

ment when the seeing man reports what he has beheld? In every age there have been souls for whom the supernatural has been the natural and the real—souls whose lives, as the consequence of that conviction, have been blessed, and have radiated blessing.

Their own lives have been blessed. Living in the higher world, the mystic is lifted above the lower.

> Rapt into still communion that transcends
> The imperfect offices of prayer and praise,
> His mind is a thanksgiving to the Power
> That made him; it is blessedness and love.

Nor, it need hardly be said, can worldly trouble reach him. In the Psalmist's phrase he is "set on high from affliction." The forces of evil are vanquished by the mightier forces of good. Mohammed, left with only one companion, flees before a host of enemies. "They are many," cries his friend, "and we are but two." "Nay," answers Mohammed, "there are three of us—you, and I, and God." So it is with all the devout souls. Their one cry is "Fear not; for they that be with us are more than they that be with them." A multitude is arrayed against them; but around them, an impregnable defence, are the fiery chariots of God. What harm can befall them? The Lord is on their side; what, then, can man do unto them? This has been the calm and conquering certitude of all the great mystics of the ages, the certitude of the spirit that has not only heard of the Supreme with the hearing of the ear, but has felt and seen Him.

I have called theirs a conquering certitude because, besides enabling them to rise superior to earthly trouble, it has helped them to win over other souls and impart to them some of their own blessedness. The incident in the Book of Numbers, which tells how the prophetic spirit pours out from Moses as in a great flood, and seizes and uplifts the men in the camp, occurs again and again in human story. What has kept religion alive through the centuries? Not cold argument addressed to the reason, but spiritual ardour leaping from one man to another. Elisha's servant sees the wonderful vision at the Prophet's prayer. In like manner, men of common clay have been won and held for religion mainly by the influence of some master-spirit. They have felt its holiness, and have surrendered. This omnipotent truth which enables it to defy and defeat the world, they have said, must be truth indeed. This beauty of character and life must be the real beauty. This vision that entrances and glorifies a human soul must be something more than a dream and a delusion. In this manner it is that religion, the belief in the unseen, has been saved. And in this manner it is being saved to-day. We say that this is an age of unbelief, and yet there are abundant signs that it is an age of religion. The paradox is easily resolved. What men want to-day is not to argue about God, but to experience Him. They need, not dogmas, but inspiration. They would get into closer touch with the great Being whom they dimly apprehend in the wonder and the mystery of the universe, and get strength and guidance from the contact with which to live their lives. Hence the new birth of mysticism at a moment when materialistic science was never so triumphant.

The Seers have preserved not only religion, but goodness—and goodness, like religion—by their example. There have been mystics who have been too self-absorbed to spare a thought for others. They have so exclusively lived in the spiritual world as to have forgotten the material world, with its woe and its call for sympathy. But the sight of the true Seer is widened, not narrowed by the higher vision; it sees earth, as well as Heaven, more clearly. Isaiah, who beholds God sitting on His throne, and the hem of His robe filling the Temple, fiercely inveighs against oppression, and demands justice for the poor and the downtrodden; Elisha, who feels himself ringed in by the protecting fiery host, restores the dead child to his mother's arms, heals the leper, feeds the hungry, makes harmless the poisoned pottage. Just because they live with God they catch some of His compassion for men. It is always the religionist that has most resolutely striven to cure the hurt of the world, to sow peace and love among its indwellers. Not the least memorable part of the story we are studying is its epilogue. The soldiers sent to capture the Prophet, are taken captive by him. He leads them, blinded for the moment, to Samaria, where they are in the power of the King of Israel, their enemy. "Shall I smite them?" asks the King. "Nay," answers Elisha, "they are at thy mercy, would'st thou so illtreat them? Set food before them, that they may eat and drink, and go to their master." And so it is always. The Jewish mystics of a later age, who suffered persecution in their own persons, and saw their loved ones slain before their eyes, consistently preach patience and forbearance. The author of the *Rokeach* is a conspicuous example. A Vital—to come down to a yet later period—as the direct outcome of his mysticism can teach that all souls spring from God, and that therefore all men, indeed all sentient things, must have our love. And of Joseph Caro, ritualist and mystic, it is told that when once a man asked him how he should act towards his son who had abjured Judaism, he answered, "Love him." How can it be otherwise? The firmer grasp upon God's existence must needs make us more just and merciful to His children; the beatific vision must needs fill us with the yearning to shed some of its splendour upon this darkened earth. The true mystic is no narrow, sour fanatic ; he is a lover of men, rejoicing in their joy, lenient to their errors, tender to their shortcomings. The Fiery Chariot does not burn or destroy ; it brings light and protection and blessing to him who beholds it, and to the souls he inspires with the tidings of its reality.

THE REVELATION OF THE DIVINE

> "And it came to pass, when the congregation was assembled against Moses and against Aaron, that they looked toward the tent of meeting, and behold the cloud covered it, and the story of the Lord appeared."—NUMBERS xvi., 42.

THESE apparitions of the Divine glory often meet us in Holy Writ. Sometimes they occur in response to a great effort of worship, as when, at the solemn consecration of the Temple, the heavenly cloud fills the holy house, descending in direct response to the music of the Levites. But they also occur at times of crisis, as on the occasion before us. The Israelites have broken out again into revolt against their leaders, charging the faithful hearts who were ready to lay down their lives for them with having slain the men who had died in and through their own sin. It is then, in that hour of consternation and despair, that the apparition occurs. Some sudden impulse turns the gaze of the assembled tribes towards the " Tent of Meeting " that stands in the midst of the camp, " and behold," as we read, " the cloud covered it, and the glory of the Lord appeared." It is a miracle, convincing by reason of its wondrousness. It shuts the mouths of the revilers—demonstrates the criminality of their rebellion. It is God's vindication of His elect. It is a token of His sympathy with them and with rectitude, and therefore His self-vindication.

What would we not give, my friends, for such an apparition in these days ? What would we not give for a sign to certify us of God's existence and of His just and loving direction of human life, so that with the certitude we might lighten " the burden and the mystery of this unintelligible world "? " Oh that Thou wouldest rend the heavens, that Thou wouldest come down "— so we cry with the Prophet. There is so much in the commonest things of experience that we do not understand. There are the problems of physical evil, of moral evil. Why is there such a thing as suffering—the suffering, in particular, of the good and the innocent? There is the existence, too, of sin—sin which blights the lives of its perpetrators no less than the lives of its victims. There is the wickedness that is marked out for prosperity, the virtue that is visited with pain and starvation and derision. There is the wickedness that requites good with evil, love with cold indifference or positive hate, devoted service, as in the story before us, with ingratitude and calumny. Life, too, seems so hard to live, goodness so elusive, duty, in spite of our struggles for it, so difficult to perform, often difficult even to discern. Why should these things be? O for an hour of the old miraculous order!—one brief revelation of God, one glimpse of His glorious Presence, to solve our doubts, to end our questionings! So we cry, and cry in vain. No sign comes from the fast shut-up heavens. Verily, in the great Prophet's words, our God is a God that hideth Himself!

And yet He does not hide Himself altogether. A corner of the veil is lifted for us. No miracle is wrought; but some revelation of Himself God does vouchsafe to the mind and the soul that look for Him. Absolute solutions of the problems that torment us are impossible; but there are alleviations of them. One that seems the most satisfying of all is to be found in the mind and the soul themselves. The very power, inborn in humanity, to conceive of the Divine, is in itself a witness to the reality of the Divine. The vision of God, which the humblest soul shares with the Prophet, can be no delusion. It is the gift of a Spirit far greater than the soul that beholds it. But I am not chiefly thinking of this fact now, eloquent and impressive though it is. I am thinking rather of the equally great and perhaps more convincing fact of human goodness. It may seem a paradox to cite the attributes of humanity in order to justify God. But the argument is strong none the less. For if rectitude is man's highest ideal, if his soul naturally turns to it as the magnet does to the pole, then surely goodness is at the heart of things, and God Himself is good. Nay, then He exists; for goodness becomes the obvious purpose of human life, the "one far-off, divine event, to which the whole Creation moves"; and a purpose implies Mind, necessitates Deity.

Well, is it not true that rectitude is the great human ideal? Do we not all confess it in our daily lives, in the aims we set before them, the assumptions upon which we base them? By the common consent of humanity righteousness is man's normal condition; wrongdoing something abnormal, unnatural, monstrous. Men may differ in their interpretation of righteousness, in their theories of its origin; but they all, from the greatest to the least of them, from the saint to the savage, acclaim it as the ideal good. And the evildoer himself adds his voice to the acclamations. Save in a few exceptional cases, in which the moral sense is a stunted rudiment, the sinner recognizes his sin, knows himself to be a sinner, perceives that he has fallen. Even children, with their limited ethical experience and outlook, know the sorrow and shame of disobedience almost from the first, and so pay homage to the principle of goodness as the norm of human conduct.

And then there is rectitude in the concrete. We are saddened by the evil that is wrought in the world day after day; but we fail to realize the enormous amount of goodness that exists in the world. The one pains us by its abnormality; the other, just because it is normal, fails duly to impress us. We forget the fight with temptation that is for ever being waged by thousands of our fellow-men. The issue of the conflict is certainly unfavourable at times. But the defeat of the fighter does not alter the fact that a fighter he is; and it is the struggle, with the devotion to goodness which it implies, that ought to count with us. But the issue is not always unfavourable. Again and again the fighter is victorious. He conquers his ignoble desires; he renounces so that others may enjoy; he suffers so that others may be at peace. Every human story has many such passages in it. The mother gives her life for her child, the friend for his friend; the moral weakling, on the brink of the abyss, saves himself by a heroic effort; the stricken heart carries its hurt with it to the grave and never loses its integrity.

What does all this mean? It *must* mean something, unless we deem the moral domain the one exception in an ordered universe. Science teaches us to see design in external Nature, though it is not the design of Paley and his "Natural Theology." The varieties of organic life, we are told, are no chance things; they are the products of the action of uniform law. So, too, are the stars in their courses. Well, what are we to say of righteousness? Is that a chance thing—an unmeaning thing? Surely something so fine and exalted must be at least as purposeful as the life-story of a beetle, or the mechanical changes that have produced a planet. Human goodness can only be an expression of the will, and therefore of the character, of Him who made humanity. He means men to be righteous; therefore He must be righteous Himself. Is there any flaw in the argument ? Evolution witnesses to wisdom and power ; how, then, can we be wrong in inferring Divine goodness from goodness in Man ? " Show me Thy glory," cries Moses to God ; and, according to the Rabbinic legend, God answers him by pointing to humanity. " Wherever thou seest the footprints of a man, there thou wilt behold my glory." For human rectitude is the clearest revelation of the Supreme.

But, you will object, there is evil in human life, as well as good. If man's rectitude is a reflex of the Divine goodness, what of his transgression ? The answer is that, as I have said, goodness, not transgression, is the natural state of man, and therefore the true key to the nature of man's Creator. Is it not true, moreover, that righteousness is slowly, but surely, triumphing over evil ? As the world moves on, it moves not only towards a higher civilization, but to loftier conceptions of duty, and to more successful attempts to realize them.

The whole matter, then, turns on goodness, on morality. The universe exists for moral ends—for these, and for nothing else. If we are sure of this, then the problem of moral evil to a large extent disappears. It is probably true that some of this moral evil will always remain as the necessary condition of rectitude, as darkness is of light. But this does not alter the central fact that goodness is the goal of life, and that therefore life and, with it, God, is good. And as to the other difficulty—that of physical evil—that, too, is turned. Unbroken ease and peace would seem to be unattainable in this life ; their opposites seem to be rooted in the very constitution of things, to be the seed of progress and well being. We must look for rest and tranquillity elsewhere, to the quiet joys of conscience, to the serene conviction that we have fought the moral fight bravely, in a temper befitting those who are soldiers of

God. We have not been placed here to bask in the sunshine, so that every intrusion of the chill shadow is resented as a deprivation of our just rights. We have been placed here to seek after the highest form of goodness of which we are able to conceive ; and according as we realize or fall short of this purpose our lives are a success or a failure.

If we can school ourselves to think so, then the world's misery or sin will no longer perturb us. Beneath all the sadness of these phenomena there is a deep-lying joy offering itself even to those who most directly suffer in consequence of them—the joy of rectitude, which swallows up all pain, the pangs of death itself, in victory, which reveals to us God in His glory, as the visible cloud revealed Him to our fathers in olden days.

FRIENDSHIP, DIVINE AND HUMAN

"Abraham my friend."—Isaiah xli., 8.

A published sermon on "Friendship" by a modern Jewish preacher[1] opens with a Talmudic story about a man who slept for a hundred years. He awoke to find himself alone in a crowded world. No one knew him, and he knew no one. In his loneliness he turned to God. "Give me friendship," he cried, "or give me death." His prayer was heard, and he died. For life without the joys of human fellowship is worthless; it is no life. No one is sufficient unto himself. Whatever a man's resources, intellectual, moral, spiritual, they must needs be reinforced, brought out, made effective, by the gifts of others, by love in its various manifestations, if he is to be a whole man, if his nature is to be saved from atrophy and starvation.

The Talmudic parable, however, like parables in general, expresses only one side of the truth. Human fellowship, rich as are the blessings it confers, is but human, and therefore not flawless. Our friends leave us. They go to the other side of the world, or fare beyond the great sea of this life; or they grow tired or cold as the years go on; or they fail when they are put to the test and, as Ben Sira says, "do not abide in the day of trouble." What is left to us then of the joys they brought? The recollection of them will be itself pain. The thought of what Louvain once was only intensifies our sense of its present desolation. Is friend-

[1] The late Dr. Israel Abrahams.

ship, then, inevitably one of those earthly boons which carry decay and disappointment at their heart? No; there is a friendship exempt from this defect. It is the friendship of God. That, *because* He is God—eternal, unchanging, supremely trustworthy—is beyond the reach of all vicissitudes. It is ours as long as we care to have it; it lasts while we last; it goes with us unto death, and beyond it. Of God it may with certitude be said, in the Wise Man's words, that He is the friend that "loveth at all times." So that if the lonely old man in the Talmudic legend had turned to God in another sense, if in the utter loss of human companionship, he had sought the company of the everlasting Friend, he would have had a happier life and death.

Abraham, whose story we have read this morning, is called by our Prophet God's "friend," and he is so designated also in the Second Book of Chronicles. It is a title given to no other Scriptural personage, and it is given for excellent reasons. The essence of friendship is whole-hearted communion of spirit. There are no reservations between friends. Each mind, each heart, is to the other an open book. Have you ever noticed how amply this condition is satisfied in the relations between Abraham and God? With the exception of Moses, no Biblical hero enjoys such intimate fellowship with the Highest. God, we read, " talks " with Abraham; elsewhere He asks Himself, " Shall I hide from Abraham that which I am about to do "; and elsewhere, again, the Patriarch daringly reminds God of His duty:—
" Shall not the Judge of all the earth do right ? " It is not the suppliant pleading here " with bated breath, and whispering humbleness," but the friend, who speaks his mind with stern candour. And with this frankness, there is united in all true friendship an equally unlimited faith and confidence. Either you trust your friend

entirely or not at all. For a friend is your other self—in perfect friendship your better self. A friend is not worth having unless he inspires you, ennobles you, makes you a better man or woman by his exhortation and example. Abraham's story exemplifies this truth also. He believed in God—trusted Him—so Scripture declares; and that trust made his life sublime. At the Divine bidding he breaks up his home, and journeys forth into an unknown land, without protest or question. God's voice gladdens his soul with the promise of a son to cheer his old age, and then kills his joy with the command to slay his child; but again there is silence. His only response is preparation for the awful self-abnegation demanded of him. For the greatest manifestation of friendship is sacrifice—not the laying down of one's life for the friend, as the Gospels insist, but the surrender, for his sake, of what is dearer than life—surrender of it, too, with a readiness, a certain blitheness of spirit, born of conscious service of the beloved.

God, then, is the friend. But the text gives that title to Abraham. He is God's "lover"—that is the meaning of the Hebrew *Oheb*; his attitude is not passive, not receptive merely, but active. But there is no difficulty here. Friendship is mutual, or it is nothing. "The only way to get a friend," says Emerson, "is to be one." Abraham was God's friend because he made a friend of God. He had the insight, the faith, the love which made that choice possible. Is it not wonderful to think of these attributes distinguishing a man in that primitive age, or, to put myself right with the critics, of their being attributed to the hero by primitive tradition? Is it not wonderful to find Deity and man walking together in beautiful intimacy in days when the gods were far off, or came down to earth only to terrify? Surely, Abraham's choice of God as his friend, like the faith from which it sprang, must be "accounted unto him for righteousness."

And we? Is not the story modern enough to have a message for us? Friends we have—most of us. Thank God for it. But can we do without the Friend? Are we certain of escaping the fate of the old man in the Talmudic legend? Human friendship may fail us in our turn. Fortunate then shall we be if we have, to console us for what we have lost, the transcendent love of God. Nay, the two boons may exist side by side. Is there any reason why the Divine friendship should not supplement the human? We can get from God what man—even our nearest and dearest—cannot give us. When trouble overwhelms us is it always the human voice that comforts? "What do these undiscerning mortals know? What do they see?"—so we cry; "Can they plumb the depths of my grief, discern the pangs of my despair?" Verily Job's protest against the futility of his friend's arguments, is true to life. They are "miserable comforters" indeed. But what if the Omniscient is with us, speaking to us words of wisdom and compassion in the recesses of our soul? Then solace and courage come to us because they come from the only source that can give it. And it is so in every situation of life. We are in moral perplexity; we know not where our duty lies; or we are assailed by temptation, and would be strong enough to resist it. Where shall we get the light or the strength we need save from the inner voice which echoes God's?

But the boon must be bought. Friendship is not to be had for the asking. We are advised to prove our friend before we trust him; and so, conversely, we must prove ourselves to our friend before he trusts *us*. Like Abraham, we must make God our friend if He is to be ours. And, for this, the old, old requisites alone will suffice. They are all summed up in one word : love—the real love that utters itself in trust, in submission, in self-surrender, and disdaining all sordid boons, asks only to be a friend and to rest in the joy of it. For the old Patriarchial story repeats itself in our experiences every day. "Go forth "—— such is the repeated command—" go forth bravely to meet the unknown that life holds for you." Shall we not seek the Divine hand to show us the way, to help us on it ? " Blessings await thee "—a child, some gleam of joy, some happy achievement. Shall we not believe, seeing that the Friend has promised it ? Shall we doubt the reality of the boon, or misuse it when it comes ? Shall not the graciousness of the promise sanctify the use of it ? And then the hardest of all demands :—" Give up, give back the gift ; put it from thee with thine own hand." Shall we rebel or murmur ? Shall we reply with a useless " No " ? For our Friend's sake, for his love's sake, evinced and proven a thousand times, we still sacrifice our best. For how else can love be requited save with love ? How can we show that we are grateful for our gifts save by restoring them ?—" My friend " ; it is God's epitaph on one who loved Him. Let us earn it in our turn, and keep it for ever when the time comes.

THE FEAR OF GOD

"But thou shalt fear thy God."—LEVITICUS xix., 14.

THE phrase occurs five times in Leviticus, and is used in each case as a sanction to enforce obedience to some great ethical command. "Curse not the deaf, nor put a stumbling-block before the blind; show respect to age; oppress not the poor"—to all these precepts, in turn, the solemn warning is attached, "Thou shalt fear thy God." The Rabbins, expounding the words, say that they are an appeal to the Israelite's conscience—"a plea addressed to the heart." These sins of oppressing the poor, of taking advantage of the weak and the helpless, are especially to be shunned because the feebleness of the would-be victim constitutes an especially strong temptation to commit them. There must be, then, no evasion, no mental juggling in the matter. There must be absolute sincerity. Hence the exhortation, "Thou shalt fear thy God"—thy God, in whose presence thou are for ever standing, whose eye discerns the most hidden things, and pierces every disguise. It is a striking interpretation. The command to fear God, it tells us, is no incitement to an abject dread of His wrath, His punishment; it is a plea for sincere and wholehearted obedience to the law of righteousness. This is what the fear of God meant to our ancient teachers. It meant a shrinking in horror from every unworthy act, even from the sophistry that dresses up evil so that it may masquerade as good. It means, as an old Jewish writer explicitly says, to fear sin—its deadening grip, its shame,

THE FEAR OF GOD

its degradation. For such fear of God is the only worthy fear of Him. It is the fear of the free man who consciously crowns his freedom by obedience, not the terror of the slave who obeys because he is afraid.

In short, the fear of God, rightly interpreted, means a vivid and abiding sense of the Divine existence, a sharing in the Divine fellowship. It means the fulfilment of the Rabbinic admonition " Let thy God be thy companion " —thy companion, thy friend, who, as a friend should be, will be thy helper, but thy inspirer too. Those who know this noble fear have learnt the secret of life in its twofold sense of a task and an ordinance. They realise the true conception of right living; they understand *why* they live. The thought of God keeps their hands clean and their hearts pure; for how can they sin with God's eye upon them, with God's hand in theirs? Their conscience is their King—a King all the more regal and mighty because deriving authority from a Divine overLord. But the consciousness of God upholds, as well as exhorts; it not only ennobles the character, but calms and strengthens the soul. " The secret of the Lord," cries the Psalmist, " is with them that fear Him." The secret of the Lord!—some would render the Hebrew word Sod by friendship, others by counsel. Whichever interpretation is right, the God-fearing man has all three boons. He has the Divine fellowship, as I have said; he is of those, moreover, whom God whispers in the ear. And so to him the great secret is imparted; he, and he only, has solved the mystery of life. Because he has seen God, he knows everything—everything that is most worth knowing. And because he knows, because there are no problems to perplex him, his spirit is at rest; the veritable peace of God is within him.

As I passed through the City one day this week I came upon an old Church, whose doors were invitingly open.

I entered, and the sudden transition from the noise of the streets to the stillness of the holy place suggested to me some of the thoughts to which I have just given utterance. "Here, and not there," I said to myself, "is the secret of the Lord to be found; not in the outer world, but in the realm within, is the truth about all things to be sought, the real peace to be attained." But what impressed me even more than the quiet Church were those I found there. Three men were on their knees, praying in the stillness. They were men, and, what is more, young men. What they prayed for, whether for moral strength or comfort, or direction in doubt or difficulty, whether they were praying for anything at all, whether they were not simply seeking after the peace and the joy of communion with the Father, content if haply they might find it, I know not. But the strength and the comfort were already theirs, written upon their upturned faces, and the direction, if they were asking for it, would surely be theirs as the inevitable fruit of their worship. It was an incident, I say, which impressed me deeply. One is accustomed to such experiences in foreign towns, but not in London, not, at any rate, in its busiest part, and at the busiest hour of the day. These men had evidently snatched a few moments from their work to be with God, to be with themselves. For them He was a reality, the one reality; and to get into touch with Him was well worth the few minutes they were giving to the attempt. Well would it be, I thought, if there were many more devout hearts such as these. The world would be all the better for it. For these men knew how rightly to value the things of the world—to value them rightly, which is not the same thing as despising them; they knew how to battle with trouble; they knew how to fight a worse evil still—the evil in themselves. One felt that one would rather trust these

THE FEAR OF GOD

prayerful souls—trust them to be truthful and honest and pure—than the many godless ones among the crowd of passers-by outside.

The incident I am describing has its counterpart, I need hardly say, elsewhere than in the Churches. In the poor Jewish quarter in the East End there are Synagogues where pious people are to be found at every hour of the day, intent upon prayer or meditation or sacred study. It may be said that these devout acts are not essential to the good life, that thousands keep themselves clean amid the grime of the world without any aid save that which they draw from their innate courage and determination. I do not deny it. But there are times when the battle grows too fierce for singlehanded struggle, when the fund of moral strength within ourselves needs replenishing, when the believer needs to have his belief reinvigorated by conscious contact with its Divine Subject. Nay, not everyone is a believer. For too many, God does not exist; and these have truly to fight the moral battle singlehanded, for they fight it not merely alone, but crippled. Must they not, then, necessarily fight it, at least now and again, at a sore disadvantage? You may say that the sense of God, the fear of Him, is a gift, that we have not all the capacity for religion, or rather the same capacity for it. But there is such a thing as the will, the determination, to believe; and we must see to it that it does not become inert and enfeebled by disuse. It is not so much the lack of the religious sentiment, but the neglect of it, that makes the Godless life. And so we must go to the Supreme from time to time to be taught of Him, to be sure of Him.

And I say this to you—to you who are worshippers—because I would entreat you to keep fast hold upon your fear of God, and to make it a living thing. Let not doubt or insidious example persuade you to give up your habit of prayer, public and private, and let that prayer be " no mechanical routine," to use the Talmudic phrase, but sincere and heartfelt. Especially see to it that you teach the fear of God to your children, that you encourage them in it, not discourage them from it by indifference or positive hostility. Let belief and trust in Him be their most precious possession, for which you willingly sacrifice all other prizes. For out of it are the issues of life—all that makes life fair and lovely, all the peace and the blessing that make it worth having. And surely you, who love your children, must needs desire for them this supreme boon, and find your deepest joy in helping them to win it.

THE CRY OF RELIGION

"Blessed be God."—PSALM lxviii., 35.

THESE are the closing words of the Psalm, and they are the Psalm itself writ small. They are at once its climax and its epitome. The Psalm is one long glorification, one long benediction, of God for His majesty and His condescension, for the awe-inspiring revelation of His might in Nature and in History, for His mercies also to sad and lowly folk, to the fatherless and the widow and to them that languish in the prison-house. It is an expression of humble submission to this august God, a song of thanksgiving for His goodness, a profession of faith in His existence and His sovereign rule. Well, then, does it end with "Blessed be God," the cry of Religion through all the ages.

"Blessed be God"—it is a cry of adoration and of gratitude. All the primal emotions that lift the human soul out of the narrow environment of this earthly life are gathered up into it. As old as the beginning of man's history, these emotions have written themselves deep upon all his history. There never was a time in the recorded life of the world when Religion, in however crude a form, was not; will there ever come a time when it will have ceased to be? We religionists cherish the belief in a revelation of God to men; will the day ever dawn when that revelation will be wholly discredited, and when the very consciousness of God will have faded out of the human soul?

Now and again we are inclined to answer Yes. The age seems to be one of expiring faith. There is less reverence than of old for sacred things ; men are turning, in ever increasing numbers, from Religion to Philanthropy, to Art, to Science, to Letters, for the satisfaction of their higher instincts. Many causes have united to produce these phenomena—the increased severity of the struggle for existence, which has diverted men's thoughts from spiritual concerns to material preoccupations ; the growth of the scientific temper, too, with its demands for rigid proofs even for the intuitions of the soul. The direct teachings of physical science have also played their part. The disclosure of the reign of law throughout the universe has tended to hide God, and to encourage the thought that man is in the grasp of a pitiless necessity, not in the gracious hands of a wise and loving Father. The doctrine of Evolution, in particular, which, substituting mechanical processes for creative energy as the explanation of the world, has powerfully helped to dethrone the God-idea from its commanding place in the human mind. Science, moreover, has helped not only to obscure the Divine, but to dwarf humanity. Men are beginning to realise their place in Nature, to understand their insignificance compared with the cosmos, and to ask themselves whether, assuming that this infinite domain has a Divine Ruler, He can possibly care what becomes of them, or heed them when they call to Him. Add to this the rise of Biblical criticism, of the comparative study of Religion, of systematic research in the domain of folk-lore—add, too, a greater sensitiveness to the tragedy of the world, to its cruelty and pain and sin, with the consequent doubt of divine goodness or omnipotence, and you will have a sufficient explanation of modern irreligion, or what seems to be such.

An explanation, but not a vindication. If men distrust the religious temper to-day it is in defiance of

THE CRY OF RELIGION

reason, though science affirms the direct contrary. The sceptic doubts—to the man of Science it sounds like heresy to say so—because of the very narrowness of his outlook. He does not understand the testimony to which he pins his faith. The teachings of Science have not really deposed God, but more firmly enthroned Him. This doctrine of Evolution, which is accountable for so much materialism, in reality proclaims and deifies the wondrous Power that could endow a primordial speck of matter, countless aeons ago, with the capacity for producing the infinite variety of life which peoples this world of ours. If, as the Creator, God is mighty, yet mightier is He as the great Being who, in the remote beginnings of things, sent the universe spinning down the grooves of change, endowed it from the first with all the grand and numberless potencies which have realised themselves by slow and majestic stages in the fullness of time. Law reigns throughout Nature ; but Law implies Mind ; and that the Divine mind is careful not only of the type but of the single life, we must believe, or deny the message of " the meanest flower that blows." The Bible, too, is not what it once was to many minds. It is human as well as Divine. But Divine nevertheless it is, the Word, as some one has said, if not the words, of God. Is it less Divine, less mighty, because it is a Moses that speaks, and God answers him with a voice, because the truths which the sacred page declares are echoed and confirmed by the mystic voice in every human soul ? Each religion, moreover, is but a phase of the religious idea common to the race ; it has been developed from some phase lower than itself by discarding some superstition or myth. But is it false on that account ? Is not the universality of the religious idea a proof of its necessity for the human mind, a proof of its truth ? Man is but an insignificant item in the totality of life ;

but is the infinite God prevented on that account from hearing him ? Is it not the very function of omnipotence to heed the smallest creature, to turn at its call, to share its pain, to thrill to its joy ? The Divine grandeur does not prevent us from believing it ; it helps us—forces us—to believe it. Nor do the pain and the need themselves prevent us. Life is not all pain ; it is happiness too. And shall we judge the Infinite God by one side only of our destiny ? Shall we judge the Infinite God at all—we finite things, creatures of a day ?

There is no reason, then, why religion should perish. On the contrary, there is every reason why it should, and must, go on living. And in truth it has far more vitality even to-day than it seems to possess. These waves of doubt have passed over the world before, without submerging it. They are always less formidable than they seem. Religion is still the overmastering force in millions of lives, still their one strength and consolation. We are misled, moreover, by narrow interpretations of our term. We identify Religion with observance, and because there is a growing impatience of observance in these times we conclude that Religion is decrepit, moribund. Whereas Religion is essentially the consciousness of God and the endeavour, no matter by what means, to give effect to that consciousness in the daily life. If this definition be correct, must we not admit that there are many more religious people in the world than we are inclined to believe ? It has been well said that, though this is seemingly an age of irreligion, never was there an age in which books about Religion were more greedily read. It is the one topic which dominates the thoughtful mind. Religion is not perishing. There is doubt rather than denial. The forces within men forbid them to deny ; the Unseen keeps its mystic grip upon the spirit. A man may be a

THE CRY OF RELIGION

sceptic intellectually ; emotionally he is still a believer. Deep down in his consciousness there is an abiding sense of God, which the crises of life, far from destroying it, only arouse and strengthen.

The truth is that Religion goes on living because men cannot let it perish. It is to the spirit that dwells in Man what his breath is to his body. A higher life is well-nigh impossible without it, and the yearning after a higher life is part of man's very nature. The joys of the mind, the solace of Art, the contemplation of the morally Beautiful cannot appease that yearning. The cry " Blessed be God " still represents the cry of the human soul. Men's one elementary need is to come into touch with Him who is the life of the universe, the ultimate reality which Art and Poetry and Music only faintly shadow forth, the master-light of all our intellectual, all our moral, seeing. They must have Him to commune with, to invoke in their perplexity, to rest upon in their weakness, to entreat in their agony, to bless in their joy. Their vaunted science does not satisfy their need as human beings ; it does not even satisfy their intellectual needs. When they have weighed a star, and resolved matter into its constituents, they feel that they are still fumbling with the lock of the everlasting doors, that the essential truth at the heart of all things is still eluding them. Behind the universe, whose riddle they claim to have solved, is its Master, its Maker, its Soul ; beyond and transcending the visible which they handle so confidently is the Unseen, whose mysteries defy their analysis, but compel their secret, their inmost homage.

The age of irreligion ? Let us rather say that it is the age of faith—faith asserting itself in the very bankruptcy of knowledge—faith, wavering and hesitating and groping its way, but faith that will be firmly established at last. What in detail its ultimate shape will be no one may prophesy. But we can discern its broad outlines. The coming religion will not be philanthropy alone, the service of man divorced from its great inspiration : the service of God. It will not be morality alone ; for morality, though it is the crown and the efflorescence of the religious life, must, if it is to be stable, acknowledge God as its source, its ideal, its law giver. Religion without the Divine is unthinkable, impossible. The religion of the future, moreover, will have its theology, but it will be of the simplest ; it will be broad and general, too, not seeking to limit the Infinite, to define the undefinable ; for " who by searching can find out God ? " It will enthrone the Supreme in the high and holy place, but bring Him also into closest touch with the hearts and lives of men. It will link itself sparingly to ceremonial ; but it will satisfy men's desire for worship. Still, as of old, it will utter itself in the words : " Blessed be God."

When such a religion prevails Judaism will triumph, Sinai find its justification. Do I mean that Judaism is no more than this, and that we are at liberty here and now to forsake it for the religion that will one day conquer the world ? No ; but that through our constancy to Judaism we are to speed the coming of that day. Our Psalm, with its final exclamation, is a proclamation of the God of Israel, a glorification of His truth confided ages ago to His people's keeping. In our turn, then, let us cry " Blessed be God," and, in the cry, voice our gratitude for our ancient religion, and our promise to keep it new by our loyalty, until its great work is done.

THE WAR AND RELIGION

THE one subject of interest for men and women at the present moment is the war; the one subject of interest for Jews always is, or ought to be, Religion. In speaking to-day of the war and Religion I may count with certainty upon a sympathetic hearing from this congregation.

For more than three years we have been the breathless, the agonized spectators of a world-tragedy. And not spectators of it only, but sharers in it. It has become part of our very lives; the woe of it is ours in the most literal sense. There is scarcely a home on which the shadow of death has not fallen. If the destroying angel has passed us by, we have heard at any rate, to use the classic image, the beating of his wings. None of us can detach himself from this far-reaching catastrophe. It may have spared us personally, but we are stricken none the less. The cry of the victims, hurt in body or soul, the cry of civilization, "wounded in the house of its friends," echoes in all our hearts. We should be inhuman were it not so. Nor is it only emotion that responds—pity, anger, shame; thought is troubled too. "There are tears in human fate, and the woes of men afflict the mind"—yes, the mind; the words of the old Roman poet are literally true. We begin to question our most fundamental convictions. We ask ourselves "Where is God in all this terrifying upheaval? Where is His goodness, His omnipotence?"

It is not my present purpose to answer this question. I shall attempt no theodicy. For the effort to vindicate

God when life seems to arraign Him, an effort always only partially successful at best, is superfluous. It has never changed a sceptic into a believer. What we have to do is not to argue about God, but to experience Him. The approach to the Highest is by way of the spirit, not of the intellect. Those who would be sure of Him, of His rectitude and His love, must assume them as the unimpeachable postulates, though life, "red in tooth and claw, shrieks against the creed." "The great venture of faith"—it is well phrased; the enterprise calls for all our confidence, our steadfastness, our courage. My purpose is not to solve the theological problems set us by this war, but to inquire how Religion has emerged from their impact. Has its empire over the practical life been shaken by the events of the past three years? This is a question to which an answer may properly be attempted; for to answer it in a way favourable to the hopes of the believer is to give him heart, and strength, and solace.

How, then, has the war affected Religion? Let me give straightway what I believe to be the true answer. The war has shaken religions; Religion it has left unmoved. Men are beginning, under the stress of recent experiences, to recast their theology, their views about the relation of God to the world; they are putting rites and symbols into their due perspective. But the sense of the Unseen, the hypothesis of Deity as the one adequate explanation of the Universe, the conviction that God lives and reigns—this seems to me as strong and as widespread as ever. In expressing this opinion I am taking account of facts. There are people whose religion the war has not touched, simply because they have virtually no religion; they have never brought religion into relation with their lives. A few days ago I discussed the subject with an intelligent observer, who has friends

THE WAR AND RELIGION

in various sections of society. I asked her whether she thought that the war had made people less religious. Her reply was " I don't think so ; most of my acquaintances never think about religion ; they go their way without it." In their case, then, religion has suffered no defeat. But a large number of persons are of a different temper. They do think about religion ; and, though their faith has been sorely tried, it has stood fast. My vocation brings me almost every day into close contact with sorrowing people in these times, and I cannot recall any instance in which the most cruel stroke inflicted by the war has extorted a cry of revolt against God or denial of Him. A sombre bewilderment, an utter inability to explain—yes, but also trust and submission. Where the blow has been most crushing there has been the greatest effort to reach up to the handgrasp of the Father, the most intense yearning to be at one with Him in prayer. This touching resignation has manifested itself in cases where I least expected to find it, where a certain worldliness or spiritual apathy has seemed most to dominate life. A short time ago I sent a message of sympathy to a mother utterly broken down by the death of her son, killed in action. " My boy," she wrote, " did not care much for the forms of religion, but he had faith—faith, particularly, in a special immortality for those who have laid down their lives in battle. And that faith," she added, " is mine too."

If we turn from the rank and file to the leaders, the evidence is the same. I suppose there are few more keen-witted men in our English life to-day than Sir Arthur Conan Doyle and Mr. H. G. Wells. The war found the former an agnostic ; it has left him an avowed believer. Whether it has made him one I do not know. But, despite the perplexing problems it raises, it has not prevented him from being one. More notable still is the second of these spiritual histories. Nine or ten years ago Mr. Wells's religion was vague, inchoate. He rejected, as he tells us in his *First and Last Things*, the idea of a personal God; the Universe, he held, was rational; there was a scheme behind it, his belief in which "not even the cruelty of nature could defeat." But he could not see his way to a Divine schemer. Now he has taken the logical step; he has taken, or announced, it during the war and, as it would seem, paradoxically enough, as the direct consequence of the war. He now believes in "God, the Invisible King," the lover and helper of men, who is busily striving to evolve order out of the existing chaos, blessing out of the horrid welter of cruelty and bloodshed. He will dry the tears of men if they will only submit themselves to Him, acknowledging His kingdom and joining with Him in the task of establishing it on earth. How Mr. Wells has come by this new and fuller faith he does not explicitly tell us in his recent book; all he says is that it has come to him suddenly as a supernatural experience. He owns, and calls himself, a mystic; in his own words, he has "found God." Elsewhere he gives another, though not necessarily an inconsistent, account of the matter. The war it is that has helped him to find the great truth he had previously missed. In *Mr. Britling* he describes a bereaved man and woman arguing about religion and the war. "Do you still believe in God?" one asks the other. "Yes," is the reply. "It's plain to me. If there was nothing else in all the world but our kindness for each other or the love we bear our dead, if everything else was cruelty and mockery and bitterness, it would still be certain that there was a God of love and righteousness. If there were no signs of God in all the world but the godliness we have seen in those two boys of ours,"

THE WAR AND RELIGION

that would be enough to prove that He lives. Here the author himself is speaking, and he speaks for countless others. We cannot detach from the great scheme of things the marvellous courage and self-renunciation which the war has evoked from both the dead and the living—from those who have gone to their death, and from those who, with equal heroism, have let them go. What is all this greatness of soul but a manifestation of the Divine? One recalls the fine saying of the Rabbins: —" Wherever "—so God declares—" wherever thou findest the footprints of men—of men at their best— there I stand before thee." Nay, more, under the shock of war the human spirit, temporarily disturbed, turns, as the magnet to the pole, inevitably to the Supreme. We look abroad upon a world convulsed, and ask if God can indeed be loving or, if so, almighty. But the doubt is momentary. Quickly the soul returns to her rest. We must have God if life is not to be utterly meaningless, a baffling, torturing riddle. And in some crisis of experience, when we are bereft of our most precious things, and hope seems to have been slain for ever, then it is that we go instinctively to the one source of strength and peace, not merely to get strength and peace, but to be alone with Him who is our one possible companion in our darkest hour. Nothing can destroy this elementary and everlasting need of the human soul. Just when logic would expel God from life the spirit irresistibly sends us to Him. Religion has survived a thousand wars; it will survive this one too. It will live as long as men endure.

So far, then, as to Religion. What of Judaism? That the war is affecting it is certain. When a world-order is passing away no religion can stand where it did. When big episodes are being enacted the personal religious outlook must needs be widened. The testimony of Christian chaplains at the front is echoed by their Jewish colleagues. Amid the clangour of the guns men come to public worship who never came before. But to ensure its appeal that worship has to be simple, intelligible, living. The old forms and the old formulas are being weighed in the balance, and those that are found wanting are being more or less openly rejected. In brief, a new Judaism is in the making, broader in conception, more spiritual, more real. Men who have looked death in the eyes are more eager to face life seriously, and, using the most appropriate means, to face it with the aid of Religion. But it *has* to be an aid, not a hindrance ; it has to be genuine Religion, an affair of the soul, not mere *camouflage*, mere make-belief. The Revolution in Russia, the work of the war, is another factor in the present situation. The establishment of freedom in that country, the religious citadel of our people, will liberate Judaism as well as the Jew. The opening of the Ghetto will set free the Jewish spirit. Out of the throes of the present conflict a new—may we not say a better ?—Judaism is being born.

We of the liberal creed may hail this new birth, rejoice to be thus vindicated. But something besides rejoicing becomes us. Personally, I confess to a regret that so much of the old order seems destined to pass away. I think wistfully of the picturesque observances that made Judaism in my youth so lovable ; nor can I forget that ceremonial is itself a bond, a factor of the religious life, as well as an expression of it. And I cannot help asking whether we are safe in trusting, all but exclusively, to less concrete things to feed and nourish the Jewish consciousness. The outlook is by no means reassuring. Surely we liberal Jews may well take thought, and resolve to keep fast hold of the Judaism we have, to save it from the enrcoaching tide of latter-day laxity. Freedom has its dangers as well as its boons. It may become a licence for religious slackness, and so compromise our right to be free, imperil the very cause to which we are pledged. Largely released from the lower service of ritual, delivered from the bonds of an antiquated creed, we are, by that very fact, necessarily committed to a more resolute loyalty to the higher observance and the nobler ideals that remain. Are we all as true as we ought to be to this implicit covenant ? At present a large number of English Jews—reform or liberal Jews among them—keep only one day holy in the year. The celebration binds them to Judaism, to Israel, by the feeblest of ties ; it can hardly guarantee them a religious life worthy of the name. But what is Israel without Religion ? You cannot, to repeat the familiar phrase, have Judaism without Jews, or Jews without Judaism. Abolish religion, and Israel's right to live disappears. Our Christian neighbours demand that we shall be a religious people, and we fall utterly in their estimation if we disappointment them. But this is a comparatively small matter. What is the world's opinion, compared with our own self-respect, our fealty or indifference, to a great historic trust ?

I commend this thought to you in all humility, but in all earnestness. Our duty, surely, is not discharged when we have nominally enlisted under the banner of progressive Judaism. A label is truly but a scrap of paper. We have to show that, in our case, it is the symbol of a sincere and deep-lying enthusiasm for a holy cause. If we claim to march in the vanguard of the Jewish host, that very fact binds us to staunchness and energy ; for shall we disconcert the ranks behind us ? Shall we make sport for them ? But we owe a duty to our liberalism itself ; we have to justify it by our Jewishness, by the ardour for Israel's creed and life-task which animates and governs our lives. The war has slain many ; let it not be said that it has killed our Judaism too, destroyed something fine in our selves—our power of self-sacrifice for a sacred ideal, our power to feel and to heed a great spiritual call.

THE WAR AND THE FUTURE

> "They shall not hurt nor destroy in all My Holy Mountain; for the Earth shall be full of the knowlege of the Lord as the waters cover the Sea."—ISAIAH xi., 9.

"THE knowledge of the Lord"—what does it mean? It means a realisation of the existence, the nearness of God, issuing in righteousness towards men. So the Prophets understood and used the expression. "Thy Father," says Jeremiah, addressing the King, "thy Father was just to the poor and needy; Was not this to know me? saith the Lord." And Isaiah, in the text, employs the phrase in a like sense. In the Golden Age the knowledge of the Lord, overflowing the world like a beneficent, health-giving sea, is to bring in the reign of Love. Violence and cruelty can have no place in the ideal human society; they are incompatible with the knowledge of God, a defiance of His will. The Messianic Era must needs be a time when the death-knell of War will have sounded, and mankind be saved for ever from its calamities, from its paralysing menace, from the nightmare of its anticipation. Loving kindness and peace are what God desires; they represent His ultimate purpose in the ordering of the world.

At first sight the passage from which our Pentateuchal reading has been taken this morning seems at variance with this idea. War is there represented as being, not contrary to the Divine desire, but in keeping with it. Nay, to make War is elevated into a positive command. If the Israelites beseige a city which makes no response to their offer of peace, then they are to fight against it and destroy it. But the contradiction is not so sharp as it appears. For the Mosaic legislator War was probably only a temporary expedient, justified by the necessity of conquering Canaan, and by the general exigencies of a primitive age. When the necessity disappeared the expedient would pass away with it. At any rate, we may fairly say that of the two conceptions, Peace and War, Peace, as the expression of the ultimate Divine purpose, as marking the final destiny of the World, represents the true Jewish ideal. Deuteronomy takes us back to a long-past, barbaric age; Isaiah projects us into an era yet to dawn, one on which the hopes and the longings of all good men to-day are immovably fixed.

War, then, is a violation, not a fulfilment of the Divine Will. Is this a self-evident proposition? No; there are powerful minds who deny it. Placing themselves at the standpoint of the fighting Hebrews of old, even surpassing them in their zeal for the sword, they not only look upon War with equanimity, but acclaim it as the essential condition of human progress. To " hurt and destroy," as the indispensable means of national aggrandisement, is, for them, as literally a command of God, as indisputably a fulfilment of His Purpose, as it is represented to be in Deuteronomy. The only difference is that while the ancient Israelites may possibly have regarded the Deuteronomic command as temporary, the modern militarist regards it as permanent. For him warfare is not merely permissible; it is a sacred duty. It is no essential evil, but a blessing. This is the theory which, following his teacher Treitschke, General von Bernhardi sets forth with equal candour and calmness in his famous book entitled *Germany and the Next War*. Those who would understand the origin and significance of the terrible conflict now raging should avail themselves of the opportunity offered by a popular reprint to read this amazing work. The author does not apologise for War ; he glorifies it. To abolish it would, he declares, be " immoral." It is the duty of a nation to be strong, to excel all others in the race for material and spiritual pre-eminence. But it can so excel only by *being* strong—strong physically—by resort to force, by victory on the battlefield, gained at the cost of no matter what suffering for the hapless foe. The nation that makes War its ideal, that prepares for it, that resolutely engages in it as occasion demands, is a vigorous nation, a nation with a future ; the people whose cherished dream is peace, is a people effete, degenerate, doomed. All nature, all experience, teach the doctrine. What is life, from its lowest to its highest manifestations, but struggle ? Insect and man have alike to submit to that ordinance. And from the conflict the finest type is evolved. The struggle " is a creator, for it eliminates "—eliminates the weak and the decadent, who do not deserve to survive. It is under the influence of such ideas—" gladiatorial " Huxley calls them—that Germany is waging the present War. She is waging it, as Bernhardi indicates, in the first place for material prizes—for empire and its attendant power, for colonies, in which to plant her surplus population, for markets, in which to sell her products, for the " place in the sun " hitherto denied her. But this is only one of her aims. Joined to it is a higher purpose. Germany has a spiritual self, in which she reposes an unswerving faith. She has a culture, a civilisation, which she believes to be of surpassing value for mankind, and which she accordingly deems it her mission to extend to mankind. This she can do by becoming a world-power, by acquiring world-wide dominion. " Force," to quote the approving interpretation of a recent English writer[1]—his, we may well believe, is almost a solitary voice in this country—" force may be necessary to establish this domination; but its ends are spiritual. The triumph of the Empire will be the triumph of the German world-vision in all the departments of human life and energy, in religion, poetry, science, art, politics and social endeavour."

This, in brief, is the theory in pursuance of which one of the most deadly wars in history has been entered upon. Those who formulate that theory are not to be charged with hypocrisy; they sincerely believe in it. " Germany above all," Germany *over* all, is a creed which they passionately hold as containing the potency of immeasurable good, not for their fatherland only, but for the world at large. But sincerely held beliefs are not necessarily true beliefs. One may not be a deceiver and yet may be self-deceived. Are these men self-deceived? Are we to accept a doctrine which regards mankind as doomed beyond escape to a periodical recurrence of the terrible episodes which are now being enacted almost before our very eyes? Are we for the doctrine of Deuteronomy, wrought into a newer and fiercer gospel of blood and iron, or for the tender, the hopeful, the ennobling idealism of Isaiah? Is the world for ever fated, like an infant, to make a few tottering steps onward, only to fall, to suffer, and with difficulty to stand erect again? Is all our boasted progress a pitiably frail structure, which war, like an earthquake or a tempest, is destined to sweep away time after time? If so, then life is unintelligible, and hope and faith are mockeries. I do not deny that war has been the seed of progress. But is it the indispensable seed? War cleanses the atmosphere. But are there not other purifying agents, more truly beneficent because unmixed

[1] J. A. Cramb: " Germany and England."

with evil? Can the well-being of the world not be assured by means that do not bring with them inevitable suffering and death? "God," says Treitschke, "will see to it that War always recurs as a drastic medicine for the human race." We prefer to think of the human race, not as a confirmed invalid, but as a healthy organism able to dispense with the aid of deadly drugs. War, cries the militarist, has been the rule ever since the world began. All the more reason, I reply, why it should cease now. It has exercised its ruinous sway long enough.

Is its complete cessation impossible? Life is a battle; but must men make the fight more bitter by their own act? Is it not their part to soften the conflict, to make it more bearable? Of what use is it to alleviate poverty, to bind up the wounds of the stricken, to dry the tears of the sorrowful, if all the moral, all the redemptive effect of the gracious work is to be undone at a blow? If we believe that progress is only possible through war, then let us openly glorify barbarism, since we have already joined its ranks. Let us admit that we have no God, seeing that we despair of Him in despairing of humanity.

No; we will have none of the hateful doctrine. If, in the eyes of some men, war seems a necessity, all the more strenuously must we fight against it. For belief in it, the preaching of it, is a menace to humanity. Once typhus, and small-pox, and gaol-fever, highway robbery and brigandage—a host of evils, physical and moral—seemed ineradicable. But, nothing daunted, we fought against them and overcame them. Shall we be less slack in dealing with the still worse evils of war and its alarms? One encouragement we have; it lies in the fact that these war-intoxicated thinkers are forced to justify their doctrine to their conscience by giving it a seemingly philosophical basis. In a more primitive age there would have been no apology, for men would have felt the need of none.

And then as to the civilising mission of nations. Granted that they have one, is force the only instrument for accomplishing it? Is it not rather the everlasting hindrance to its accomplishment? Think of it. To slaughter men in the name of progress, make homes desolate in the name of civilisation, multiply widows and orphans in the sacred cause of culture!—was there ever such a glaring self-contradiction? How can those who do such deeds justify their right to the spiritual leadership of mankind? What sort of place in the sun *do* they deserve—they who have soiled themselves by dark deeds which will not bear the light? Their vaunted civilisation is tainted; it stands self-condemned. No; force can achieve nothing worth having. Whatever has been accomplished for the good of mankind hitherto has been accomplished by totally opposite methods. Justice, compassion, love—these are the true levers of the world, the sole justifiers of men. " Not by might nor by power, but by my spirit, saith the Lord of Hosts."

Culture, ideals—all the great nations have them, and these spiritual possessions of theirs are all needed to ensure the progress of humanity. But they must be used in the spiritual temper that befits them; they must be used, not to curse, but to bless. Let all the nations, laying aside their murderous weapons, cultivate the rivalries of peace. Bringing their higher endowments into one common stock, let them vie with each other in the effort to make the richest contribution from that joint spiritual fund to the well-being of mankind. Thus, and thus only, will they attain to true power, avoid the degeneracy which the modern war-maker so greatly dreads. It is no untimely lesson, though the cannon are roaring at this moment, and would deafen our ears to all but warlike teachings. We have to think of peace even now, to resolve that, as far as we can help to ensure it, this conflict shall prove to be a war against war, that when it has reached its end at last a brotherhood of the nations shall take the place of a world in arms. Then Peace will have achieved a victory more renowned than War. Then one great stride will have been made towards the halcyon time of which our prophets dreamed, when "men shall not hurt nor destroy, seeing that the earth shall be filled with the knowledge of the Lord as the waters cover the sea."

CHRISTMAS AND WAR

I HAVE read that Anton Lang, the impersonator of the Christian Saviour in the Oberammergau Passion Play, was killed in battle a few weeks ago. The event was symbolic. According to the old Apostolic idea the recreant Christian, who has "tasted the good word," and "fallen away," crucifies his Lord afresh, and "puts Him to open shame." And what faithlessness to the "Prince of Peace" can be more flagrant than that which has plunged twentieth-century Christendom into the worst horrors of war? Among the many wounds inflicted upon the Master by his followers none has been more cruel or more deadly. The Gospel of Peace and Goodwill, which he claimed to have been divinely chosen to preach, has been flouted, derided, falsified by its plighted adherents. Verily Christ has been slain in this war.

To-day is His birthday. In thousands of churches they are rehearsing the story of the Nativity, with its account of the angelic choir who sing their promise of a glorious era about to dawn on a sorrowing world.

> Yea, Truth and Justice then
> Will down return to men,
> Orb'd in a rainbow; and, like glories wearing,
> Mercy will sit between,
> Thron'd in celestial sheen,
> With radiant feet the tissued clouds down steering:
> And heav'n, as at some festival,
> Will open wide the gates of her high palace hall.

But that Golden Age did not come then, nor has it ever come. On the contrary, the lapse of nineteen centuries finds mankind not at peace, but at war ; not the gospel of love, but the gospel of hate dominates the world. Christmas Day, which should be the festival of peace and goodwill, falls in a time of general carnage and rapine ; the birthday of the Master becomes a day of mourning at his murder.

The thought will find utterance in many a Christian pulpit this morning. For to no one is the painful disparity between the doctrine and practice of his communion more evident than to the devout Christian himself. The seeming failure of Christ !—a thousand preachers will discuss the theme. As for us, let us be just. "Christianity is bankrupt," men cry, and point, as evidence, to the present state of the world. Shall we not rather say that Christendom is bankrupt ? What is good, and true, and mighty in the Christian religion is good, and true, and mighty still. It will bear fruit in God's good time. Why should we not acknowledge it, as great Jews, like Maimonides and Jehudah Halevi, acknowledged it ? When the simple teaching of the Gospels, as distinguished from St. Paul's pagan travesty of it, triumphs, when men turn to God, the Father, and serve Him with one consent, when they practise righteousness and love towards each other all the world over, then Israel's hope, cherished through the ages with pathetic persistence, will be fulfilled. The Gentiles will have been led along the way of their own religions to the one Religion which Judaism enshrines. No ; it is not Christianity—true Christianity—that has failed, but its self-styled adherents. The call to God, to rectitude, to peace and brotherliness, has come to them, but they have been heedless of it. Theirs is the defeat.

But, you will say, is this not an admission of Christianity's failure ? The very fact that it has pleaded with men in vain proves its impotence. It should have been strong enough to break down their stubbornness, to capture their souls by the sheer beauty of its doctrine. But see where the argument leads us! God himself has been pleading with men for much more than nineteen centuries, and too often pleading in vain. Sin still holds sway; one of the deadliest wars in history is raging. But dare we say on that account that God has failed, that His hand has waxed short? Nay, let us look at home. We Jews, by the theory of our religion, are " a kingdom of priests and a holy nation," bound to be the world's exemplars in rectitude and sanctity of life. Is not the title a mockery, the bond a dead letter? But shall we say on that account that Judaism is bankrupt? When Israel has gotten him " a new heart and a new spirit," a soul sensitive to the appeal of his God, alive to the splendour of his mission, then the vitality and the power of his religion will be revealed to himself and to mankind.

No; Christianity, in its essence, is still a living religion. In its essence, I say, because, as I have already suggested, we must discriminate. The old theistic and ethical ideas of its Founder are indestructible. We Jews must necessarily believe it because those ideas were derived from the Judaism in which he who taught them was born and nourished. The pagan teachings grafted upon them will perish. And it is to these later accretions that we must look for the causes of the failure of which Christianity seemingly stands convicted. Why is the message of peace and goodwill set at naught by the nations to-day? Why is brotherhood fled from the earth, and war still the favoured arbiter of international disputes? Why is the Master wounded, slain, in the house of his friends? Let a Christian minister answer the question. "Christianity," he declares, "has never dared to call any war wrong." By Christianity he clearly means the Church; and the accusation is true. Not content with tolerating war, the Church has blessed it. Nay, it has made itself a secular power even more than a religious one. "Do you submit to the Church Militant?" said the ecclesiastics to Joan of Arc when they held her life in their grasp. "I submit," she replied, "only to the Church triumphant above." The Church Militant, not the humble, peaceful Church of the Founder, with a kingdom not of this world—*there* is the origin of half the wars that have devastated the earth. The Church has strained after earthly power and dominion even more eagerly than after spiritual supremacy. It has emphasized the religious differences of men instead of reconciling them, seeking its victories not by conciliation, but by persecution, as we Jews know to our cost, triumphing not by love, but by destruction and death. In one hand it has held the crucifix, in the other the sword. Can we wonder that the world, morally speaking, stands where it does, that the earth is being drenched with blood in this year of grace?

But again let us be just. This conception of the character and mission of the church is old and well nigh outworn; it is fading away before the uprising of a nobler vision. In all the civilized world Religion is being regenerated by the infusion of humanitarian ideas. The signs of it are unmistakable. War is far—very far —from obsolete, but it has lost much of its ancient glamour and glory. It is something of which to be ashamed, something to be apologized for. Even our chief enemy in this present conflict, while extolling war as the maker and preserver of a people's vigour, inconsistently excuses this particular war as one of self-defence. And we, his antagonists, though believing and declaring that our cause is just, confess in our inmost hearts that the means we have chosen to vindicate it are at best a necessary evil, a huge blot on our civilisation. On both sides the confession is translated into action. This day last year a truce in the gigantic fight was called, out of respect for the day's sacred associations. It was a striking self-contradiction. For if warfare is a glaring anomaly on any one day, it is that always. Is not God ever near us, His word for ever calling to our hearts? Ought not every day, every hour, to be consecrated to Him? Nay, are not men always brothers? Is the duty of forgiveness and compassion subject even to a moment's moratorium? No; for the Christian to think of honouring his Master by a Christmas truce is in effect to dishonour him, to accentuate the sin against love which all war involves. He sees the better way, but deliberately chooses the worse. And yet all such inconsistencies have their good side, for they betray a conscience disquieted, the first stage on the road to repentance. They contain the promise and potency of recovered sanity for mankind. They foreshadow the time when the veil that is spread over all nations, hiding from them the higher truth, shall be rent, when the clash of arms shall cease not for a day, or for a century, but for ever. Let us join our supplications to those of our brothers of all creeds and all nationalities for the speeding of that time. With the English poet let us pray:—

> Oh! let Thy Word prevail, to take away
> The sting of human nature. Spread the law,
> As it is written in Thy holy book,
> Throughout all lands; let every nation hear
> The high behest, and every heart obey,
> Both for the love of purity and hope
> Which it affords to such as do Thy will
> And persevere in good, that they shall rise
> And have a nearer view of Thee in heaven.
>   Father of good! this prayer in bounty grant,
> In mercy grant it, to Thy wretched sons.
> Then, not till then, shall persecution cease,
> And cruel wars expire.

CHRISTMAS AND WAR

           Shall enmity and strife,
Falsehood and guile, be left to sow their seed
And the kind never perish ? Is the hope
Fallacious, or shall righteousness obtain
A peaceable dominion, wide as earth
And ne'er to fail ?
           The law of faith,
Working through love, such conquest shall it gain,
Such triumph over sin and guilt achieve ?
Almighty Lord, Thy further grace impart !

To this lovely petition let us cry, with all hearts, Amen ! Amen !

PEACE AND GOODWILL

" He was wounded through our transgressions ; he was bruised through our iniquities. But the chastisement of our peace was upon him, and with his stripes we are healed."—ISAIAH liii., 5.

THIS, for our Christian brethren, is the season of Peace and Goodwill. The birthday of their Founder recalls them to reverence for the large-hearted love which he is said to have set in the forefront of his teaching, and to have practised not only during his life but in the agony of his death. The glaring contrast between the message of the season and the present state of the world leaps to the eye. Five years of war, attended by anguish almost unparalleled in extent and poignancy, have been followed, not by peace—the true peace that is rooted in goodwill—but merely by a cessation of strife, itself but partial, by civil turmoil only one degree less disastrous than internecine conflict. The nations are still bleeding from the wounds dealt by the war. Mutual distrust and animosities keep them apart—nay, divide them against themselves. Widespread economic instability has, in places, deepened into financial ruin, into direst poverty, into famine, and disease, and despair. In Russia a blood-stained tyranny masquerades as ordered government ; in Eastern Europe, generally, our people are trembling for their lives ; in Vienna little children are dying of hunger by thousands. At home, as well as abroad, the situation is charged with disquiet and danger. Martial law strives in vain to keep the peace in Ireland ; murderous outrage makes a mock at it every day. The awful irony of it is the torment of all faithful adherents of the Christian creed. " Why," they ask themselves, has Christian precept so signally failed to mould after its noble pattern the public life of Christendom ? Is it not time that the doctrine and example of the Master received the one real homage of obedience and emulation ? Is it not time that we Christians should admit that the assumed order of things has been reversed, and that the sceptre, supposed to have departed from Judah, and to have been transferred to themselves, has been regained—if it were ever lost— by the hands to which it was originally entrusted."

So some of them are asking. It is no mere flight of fancy on my part. A week ago, on opening my Sunday newspaper, I read the following remarkable words from the Editor's pen :—" During the last twelve months, amidst the barbaric screaming and droning of jingoist hate and egotist stupidity, it has sometimes seemed that the effective Christians were Jews—those best Jews who smooth animosities, unravel tangles, and hate the disorder of injustice as much as its wrong. Also we must not forget the Quakers, answering, as always, to every bitter cry for human help. But every other Christian body, as a body, has been backward in its due work. The frightful tragedy of Europe . . . might well give a cue to Christmas pulpits. That is if our echoes of the angelic song are not a traditional mechanism or a mumbled hypocrisy." These, I say, are remarkable words. The journal which published them is one of unquestioned standing and influence. I have read it regularly for many years, and never, in my recollection, has it printed one unjust or ungenerous word about the Jew. This negative virtue is now crowned with positive appreciation. The *Observer* has had the courage to admit the possibility of the Jew, rather than the Christian, being the real exemplar of the excellences which are usually deemed exclusively Christian and are so, specifically, designated. "It has sometimes seemed that the effective Christians were Jews"—so says the Editor. Notable as the utterance is, it does not stand quite alone. I seem to remember how, when a Jew,[1] who had gone into residence at Toynbee Hall some years ago, distinguished himself by the exercise of one or more of these virtues, the Rev. Canon Barnett, the Warden, or one of his staff, declared that this Israelite was the best Christian of them all! On the other hand, we shall agree that the editorial utterance, more public, as it was, and therefore calling for the greater courage, intended to have a far wider application, was much the more striking of the two testimonies to the Jewish character. When one thinks of the totally different estimates, of which certain other English newspapers have recently made themselves the mouthpiece, one can only say "daily papers, please copy!" At any rate, this voluntary tribute of the *Observer* comes as a timely reminder that truth and fair play are not extinct qualities in England to-day, and that there are Christians ready to do justice to the Jew even at the cost of doing violence to their most tender susceptibilities. All honour to them!

"It has sometimes seemed that the effective Christians were Jews—those best Jews who smooth animosities, unravel tangles, and hate the disorder of injustice as much as its wrong"—the words are not mere rhetoric. They have history to justify them. The 53rd chapter of Isaiah, from which I have taken my text, suffices in itself to prove the statement. Christians of the old-fashioned type see in this wonderful passage a prophetic picture of their Saviour, who bore the griefs of men, and was wounded for their transgressions, upon whom

[1] The Rev. Harry S. Lewis, now of New York City.

was laid the chastisement of their peace, and by whose stripes they are healed. By Christians of the new type, however—scholars and divines among them—it is admitted that the Person here portrayed is not the Jew Jesus, but the ideal Jew of every age—those "best Jews," of whom our Editor speaks, who "smooth animosities and hate injustice." It is they who have carried in their hearts peace and goodwill towards all men, not merely preaching these lovely qualities, but practising them. It is they who have suffered the death agony, not for a few brief hours, but for centuries; it is they who have been pursued with the unrelenting hatred of powerful enemies in the sacred name of religion; it is they who have known an age-long Calvary, they who are the historic Christ, the suffering Messiah, suffering by, and for, the sins of the world. Yes, the parallel is absolutely exact. For though they have suffered, they have blessed the hands that smote them. Wounded by men's transgressions, bruised by their iniquities, the chastisement for the world's peace has been upon them, and by their stripes it has been healed. They have given themselves as a sacrifice so that men might be reconciled with God and with each other, so that peace and brotherhood might prevail over strife, and disunion, and hate. A great Jew of the 11th century—Jehudah Halevi—as we all remember, called Israel "The heart of the nations." Even, he said, as the heart feels all the ills of the body, so the Jew re-acts to all the woe of mankind. If there is war, or political commotion, or civil conflict, though it is not of his making, he experiences its dread effects in his own person—he, more certainly than all others. Whoever may suffer or escape, he will assuredly have to pay. But in another sense the saying is true. For the heart is the seat of all tender emotions—of mercy and compassion, of forgiveness and love ; and so the Jew is the heart of humanity, seeing that, moved by such feelings, he has been the mediator of mankind, striving to reconcile man with his brother, giving himself to the noble task of healing the world's hurt, of finding expiation for the world's misdeeds. This, again, I say, is history. For history paints on its canvas the figure of the wandering Jew—not a fugitive outlaw, dowered with a curse, but a pilgrim seeking a shrine, a spiritual trader carrying knowledge and civilisation from land to land for the enrichment and the blessedness of men. It depicts his very skill in finance, in international commerce, which it is the fashion to throw up against him as a crime, as a unifying instrument fashioning the solidarity and the progress of humanity. It pictures something more. It tells us that it is always the best Jews who smooth animosities and hate injustice—the best Jews because they hold up to admiration the noblest ideals of both Judaism and Christianity. For who but the Jew, together with the Quakers, whom my Sunday newspaper, to my great delight, includes in the category of humanity's true servants, dared to preach peace during the past period of strife when most other men were for war—for war alone, as the one proper pre-occupation of wartime to the exclusion of amity and brotherhood? That this pulpit, from which I am now speaking, was consecrated to the preaching of it throughout those five awful years will always be a precious memory for at least one of its occupants. And now that the dread conflict is ended, and our thoughts are bent upon making further wars impossible—those wars which, we are warned, will annihilate navies, and cities, and whole communities in a few days or hours—with whom but the Jew has the idea of a League of Religions originated which is to deliver mankind from those horrors, and to weld it together in an enduring bond of peace and goodwill? A League of Religions!—a dream you will say. But such dreams are the stuff the world's life is made of. And, if you ask for concrete facts, let a Montagu and a Reading, messengers carrying the gracious offer of goodwill and brotherhood to distant lands, be the convincing answer. No wonder that one of the latest of our critics can speak of our race as "challenging civilisation with the renewal of faith in humanity."

Let us thank, then, this Editor of an important English newspaper for his brave words—as true as they are brave. The best Jews do smooth animosities, do unravel tangles, do hate injustice; and they do it in spite of the suffering which detraction, and contempt and persecution entail upon them. And in thus working for peace and goodwill what is the Jew doing but recalling Christians to their Christianity, entreating them to be true to themselves by faithfulness to the doctrine of their Master. And he asks them for this loyalty, not only for his own sake, not only to secure him his bare rights as a citizen and a human being, not only for the sake of his personal welfare, his very safety, his very life, but for the sake of the world at large and its deliverance from its present miseries, nay, for the sake of the good name of Christendom itself. This is the age-long appeal of the Jew to his Christian brother. Our Editor recognizes the fact; and, so recognizing it, he, and all the best Christians with him, are helping to fulfil that ancient prophecy of ours which foretells how the nations, rightly interpreting the Jewish life-story, will envisage Israel, wounded and bruised by man's inhumanity, nobly retorting upon them with the proffer of moral health and salvation. "The chastisement of our peace," they cry, "has been upon him, and with his stripes we are healed."

THE POWER OF THE BIBLE

"It pleased the Lord for his righteousness' sake to make the law great and glorious."—ISAIAH xlii., 21.

AND by Torah, the word here translated "law," the speaker probably meant not the contents of any book, but the whole body of religious doctrine orally handed down from the past, and taught by the Prophets. That teaching, always effective, was to grow in power. History would vindicate its truth and, with it, the righteousness and the trustworthiness of God.

Last Sabbath we began anew our annual cycle of readings from the Pentateuch, the first of the three great sections of the Bible. Like the Prophetic teaching which it embodies, the Bible, too, has proved itself "great and glorious." It is wonderful to think how, after the lapse of centuries, the Jew still goes back year after year from Deuteronomy to Genesis with unabated zest for his Sabbath readings. Something new he always seems to find in the Divine Word. The Torah, with its discipline, its idealism, its consoling promises, has been, from first to last, the "secret bread" that has comforted the Jewish heart, nourished the Jewish spirit. For the Torah let us substitute the Bible, for the Jew civilised humanity, and we shall set forth the truth in its fullness. The "People of the Book" have discharged a part, at least, of their mission. They have given their sacred Scriptures to the world with blessed results, and thus proved themselves, in our own Prophet's words, "a light of the Gentiles." Even more wonderful than the place which the Pentateuch keeps in the life and soul of the Jew is the sway which the whole of Scripture exercises over mankind. They used to speak of the Seven Wonders of the World ; the Bible is the eighth, and the first—the first in degree. It is the one book in all literature which promises never to become obsolete. Time, instead of diminishing, has thus far only increased its significance and its power. And the shock of this world-shaking war, far from dethroning it, has only rooted its empire deeper.

A few weeks ago our chief English newspaper had an article on this subject. It began as follows :—" An extraordinary demand, we are told, has been created by the war for Bibles in the United States. Presses are running from fifteen to eighteen hours a day, but are still several weeks behind orders received. What is happening there has its counterpart here in the work of the Bible Society and other agencies. Throughout the war, and in practically every place where our armies are on active service, devoted men and women have provided copies of the Bible for the troops. Many of the men have joined themselves into leagues for the regular reading of the Scriptures, and frequent testimonies have been offered to the benefit derived from this practice." And the writer went on to account for this striking fact. " When men," he said, " are engaged on great ventures which test all their resources of body and soul, the Word of God is found to match their spiritual needs with supreme completeness. The Bible is a great book for those engaged in great tasks. . . . It insists on the supremacy of moral forces, and shows with unique impressiveness how naturally wellbeing depends on righteousness and the fear of God. One after another the great nations of antiquity are brought before the bar of the Most High, and their fate is seen to depend on their obedience or disobedience to His laws. Great armies are employed to execute His judgment in the world.... The true soldier, moreover, has the sense of an appointed destiny. He is no longer the sport of fate. In defeat or victory, in life or in death, he is in the hands of God, who never forsakes those who put their trust in Him. This assurance is found throughout the Bible. It is the declaration which rings out everywhere in Holy Writ. No wonder the valiant soldier finds the Book a *vade mecum* of strength and good cheer."

" The Bible is a great book for those engaged in great tasks "—it is well said. If we analyse the Hebrew Scriptures we shall find that the chief secret of their imperishable power is their human interest and especially their ability to nerve men for the crises of life. Whether the scene is a battle-field or a man's private chamber, the capacity of the Bible for evoking the best from brave spirits is always the same. It gives strength to the battling soul, for it gives it the assurance of God—the assurance of eternal justice, which will bring right at last out of wrong, the assurance of love which visits and vindicates the strong hearts that keep their faith in it. The Bible, it has been said, helps men to find themselves; but it does so because it helps them to find God. He sits above the flood, on heights where earthly catastrophes are dwarfed, and He presses all events into the service of His majestic and righteous purpose. Therefore let good men be brave and strong; for all the forces of the Universe are on their side. This is what the Bible, with its big picture of all life, individual and national, teaches us. And this is the main source of its power. One of the great masters of modern French fiction, Romain Rolland, has made good use of this fact. He tells how his hero, momentarily beaten down in the conflict of life, goes in his anguish to his Bible, and,

THE POWER OF THE BIBLE

" opening it at the most sombre words of all," the 7th, 13th and 19th chapters of Job, finds his ability to struggle on renewed. " What casts down, and overwhelms, and blasts the soul beyond all hope," is, he sees, " the niggardly suffering which has not the strength to forgo ease, and pleasure, and self-gratification. He is braced up," the author tells us, " by the bitter savour which he finds in the old Book, by the wind of Sinai coming from vast and lonely spaces, and sweeping away the steamy vapours. He reads over again the words of Job : ' though He slay me yet will I trust in Him.' He rises ; he is ready calmly to face the fight anew."

A brave book for brave men, whose hearts are flung open to the message that comes from the eternal source of strength—such is the Bible. In this respect it has no equal among the other Scriptures of the world. They are great in their way—wise in counsel, with a certain mythological grandeur. But they are not so virile, so direct in their appeal, so human. They have less power over life because they are less living, have less power to renew their own life from age to age. " They have mouths, but they speak not ; feet have they, but they walk not." In the agony of the soul they are dumb ; when the world is moving on with great strides they stand where they did when it was but a tottering child. But the Bible, in virtue of some unique attribute, keeps pace with men's thoughts and acts. Like the greatest of its Prophets, its eye is not dim, nor its natural force abated.

Great in its religious quality, the Bible is also great as literature. Even the agnostic reads it with delight as a classic ; he pays homage to the beauty of a book whose one theme is the God he knows not. Think of it. Where is poetry finer than the Psalms, drama more thrilling than the career of Joseph, romance more wonderful than the story of Israel in the wilderness? What tale of conflict surpasses in impressiveness that of the contest between Moses and Pharaoh? What epic transcends the great saga of Samson? Would you read the history of a soul? Then turn to Jonah or to Job. A couple of years ago a series of leaflets or broadsheets was issued for distribution among our soldiers at home and abroad. They contained some of the finest gems of English literature, and holding the pre-eminent place among them were extracts from the English Bible.

The war has enhanced the value of Holy Writ in men's estimation. There was room for it. The days of peace had been marked by a certain decline in the influence of the Bible, among thinking minds more particularly. This was largely due to two causes, the growth of the scientific spirit and the increased attention given to Biblical criticism. But even before the war came to restore the balance thus disturbed thoughtful men had begun to regain their sense of proportion. They had begun to see that the real greatness of the Bible was to be sought far less in its individual, than in its general characteristics. It was, as James Martineau had well said, the word of God rather than the words of God. What did it signify that its science was antiquated? Its proclamation of a Divine, overruling Power, its affirmation of a moral order in the Universe, its testimony to the heavenly origin of man and of his corresponding responsibility at God's judgment-seat, were precious facts which gave it a supreme and an everlasting value. And as to literary criticism, that, instead of shaking the authority of the Scriptures, has in reality enhanced it. At first seeming to create problems, it has resolved them. A due perspective, the recognition of the human element, side by side with the Divine, in the Bible, has made everything clear. Legend, apologue, poetry—these, we

THE POWER OF THE BIBLE 231

discern to-day where the men of old saw prosaic fact. But, underlying them all, we know that there is still fact—the supreme fact of God's existence and Providence—and that suffices us. The witness of the Bible to the Divine remains no less mighty because we recognise many hands at work in the Pentateuch, because more than one Prophet speaks to us in Isaiah, because David may never have written one of the Psalms. The spirit of God still speaks as clearly as of old from the inspired page to the kindred spirit of man.

And then, finally, apart from its religious and its literary grandeur, the Bible appeals to men as law. Old enactments it contains which have lost their force by the effluxion of time. But the sanctity of law as a principle, the paramount need of obedience, of self-discipline, as the essential condition of human well-being—these ideas the Bible still upholds, and their worth will last as long as the race endures. But even individual laws of the Bible still hold undiminished sway over the minds of men. The Decalogue and its amplifications, thousands of years old though they are, remain the immovable basis of civilised legislation. Nay, even some of those same obsolete laws are re-conquering their place in human estimation amid the upheaval of war. " Let us go back to the old Mosaic rule of ' an eye for an eye and a tooth for a tooth ' "—so cried a British statesman the other day in advocating reprisals on the German enemy. He would have us revert in this 20th century to the primitive teachings of the Hebrew Bible, addressed to a rude age and meant for that age only. Nay, more, he would have us better the instruction. For while the Mosaic law exacted retribution from the guilty, this modern statesman, voicing the latest word of civilisation, would exact it from the innocent ! Verily, who shall dare to say, even in these latter days, when even moral values are in the crucible, what is really antiquated in the old Book ? Who shall say of its mandates and its mission " Thus far and no farther ? "

But I must close. I have said enough, I trust, to establish the unmatched greatness of Israel's spiritual heritage. Let us rejoice that we share in it, that we belong to a people who have given its best possession to men at large, to be their best possession in their turn, the source of their strength, the guarantee of their happiness, the potency of all the world's good that is yet to be. Let us praise God whom " it hath pleased for His righteousness' sake to make the ancient teaching great and glorious."

MORALITY AND RELIGION

"Ye shall fear every man his mother and his father, and ye shall keep my Sabbaths; I am the Lord your God."—
LEVITICUS xix., 3.

"I AM the Lord your God." The phrase recurs in this great nineteenth chapter of Leviticus with almost rhythmical regularity, like the refrain of a noble song. " Ye shall fear every man, his mother and his father, and ye shall keep my Sabbaths; I am the Lord your God. . . . Thou shalt not curse the deaf, nor put a stumbling block before the blind; I am the Lord. . . . Thou shalt love thy neighbour as thyself; I am the Lord. . . . Turn ye not unto them that have familiar spirits, nor unto the wizards; I am the Lord your God. . . . Thou shalt rise up before the hoary head, and honour the face of the old man; I am the Lord." Every phase of personal duty is enforced by this solemn affirmation—deference to parents and the aged; tenderness for the infirm, and the stricken, and the helpless; ceremonial conformity; the sanctification of God's days; the avoidance of superstition; love for the stranger and for the enemy.

What does the declaration exactly mean? It may be interpreted in many ways. We may understand it, with the Rabbins, as setting forth the great idea of Divine recompense. God, the Just and the All-powerful, calls sinners strictly to account; His promise of blessing for the righteous is sure. Or we may see in it an appeal from the great heart of God to the conscience of His human child :—" I am thy Heavenly Father who loves thee ; do this for My sake." Or, again, it may be construed as a stern behest : " This is My will—Mine, Who am the august Lord of the universe ; bow before it, O man, in awe and submission." For each different nature, for each of life's varying circumstances, it has its various application. But deeper than these different conceptions, and comprehending them all, is one fundamental idea—the idea, namely, that the laws here formulated have " proceeded out of the mouth of the Lord," that they are Divine in origin, that Duty comes from the same source as the universe, and is as majestic and enduring. Addressing the heavenly bodies, " What are ye orbs ? " cries the poet ; and he answers, " The words of God, the Scriptures of the skies." But the converse idea is also true ; the precepts of the moral law are like stars of light, eternally set by the Divine Hand in the firmament of the human soul for man's unerring guidance.

Duty, then, is Divine—that is the thought which the text chiefly inculcates. Whoso sins rebels against the Sovereign Will opposes himself to all the forces of the universe ; whoso keeps the Commandment puts himself into harmony with that Will and with the universe which is its expression—ranges himself on the side of Omnipotence. Thus every virtuous act is, in Rabbinic phrase, " a crowning of the Creator." Every base desire overcome, every noble aspiration realized, is homage paid to Him who has made goodness, even as He has made the world. We frame some high ideal, and strive to be true to it ; why ? Is it not " because of the divinity that stirs within us," because of some sense of obligation, perhaps only partly discerned, to the Supreme Lawgiver ? In lower natures this sense, it is true, is often non-existent, or too fast asleep to be roused; only fear of the policeman, dread of social penalties, compels obedience. Even in seemingly higher natures morality may be but thinly veiled self-interest. Honesty is the best policy; health rewards temperance; to be open-handed in charity is to get reputation, rank, social power. But these calculated decencies are not morality; they are only the semblance of it. True morality is an affair of the Conscience, and Conscience, in the ultimate resort, is the voice of God. It is the old solemn declaration, " I am the Lord your God " ringing and reverberating in the soul.

At first sight it does not seem so. Conscience, it may be said, is the product of education, of environment, of chance. It may be warped, drugged, slain. But Conscience is a fact none the less; and the fact points to a paramount Will outside ourselves, of which Conscience is an echo, however feeble or distorted. Beneath its muffled tones sounds the call, " I am the Lord your God." But in many cases the call is thunderous, and proclaims its divinity. There are thousands and tens of thousands of men and women to-day for whom God is a reality and His voice an everlasting exhortation. " How can I do this great wickedness," cries Joseph in the hour of his greatest temptation, " and sin against God? " It is the cry of many a living soul. "I cannot sin," it protests; "for to do so, would be revolt against the Highest. How could I live in His sight, in His company? He would see this unclean thing, and turn away from me." Or, contrariwise, " This goodly act clamours for performance; shall I refuse? No; for what will God think of me? How, if I refuse, can I look up into His face? " The cry may not take precisely this form. It may word itself thus :—" How can I sin against *myself?* I have a soul; how shall I defile it? " But even then God is not excluded. For whence this thought of sin as a degradation? Why do I fall in my own sight when

I have done wrong? Is it not because I have fallen in God's sight? Is it not because I have consciously become unworthy of my sonship, because I have defaced the divine image in my soul, because I have shown myself ungrateful and rebellious when I should have been nought but dutiful and loving?

The God-idea, then, is the root of the moral life in every sense of the word. It is the origin of it, as well as its foundation and inspiring force. As soon as primitive man felt God, however dimly and crudely, he began to be moral. With the conception of an All-powerful Being in, and above, Nature, speaking in the babbling stream, in the murmur of the sea, in the mystic whisper of the forest, now smiling in the sunshine, now frowning in the storm, there was simultaneously born within his soul the conception of Duty. The Supreme *was*, and therefore His will was supreme. "I am the Lord your God"—the thought embodied in the phrase is the source of the moral law. It is its one bulwark too. Destroy Religion, and the whole fabric of duty is jeopardised. Experience, you may say, refutes the assertion. You have known, you may tell me, many an excellent man who has had no religion. But how do you know that he has had none? He has told you so? But was even he a trustworthy witness? What is Religion? Is it always something that expresses itself in clear-cut dogma? An intuition, a vague yearning after something higher and better than oneself, even a superstition, may be religion, and many a man is under the influence of such a force and yet deems himself an agnostic. Nay, he may fancy that his morality is absolutely detached from the supernatural when it is in reality its product. What Renan calls "the sap of the old beliefs" still flows within him; his early religious training still produces its effect.

If experience is to count for anything we must say that thus far a godless morality has not succeeded. It cannot succeed because it has no sufficient sanction, no effective driving power. Why should we be moral? "Because," the agnostic moralist will say, "righteousness is a debt we owe to our fellow-men, to Society at large." But social duty does not cover the whole ethical domain. There is duty to oneself; how is that to be enforced? What, if morality is based on a godless foundation, is to prevent a man, shipwrecked on a desert island, from drinking himself to death? "Morality pays," we shall be told. But what if a man says, "I prefer to be paid in a different coin; a short life and a merry one for me"? Take away Religion and you rob virtue of its one foundation, its one efficient plea. "Be good," you say to your child. "Why?" he will ask, and you must answer him. Your best answer, apart from the religious one, is "for love of me"; and it will serve, perhaps, for many a day. But the years come "that bring the philosophic mind," and the child, now a man, will ask the question of himself. Then filial love will not suffice. "Why," he will ask, "did my parents commend these acts to me and forbid those?" If there is no God in all his thoughts, it may go hard with the parental doctrine. Sometimes these obstinate questionings will come even in youth. I have known children, carefully brought up on agnostic ethics, rebelling against the teaching on the ground that it was unsatisfying. Then they were sent to a religious teacher, and their revolt ceased. To-day they are parents themselves, and having their own children taught of God. An agnostic morality has been aptly compared to a flower in water; it may expand, but it does not propagate itself. The godless man may save his own morality; he cannot, with anything like certainty, at any rate, transmit it to his children. And even his own morality must be frigid and mechanical, compared with the ardent virtue of the religionist, warmed and fired by the thought of God, the Sovereign Lawgiver who has ordained righteousness as the law of men's being, and asks them to cling to it for His sake and for their own. Well, then, does this great chapter of ours end as it began—with an appeal to the religious Conscience, but with an appeal on behalf of the entire law, and not merely of single enactments of it :—" And ye shall observe all My statutes and all My judgments, and do them ; I am the Lord."

FAITH AND REASON

> "Lord, my heart is not haughty, nor mine eyes lofty; neither do I exercise myself in great matters, or in things too wonderful for me. Surely I have stilled and quieted my soul, like a weaned child with its mother; my soul is with me like a weaned child."—
> PSALM cxxxi., 1, 2.

THE childlike heart—this is the Psalmist's happy possession—happy because it is a heart at peace, which neither the sorrows nor the problems of life have power to disturb. But it is happy, too, because the temper it betokens is the wise and right temper, one which befits the denizen of earth, the child of God. So becoming is it that the Psalmist can urge it as a merit in his pleading with God. "Lord," he prays, "look into my heart and see how lowly it is. I do not attempt, I do not claim, to solve the great mysteries; I acknowledge that they are too hard for me. What is my intelligence measured against Thine infinite wisdom. My part is not to understand, but to trust. A babe in knowledge, I make myself as a babe in quiet trustfulness. To be with Thee, to feel Thy nearness, to rest in Thee as a child on its mother's bosom—that is enough for me; it is peace, blessing, life itself."

We are entitled to rank this Psalmist with the mystics, with those religionists who, disdaining, or distrusting, all attempts to prove God, are content to experience Him, or who find the very fact of their experiencing Him the one irrefragable proof of His reality. Both methods, the intellectual and the spiritual, have had their vogue in well-nigh every age, though probably the Psalmist's is the older. Primitive men heard God in the rushing stream before they deduced Him from the periodical wonder of its renewed flow in the springtime. They felt Him before they began to reason about Him. He was in their soul, a conscious part of their very being, when as yet their minds had not opened to admit Him from without. Nay, it was the instinctive sense of His existence which impelled them to reason about Him, and moved them to seek in external Nature voices that should echo and corroborate the testimony of their souls. This mysterious Being within themselves, whom they apprehended but could not define—how congenial a task it was to discern His footsteps in the world outside them, in its alternate frown and smile, its grandeur, its miracle! Without doubt the mystic preceded the thinker. The child has God in his heart long before he has enthroned Him in his mind, and the evolution of the child is a miniature of the evolution of the race.

Is the Psalmist's mystical temper discredited because it is primitive, because it is the temper of the child? Let us beware of thinking so. We must distinguish between the childlike and the childish. Innocence, trustfulness, freedom from self-consciousness, large-eyed wonder—these are the child's characteristics. Do we decry them as childish? Do we not set them among the precious things of humanity, love them when we see them, sigh for them when we ourselves have lost them? How, then, shall we distrust the child's unconquerable faith in God, his simple acceptance of Him, that feeling for the wonderful which is fed and satisfied by the thought of Him. The child can teach us many things; to realize the Unseen, to behold It, as the old Jewish poet says, when the physical eye is dimmed—this he can teach us best of all.

Or shall we distrust the childlike temper because it

FAITH AND REASON

is that of primitive man? All the old things are not dead or antiquated, certainly not all the old ideas. They live exactly as long as their power of appeal lives, as long as they have a message for human souls. And the doctrine of God has an inexhaustible message—a message which men need most to hear, one addressed to the spirit in man which, like God himself, its fountain-head, is essentially ever the same. Preach the good tidings—declare that God lives, that He judges the earth in righteousness, that all is for the best—and " though Nature, red in tooth and claw, shrieks against the creed," the heart responds to the message as eagerly in the twentieth century as in the first. The great basic concepts of Religion are ever new because they are born of man's soul, and that renews itself again and again throughout the ages. Its witness to God is always valid; it is the one supremely authentic witness to Him.

It is a hard saying; but history seems to prove it true. The appeal to the soul on behalf of the great verities of Religion has, thus far, been more successful than the appeal to the intellect. To which books of the Bible have men turned by preference for the higher nourishment? Not to the so-called Wisdom Literature—to Ecclesiastes, with its keen discussion of the value of life, or to Job, with its reasoned arraignment of the Divine justice—but to the Psalms, with their exhortation to faith, their proffer of solace, or to the Prophets, with their proclamation of God's providential rule of the world, their portrayal of life, individual and national, as a majestic moral pageant. Who are the later Jewish authors that have been most lovingly conned? Not Maimonides, the Hebrew Aristotle, but the medieval mystics; not Jehudah Halevi, the philosopher, but Jehudah Halevi, the God-intoxicated poet. And so it is to-day. Wordsworth, a century old, still enjoys the youth of his influence—Wordsworth, shaking off the pessimism produced by the Napoleonic conflict in mystic communion with Nature. And we are not merely listening to him, but following his example. Face to face with the present cruel struggle, we deliberately crush out our doubts of Eternal goodness by passive surrender to the instinctive conviction of its truth. War humbles us before the dread Power it discloses; but that Power we feel, though we cannot prove it, is benign. Forty years ago, when physical science arrogated to itself the right to expel God from the universe, the favourite books were those that tried to prove, on purely scientific grounds, that He ought to remain. To-day, when we see that God's secret is not with those who argue about Him, but with those who fear Him, such arguments are obsolete. Only this week I was told by an official of one of our greatest libraries that the books now most in request are those like Von Hügel's "Mystical Element of Religion," a work extending to eight hundred closely printed pages of solid difficult reading. Another decade may see another change in the public taste. For, as my librarian said, there is a fashion in religious studies as there is in neckties. But the significant fact remains that, in this the latest century, thoughtful people have gone back to the old ways of approach to the Divine, that the childlike heart, which was the joy and the pride of the Psalmist, still survives in adult mankind, still makes its confession of God, still humbles itself before Him in unquestioning submission.

And is this not quite intelligible? A reasoned faith is a blessed acquisition. But reason is its buttress, not its foundation. The man who depends upon reason alone for his faith is lost. As to the superstructure let there be free inquiry; but for the foundation we must fall back, in the last resort, upon intuition alone. Even

FAITH AND REASON

the sacred search for truth has its limits. Or rather let us say that, to this particular kind of truth, the soul, as compared with the intellect, has a paramount claim to be heard as a witness. Spiritual things are spiritually discerned. Justification of God—of His goodness, His power, His love—are never convincing. The solution of one problem is the suggestion of another. When you have disclosed the core of good in things evil you have still to explain why the seed should not have been good, too, why it should be necessary for the world, as a condition of attaining to well-being, to reach it through pain and sin, through pestilence, and earthquake, and desolating wars. No ; there is only one way of being sure of God ; it is the way of implicit trust, the way of prayer, of lowly contemplation—the way of the Psalmist, with stilled and quieted soul, like a child with its mother.

This temper is the one thing needful. Its necessity grows as life becomes harder to live, its tragedy more oppressive, its riddle more perplexing. To be at one with the Supreme through the spirit, to put all our doubts mechanically from us, and to cast ourselves utterly upon the Everlasting Arms, is to pass unscathed through the troubles and perils of life. It is to build up our higher selves out of pain and sorrow and struggle. For God we *must* have if the universe is to be intelligible, if we are to be saved from heartbreak, if rectitude is to be safe. The more life seems to hide God from our sight the more do we need Him, the greater becomes the need of postulating and grasping Him. The religious edifice may have to be reconstructed again and again—it may even be overturned and never effectually reconstructed— but the foundations remain, an immovable rock, and that is everything. Amiel could say towards the close of his life, " My creed has melted away, but I believe in God, in the moral order, and in salvation ; Religion for me is to live and die in God, in complete abandonment to the Holy Will, which is at the root of Nature and Destiny."

I commend these thoughts especially to the mourning hearts, who are worshipping with us this morning. Make yourselves as children, dear friends, to the Heavenly Father; trust yourselves to Him. Be sure that the wounds He deals are faithful as are the wounds of a friend. For so the cherished one who has left you will, in his death, have left behind for you his richest gift, his most precious blessing.

CHARLES DARWIN

"I saw the Lord sitting upon a throne, high and lifted up, and His train filled the temple."—ISAIAH vi., 1.

YESTERDAY[1] was the hundredth anniversary of the birth of Charles Darwin. It would be superfluous to dwell upon the greatness of the famous naturalist. His name is familiar to every man and woman with the slightest pretensions to culture, or indeed to a knowledge of the forces that have chiefly fashioned the intellectual life of our age. The doctrine with which Darwin's memory is most intimately associated has written itself deep in the annals of modern scientific thought. His theory of evolution, acting chiefly through natural selection, has profoundly modified men's conception of the history of organic life upon this earth.

But—and here we reach the especial interest of this centenary for the religionist—Darwin's main conclusions, besides being of incalculable significance for physical science, have exercised a far-reaching influence upon religious thought. Those conclusions were two in number. Darwin affirmed, first of all, that the varieties of living creatures peopling this globe are the result of certain natural causes operating automatically. Instead of being the product of special and separate activities on the part of the Creator, each species has been developed from a lower form through a process of adaptation to environment forced upon the organism by the struggle for existence. Secondly, Darwin taught that this mechanical process, affecting the life-story of the lowest

[1] 12th February, 1909.

animals, has played its part in the history of the very highest, of man himself. The human species is the last term in a long series of changes, of which the simplest organic forms are the beginning. The weak points of this doctrine are recognised by scientific thinkers to-day, but it is easy to understand how deeply it moved devout minds when it was first promulgated fifty years ago. Evolution—no new thing then for the man of science, seeing that Darwin claimed to have discovered not the great principle itself, but the manner in which it works in the animal world—Evolution was made familiar for the first time to the average man. His Bible taught him that this world and all it contains had been made in six days by special acts of creation. He was now familiarized with the idea that they had been slowly evolved through countless æons under the influence of rigid, mechanical law. His Bible taught him, further, that man, the crown of Creation, was gifted with distinctive attributes which, exalting him immeasurably above the brute, brought him very nigh in nature to Deity. He was now told that Man was descended not merely from the ape, but from a creature far lower in the scale of being, so low as scarcely to be distinguished as a living creature.

The consequences are matters of history. The Darwinian doctrine, in this respect sharing the fate even of the law of the attraction of gravity, was banned by a certain section of religionists as false and pernicious; by others it was accepted at the cost of an utter surrender of their religious faith. That was at the beginning. To-day juster judgments prevail. We see that the doctrine of evolution—even assuming it to be a true doctrine—ought never to have destroyed the religion, or disturbed the equanimity, of one single believer. Evolution is certainly irreconcilable with

Creation as usually understood; but, as we have come to perceive, it is not irreconcilable with the God-idea. On the contrary, it affirms that idea anew—supplies it with fresh and, if possible, stronger arguments. For what does the doctrine teach? It teaches that, at the beginning of things, the primordial organic atom was endowed with the capacity of evolving the countless varieties of animal life that fill the world. That long, orderly, and majestic process has taken place without direct intervention of God; but it was carried out none the less surely and triumphantly. Is not this at least as Divine, because as wonderful, a process as Creation? Is it not at least as eloquent of Omnipotence? He who made the law of Evolution, and then stepped aside to let that law work—is He not at least as majestic, as real a Being as the God of the old religionists, who, with the hand of the magician, called the world and its in-dwellers into existence in six short days?

And Man—has Darwinism robbed him of any particle of his dignity? Is he less great, less divine, because he has to own the lowest organism for his first ancestor? From whatever source his high potencies, his mighty faculties, have sprung, they are facts. His scientific skill which "charms her secret from the latest moon," his perception of the beautiful, his self renunciation for Duty's sake, his power to lift himself to God in thought and being—these, the chief gems in his crown of glory, still remain to him untarnished by his descent. They are no less genuine, no less splendid, because, like his physical nature, they have been evolved. The human soul is still a real thing in spite of half-a-century of Darwinism; Man may still be said to be fashioned in the Divine image.

Nor, again, is God's greatness impeached any more than Man's. The human soul was not placed in the first man with its full stature attained. It has grown in the long interval by small degrees. But the capacity for growth was given to it from the first; the heavenly pattern was held before it, after which it might and must slowly mould itself. Once more, then, we have a witness to the power, to the existence of the Supreme. What but Omnipotence could have endowed that prehistoric speck of sea-slime with the ability of ultimately developing into an Isaiah, who could " see," with the eye of the Spirit, " the Lord sitting upon His throne," or a Darwin, who, awed by the wonders of the great pageant of life on this planet, could, though with dimmer vision, discern " His train filling the temple " of the universe? A Darwin, I say, for even the great apostle of Evolution protested against the notion of " blind chance " being the origin of life. " The understanding," he cried, " revolts at such a conclusion."

We see these things more clearly to-day than did the men of fifty years ago. We recognize that Religion, like the animal organism itself, must change in its outward manifestations in response to a mutable environment of thought and knowledge; but it lives on notwithstanding, and lives on all the more vigorously for its power of adaptation. Modern scientific thought has compelled us to look at the Bible from a new standpoint. For us it is not the last word on anthropology or astronomy, but a great and precious text-book on God and duty. From that eminence science cannot depose it; for its appeal is to the human conscience, to men's instinctive love of the morally beautiful, over which science holds no jurisdiction.

And if we understand better to-day what Religion really is, we also perceive more clearly the limitations of human inquiry. Science, once an autocrat, assuming through the mouths of some of its votaries the right to be the touchstone of all truth, claiming to explain the Universe without recourse to the hypothesis of God, now speaks more humbly, more becomingly. She has learnt to know her place. Supreme in her own realm, she confesses that it has boundaries, that beyond it stretches a vast realm of knowledge unexplorable by her methods. Nay, the farther the man of science advances in his own domain, the more deeply conscious is he of the impenetrable mystery that enfolds all things—" the thick darkness," in the words of our Pentateuchal lesson, " where God is."

Finally, we see, too, that physical science is only a fragment of the great totality even of science, the knowledge of physical man only a fraction of the knowledge of the entire man. Darwinism, in its earlier years, turned many believers into sceptics. " Man," they said, " is no more than the breath of his body ; what room is there for immortality in a creature of such lowly origin ? " But since that time a new science has been born, or rather a larger view has been born of what science means. Psychology now shares the field with biology. The scientific materialist has to reason with the scientific believer, of whom a James and an Oliver Lodge are the types. For these men the phenomena of the human spirit are equally deserving of being taken into account with those of the physical life ; the facts of religious experience are as eloquent as the story of the development of the human species. The whole wonder of the life of Man is not explained when we have talked of Evolution and Natural Selection. The " beatific vision " has yet to be accounted for—the intuitions and up-leapings of the soul, the ecstasy of the religious heart, *of low as well as high degree*, that in every generation " has seen God sitting upon His throne, high and lifted up." For these are facts no less real than the wondrous procession of life which physical science loves to disclose to us. And without the theory of God they defy explanation.

And so to-day we are able to give their due place to the firmly-grounded teachings of the biologist and the naturalist among our intellectual possessions. We may acknowledge their value, and yet keep our hearts open to the message that comes to us from other domains, of which the human spirit alone holds the key. And so, too, believers though we are, we shall join in crowning the memory of the great student who, with singular patience and sincerity, laboured for the truth, and with equally singular courage and humility revealed his conception of it to a world more sceptical and unsympathetic than ours. For every earnest seeker after truth, whether he find it or not, is a seeker after God, of whom truth is the mirror and the manifestation.

SUPERSTITION.

"O my people, remember now what Balak King of Moab consulted, and what Balaam the son of Beor answered him . . . that ye may know the righteous acts of the Lord."—
MICAH vi., 5.

THE story of Balaam, whatever the reason for its inclusion in the Sacred Narrative, serves one valuable purpose. It teaches us the folly of superstition. Balaam, the renowned magician, is summoned from his Eastern home by the King of Moab in order that he may accomplish by his sinister arts the task of arresting Israel's victorious progress which honest warfare has failed to achieve. Nothing loth, he consents, but he employs his wizardry in vain. Opening his mouth to curse, he is constrained to bless. Some Power, infinitely mightier than his puny magic, overmasters him, and he has to confess himself beaten. "How shall I curse," he cries, "whom God hath not cursed? . . . Verily there is no enchantment against Jacob, neither is there any divination against Israel." The Almighty, he feels, is the one Lord of the universe and of life. Everything happens in accordance with his will. Where is the power, human or superhuman, that can deflect His purpose by a hairsbreadth, that can fashion men's destinies for good or for evil in His despite.

Superstition could receive no more impressive rebuke than this one, uttered by the high-priest of superstition. For what is superstition? It is the temper that imagines the world the sport of disorder, instead of being ruled by law. What happens to men, it holds, is the outcome not of any rational purpose, but of the action of tricksy forces, which imagination exalts into gods, even if it does not consciously deify them. These forces have to be propitiated—their goodwill purchased, their ill-will bought off ; and the methods used for propitiating them are as irrational as they themselves are. Grotesque, even cruel and immoral rites, take the place of sane worship ; conformity to arbitrary and un-moral rules of conduct supplant the righteously-ordered life. And the mind is ever on the watch for hints of the favour and the disfavour of the dreaded Powers—for signs, and omens, and portents. There are lucky numbers and unlucky ones, fortunate days and unfortunate ones. The most trifling incidents of everyday experience become fraught with prodigious significance ; out of them are the issues of life and death. Even the ceremonies of religion are pressed into the service of superstition. They are distorted and degraded. Instead of exalting and purifying the soul, they are used to minister to its craven fears, its ignoble yearnings.

The early history of mankind is a record of superstitions. If you read Professor Frazer's fascinating book, *The Golden Bough*, you will see how large a place these false beliefs occupy in the lives of existing savage tribes. And what those tribes are to-day the progenitors of civilized man were ages ago. The nearer men are to barbarism, the more superstitious they are. And the cruder their theology, the more superstitious they are. It is only as they advance in the religious scale, only as their conception of God and His relation to the world becomes ennobled, that their superstitions fall from them like an outgrown garment. No doubt the advance is partly intellectual. The ennoblement of religion—let us be just and acknowledge it—is due in great measure to the spread of scientific ideas. The great achievement of physical science is the demonstration of the reign of law throughout the universe. Acknowledge that reign, and superstition vanishes. Believe that you live in a duly ordered world, in which caprice has no place, and you can have no faith in magic or enchantments, or in attempts to propitiate powers that are the very incarnation of lawlessness. But not to science does all the credit belong. The wondrous intuitions of men like the old Hebrew Prophets are entitled to part of it. In an unscientific age these great souls soared to the truth by their own innate strength. They saw God sitting on His throne, the indisputable ruler of the universe and of the lives of men. From the failure of a Balaam and his incantations they could deduce " the righteous acts of the Lord," His trustworthiness, His just and benign and orderly disposition of human destiny.

We live in a scientific age, and it is our boast to possess an enlightened religion. And yet we are not altogether emancipated from the bondage of superstition. We still stand too near to the world's childhood for full intellectual freedom. There is a great deal of the primitive man in modern men. We are not comfortable when we walk under a ladder, or spill the salt at table. We hastily straighten crossed knives, avoid a dinner-party of thirteen, and hope to conciliate the jealousy of the malign Powers by crying " Unberufen ! " Even the acts we do in the name of Religion are apt to take on a superstitious hue. Our prayers, though addressed to God Himself, are not infrequently employed as purely mechanical means of getting our desires. Too often we are afraid to omit our devotions lest the very omission should tell against us in the dispensation of the heavenly bounty. This only goes to show how hard it is even for the educated mind to shake off the yoke of primeval ideas. We submit to their thraldom while recognizing and condemning the folly of it in our inmost hearts.

The truth is that as long as any remnant of these old superstitions clings to us we show ourselves imperfectly civilized, imperfectly religious. True religion cannot exist side by side with superstition. Hence the repeated prohibitions of magic and witchcraft in the Pentateuch. The "statutes of the nations," against which the Israelites are warned in Leviticus, include not only immoral, but superstitious practices—attempts to communicate with the dead, divination by omens, traffic with wizards and soothsayers. For superstition really means idolatry, homage to many divine Powers instead of one; and it was upon idolatry, with its debasing effects upon the mind and the character, that the old Pentateuchal legislation most persistently made war. It means the enslavement of the credulous to the wonder-worker. It means, moreover, a gloomy outlook upon life, the conception of it as the sport of chance incidents, not as a moral ordinance rooted in wisdom and equity. It means the dethronement of God. For what sort of affair does life become if I am to be visited with misfortune simply because I happen, in all innocence, to look at the new moon through a window? What sort of being does that god become, who works or tolerates such cruelty? Superstition is the parent of despair, the ruin of religion. Significant it is that Saul, a mental and moral wreck, has recourse to one of the witches he has sought to exterminate in his saner and nobler days.

And so if superstition and religion are incompatible, especially incompatible are superstition and Judaism. Some years ago I was asked by a Jewish friend to take part in a spiritualistic *séance*. He knew, he assured me, a highly-gifted medium who had a special faculty for getting into contact with the realm of the shades. I only succeeded in putting an end to his importunities when I cited the Mosaic precept against consulting those possessed of a familiar spirit. He could not, in the faec of that prohibition, persist in his request to one like myself, who reverenced the Pentateuch. For the superstitious man cannot be a good Jew, seeing that Judaism, when at its best, has been the very negation of superstition. The Bible ; the finer spirits of the Talmud, with their warnings against " the ways of the Amorites " ; the medieval teachers, of whom Maimonides is the type, demonstrate the truth of the assertion.

Nor would it be true to say that, since superstitions have always eagerly fastened themselves upon religions, the disappearance of Religion is all that is needed for their final extinction. The superstitious are not confined to the ranks of the religionists. Some of the most superstitious persons I have ever known have been avowed agnostics. The East End Jew, with at once too much and to little religion, scribbles Hebrew verses on the door of a sick-room to charm away malevolent spirits ; he hangs an amulet against the Evil Eye round the neck of his child, he swings a cock about his head in expiation for his sins, on the eve of Kippur. But is he much worse than his West End brother who seems not to have God in his thoughts all the livelong year, and yet makes a point of attending synagogue on the Day of Atonement, moved by some indefinable impulse of dread ? Both men alike feel the great Mystery that lies behind life ; bow before it ; strive to conciliate it. But both do it in the wrong way ; both are superstitious. The avowed Agnostic, too, feels a like impulse. He is forced to put something in the place of his lost belief. No ; the remedy for superstition is not less religion, but more—religion of the right kind, the religion which, freeing the soul from the tyranny of degrading beliefs, sets it in true submission at the feet of a just and living God.

One difficulty may occur to you, which I would notice in conclusion. It is the difficulty involved in prayer. Balaam attempts to coerce the will of God, and fails. But do we not, it may be asked, make the same attempt in our prayerful requests ? And, if so, is not all petitionary prayer superstitious ? The answer is simple. No petition is superstitious that is offered in the right spirit and with the right intent. The common mistake is to think that prayer is intended to alter the purpose of God ; it is intended, on the contrary, to effect a change in ourselves. If we ask for our needs, thinking that by the mere asking we shall get them, we degrade prayer into a superstitious act. But if what we aim at is to prepare our hearts by our fervour, by our submission, for an inflow of the Divine grace, and so to make them worthy of the boons we seek, then our prayer is justified, and no taint of superstition clings to it.

"He," says George Meredith, "who rises from his prayer a better man, his prayer is answered." This is the essential truth of the matter. It was proclaimed by the great Prophet of Israel ages ago. Protesting, on the one hand, against the wizardry of a Balaam and the rites of a mechanical worship, on which their own people staked their hopes of salvation, these noble teachers upheld, on the other hand, the saving power of the righteous life. " Shall I come before the Lord," asks Micah, " with burnt offerings, with calves of a year old ? . . . He hath shewn thee, O Man, what is good, and what doth the Lord require of thee, but to do justly, and to love mercy, and to walk humbly with thy God ? " These are the forces which, lifting men on to the highest plane of being, place them in sure touch with the Supreme and with His mercies. These are the forces which alone possess the true magic—the magic that transfigures human life, and evokes the grace and the blessing of Heaven. Between the superstition of a Balaam and this great utterance of Micah, a wide gulf is set; but the Israelite soul, with wondrous insight, knew how to bridge it more than two thousand years ago.

OPTIMISM

"Though a sinner do evil a hundred times and prolong his days, yet surely I know that it will be well with them that fear God."—ECCLESIASTES viii., 12.

THIS is an optimistic utterance, and paradoxically it is to be found in the one pessimistic book of the Bible. The Talmud tells us that it was proposed to keep Ecclesiastes out of the Scriptures because of its pessimism, but its epilogue saved it :—" Fear God and keep His commands, for this is the whole duty of man." But, in truth, there is much sound doctrine scattered all through the book. Ecclesiastes is the picture of the philosophic mind, of the average mind, for ever halting between two opinions, the goodness and the badness of life. Changing mood and circumstance, even shifting states of health, make a man a pessimist one moment, and an optimist another. Hence while the author of Ecclesiastes can cry " Vanity of vanities, all is vanity," he can also declare, despite the teasing fact of the sinner's prosperity, that it will ultimately be well with them that fear God.

Apart from Ecclesiastes—nay, together with it—Holy Writ is essentially optimistic; it is the hopeful man's Bible. All seeming evil, says Scripture, is overruled for good. The world would be all right if man would make it so; God, in spite of man, is going to make it all right in His own good time. God saw all that He had made and behold it was very good—this is the first judgment on the scheme of things, and it is the final one. The story of the journey to the Promised Land is an allegory as well as a fact; life is a pilgrimage to something better, not only hereafter, but here. "The best is yet to be." Righteousness, so sorely persecuted, so fraught with suffering, is the only real wellbeing, and it will triumph at last. All who deny this creed are in the opinion of the Biblical writers, transgressors, blasphemers. For to say that the world is all wrong, and life incurably evil, is either to say that there is no God, or to assert that He is cruel, or careless, or powerless, willing human misery, or indifferent to it, or unable to remedy it—which is virtually the same as saying that there is no God. Pessimism, then, is the one heresy. The spies, who brought back a gloomy report about Canaan, were pessimists; but their sin is called want of faith. And rightly so; for the two things are one. You remember how a Prophet foretells, in a season of famine, that a measure of flour shall be sold almost for a song on the morrow. One man doubts. "Yes," he says mockingly, "if God were to make windows in heaven, then this thing might be." "Behold," retorts the Prophet, "thou shalt see it with thine eyes, but shalt not eat thereof." And so it was. The eager crowd, pushing to get the abundant food next day, trampled him under foot. He almost deserved his fate. For he was a pessimist, a denier of God, of His mercy, His power, His providence.

That is why, I suppose, the Jew has always been an optimist. He has laughed at his troubles to save himself from tears; but he has laughed at them, too, as an act of faith, because if he had done otherwise he would have been false to his mission as a witness to God. What! Should he, the chosen truth-bearer, turn his back on the truth—be an apostate? Though he himself might suffer, the Messiah would put everything right at last for Israel and for mankind. The Jew mourned for his lost national glory; but a greater glory would eclipse it and obliterate its very memory. He looked back sometimes, but forward far more often, and if he looked back it was the more hopefully to look forward. Recalling past mercies, he felt surer of coming ones. To despair of the future was to despair of God.

All religion is essentially optimistic, as all the Bible is, though some religions are more optimistic than others. The religionist accepts the Law, sings with the Psalmists, predicts with the Prophets. He accepts God's stern decrees as a holy and righteous ordinance, to which he bows dutifully and submissively; He sings like any Psalmist of the defeat of sorrow, the destruction of sin; with the Seers of old he cherishes in his heart the vision of a golden age. Take religion from a man, and you take from him his hope, his joy in life, his belief in it. You kill his soul. So let us be optimists—for our own sake, and for the sake of others. To go about with long faces is a sin against our fellow-men. There are people who do so, and they are like a sudden thundercloud coming between us and the sunshine. The former times, they insist, were far better than these. The former times!—they forget that, in former times, epidemics went their deadly way unchecked, innocent women were tortured and killed as witches, men were hanged for a small offence, and for no offence—burnt for their very virtues; demented people were whipped to drive the evil spirit out of them. Would the pessimist really like to have lived in those good old times? Would he be happy in the best of times? Of course not. For pessimism is a frame of mind, a way of looking at things, not a reflection of the things themselves. Put the pessimist in the garden of Eden, and he would declare it to be anything but a Paradise. His spectacles are wrong, or rather his eyesight is. If he looked at things truly—looked at life, not at little bits of it—he would alter his judgments. The optimist also sees the dark side of life, but, unlike the pessimist, he sees the bright side too, and that encourages him to believe that the bright side is the right, the winning side ; it encourages him to work, and prove it to be the winning side. For optimism is not the ignoring of evil, but the courageous determination to look it steadily in the face and to quell it with the very courage.

Thus the pessimist stands self-condemned ; he denies that there is a soul of good in things evil, and therefore desists from seeking it. He helps to bring about the disasters he fears. Whereas to believe the best is half way to achieving it. It is the one conquering force. You remember Watt's picture of Hope. A blind figure, with a harp of which only one string remains, sits above the globe. For hope persists in spite of evil fate, when well-nigh all the music of life is hushed, and wins—wins the whole world. Every benefactor of mankind, every promoter of its progress, has been an optimist.

All the world's story justifies the optimistic view. The world is not only a good place, but is getting to be a better one, though a thousand voices seem to shriek against the creed. A strange time, you will say, in which to preach it, when war is mowing down precious lives every day and torturing countless hearts. But some wondrous alchemy is winning the gold from the seething crucible—evoking a new order, social and moral, a better day for the poor and the downtrodden, larger conceptions of personal duty, and mightier efforts to fulfil it, a new international covenant based on equity, and justice, and brotherliness. This new order is already in the making. England, we said, is declining ; she is losing her proud place among the nations ; she is sinking ever lower into materialism, and sloth, and selfishness. But at the clarion call of a great emergency she has nobly proved her mettle—shown that her spirit is sound, that she is as great as ever. Moreover, stained by cruelty as this war is, it still bids us hope. For the cruelty seeks to excuse itself to the moral law, to the conscience of mankind. In olden times there was no attempt at excuse, nor any collective conscience to which to offer it. We are ashamed of war as a blot on our civilization; that shame is a new thing, the potency of lasting peace, the herald of a better time.

The hearts of men are changing, but their souls too. Human nature, instead of being vile, is proving itself nobler. It is a time of self-sacrifice, of religion. Do not believe that faith is dying; it is only seeking new forms in which to express itself. Men are trying to find a common spiritual bond, to make religion the force that unites, not separates and estranges. Do not believe that Judaism is perishing; it is only changing its manifestations, the better to do its destined task. Do not believe that wrong is going to triumph. "Though a sinner do evil a hundred times and prolong his days, yet surely I know that it will be well with them that fear God." It is a conviction that springs eternal in the human breast. The modern poet affirms it too; he must needs trust

> . . . that good shall fall
> At last—far off—at last, to all,
> And every winter change to spring.

Would you be assured that the message is true? Then listen to your own hearts, and you will find it echoed there.

MAKING THE BEST OF THINGS

"And it came to pass after these things that Naboth the Jezreelite had a vineyard, hard by the palace of Ahab, King of Samaria."—1 KINGS xxi., 1.

I ONCE preached, and have since printed, a sermon on making the best of people. This morning I should like to speak about making the best of things. Both are aspects of the same optimistic temper. By making the best of things I mean not making the best of bad things —or what we usually think of as bad things—though that is a virtue and a duty. What I mean is making the best of good things. It is wise and noble to meet the troubles of life with courage and resignation, to make the best of what seems like a bad bargain with fate, and if we cannot get what we like, to school ourselves to like what we get. But what I have in my mind just now is the happy temper for which there are no such things as bad bargains with fate. I call it a happy temper because those who are fortunate enough to possess it succeed in getting the most out of life, and have within them an unfailing source of good health, both bodily and mental. Whereas those who lack it have within them the fruitful seed of untold miseries.

This, as you will have recognised, is quite up-to-date doctrine. There has been a revival in recent years of the old idea which establishes an intimate connexion between mental and physical wellbeing. The "new thought" and the "higher thought" are modern bits of phraseology—I had almost said modern jargon—

dressing up in new guise truths as ancient as the Book of Proverbs, with its warnings that " a tranquil heart is the life of the flesh," but that " envy is the rottenness of the bones." If you would be well, we are told by the modern, as well as the old world teacher, give heed to your thoughts and your feelings. Cultivate purity of mind, cheerfulness, an even temper, contentment, and all the rest of these simple, but not very common virtues, for your life's sake. In Scriptural teaching and phrase " they are your life and the length of your days." Make the worst of things and you will suffer; make the best of them, and you will be at ease—not only in mind, but in body. " My flesh also," exclaims the Psalmist, " shall abide in safety."

These two opposite tempers are aptly illustrated in the familiar story of Naboth and his Vineyard. On the one hand there is Ahab, a King, living in a palace—a a man who, humanly speaking, has everything to make him happy. But there is one bitter drop in his overflowing cup which spoils all its sweetness. Hard by his palace is a vineyard, no great thing in itself, but because it belongs to somebody else it robs his royal domain of all its charm for him. Just for the lack of those few yards of land his magnificence is non-existent, and he is a miserable man. Now, contrast with Ahab the owner of the vineyard—Naboth. His little property lies close to the palace, which is for ever challenging comparisons with it. Does the fact make him discontented? Does it make him value his vineyard less? Not at all. There is nothing he values more. The King has tried to coax him into selling it, offering him a better vineyard in exchange. But Naboth refuses; for him there is no better vineyard in all God's earth. " The Lord forbid," he cries, " that I should part with the inheritance of my fathers." The inheritance of his fathers!—there you

MAKING THE BEST OF THINGS

have it. This poor vineyard of his is something so precious that nothing can buy it. It is of small intrinsic worth; but, as his ancestral heritage, the embodiment of cherished memories and associations, it is priceless. For Naboth it is the one desirable vineyard. It is so for Ahab too. Only while for him it is desirable because it is another man's possession, for Naboth it is desirable because it is his own! There is a world of difference between the two tempers.

There are many Ahabs in the world, too few Naboths. Life is not overstocked with joys—let us make the most of what joys there are. And we can do it if we choose. Happiness, as I doubt not you have more than once been reminded, depends less upon the incidents of life than upon the way we look at them, the spirit in which we meet them. The Ahabs, in spite of their good fortune, will always be wretched; the Naboths, in spite of their fewer blessings, will always be happy. And the great point is that the magic power which transforms seeming evil into good, and the good into the best, is within reach of us all. It is a matter of self-discipline. There are people—I do not deny it—who are born optimists, just as there are people who are born pessimists. I have a friend of whom it has been said that if she came upon a daisy in a field, she would be sure to say, "this is the finest daisy I have ever seen!" For her the good that happens to come her way is always the best. "Sir," said an old omnibus driver to me, on my condoling with him after three weeks of continuous rain, " Sir, it is my belief that we always have the weather that is best for us." No doubt my friend and my omnibus driver are born optimists. But I am quite sure that they would have lost their optimism long ago if they had not assiduously cultivated it. And, in like manner, it is quite possible for the born pessimist to change his dreary creed if he will only take the trouble. But then taking trouble is just what most of us detest.

There are people, to be sure, who would like to be optimists, only they don't know how to set about it. Well, our Scriptural story will help them. Let them begin by thinking about their own vineyard, and trying to find reasons for believing it to be the best vineyard in the world—unique in situation, its vines the most fruitful, its grapes the largest and the most luscious. They will idealize life no doubt ; but, in spite of that, they will be far nearer to the truth than the pessimists are with joyless depreciation. For joy—by whatever mental process we attain it—is real, and life is worth exactly what we get out of it. Suppose we do see things rose-colour, when they are only pale-pink, that they are rosy to our eyes is a fact, and the fact is everything. What matters it if my lot is not so fortunate theoretically as that of my neighbour next door, or of the millionaire I read about in the newspapers, or of the King on his throne, so long as I hold myself to be the most fortunate person in the world ? If I feel the happiest of men, I *am* the happiest. All the wealth of the millionaire, all the royal state of the King, cannot make either of them more than that. And on the other hand it may make them less. Even a King, as Ahab's story teaches us, may be far from happy. His very magnificence may help to make him wretched. We know what a crumpled rose-leaf may do to make even a royal bed intolerable. Of life the so-called " fortunate " man may say

> What care I how fair it be
> If it be not fair to me.

Making the best of things—of the good things—it is the secret of happiness. I do not forget that dissatisfaction is a condition precedent of all progress, that no one can better his condition who is not discontented with it. But there is a right and a wrong discontent. The discontent which is the germ of wellbeing is by that fact justified. The explorer, the inventor, the energetic man of business, the student, the social worker—each knows that wholesome discontent, and blessing comes of it. But the man who, like Ahab, is dissatisfied from sheer greed and covetousness, who pines for what is not simply because it is not his, who depreciates his possessions just because he has them, will always be longing whatever he has, and the things upon which he has set his heart will cease to satisfy him as soon as he has gained them. Such a man does no good either to himself or to anyone else. His is a sterile discontent, and therefore foolish and bad.

Let us beware of this temper. "Who," asks the old Jewish sage, "is truly rich?" and he answers "he who rejoices in his lot." Rejoices, you will observe, not shows a mere sombre acquiescence. To price the gifts of life at something more than their face value—this is the part of goodness and of wisdom. There is much to be done in this direction. We are the recipients of boons of which we have not sounded all the blessedness; we have opportunities for happiness of which we have not realized all the magnitude. We long for the joys we do not possess, when we have not exhausted, or even measured, the joys we have. We are always coveting our neighbour's vineyard to add to our own domain—a domain so vast and so rich that we have never properly appreciated or explored it. We sigh for the pleasures of the country, and take an infinite deal of pains to capture them, forgetful of the joys offered us by the town. At this time of year the gardens and parks of a great city like this are a dream of loveliness; they spread for us a feast of pure delight. Yet comparatively few enjoy to the full the pleasures thus offered to them. Many travel miles in search of pleasures which, if they will only look for them, they will find awaiting them at their very doors.

And so it is throughout. We rush after the newest of new books just because they are new. The old ones—those stowed away for years at the back of our bookshelves—would afford us equal, probably greater enjoyment. I like to think of my late colleague in the ministry who lived almost to be a hundred, asking somebody to read to him over again his well-thumbed Dickens shortly before he died. Years of friendship with the old books had only tightened its bonds. It is Naboth's love for his ancient patrimony over again.

We may well take the lesson to heart. How good it is for the mind and the character to turn the most familiar objects into reasons for joy, to prize one's own vineyard, even though it is hard by a palace which is always challenging comparisons with it—to prize it as the finest of all domains—to think of one's daisy as the most beautiful daisy that grows! There are joys enough in the average life to satisfy the most exacting. Think of the inestimable boon of health, the glorious capacity for work, the power of helping and blessing others, the inexpressible delights of home-life, the love and devotion of our dear ones. These are priceless gifts, which no other joys can match—none, at least, of those that we usually associate with the lives we envy.

Let us cultivate the thought. For there is happiness in it—happiness more real because more abiding than that yielded by worldly goods and the lower pleasures. It is the happiness of contentment, of peace, of general wellbeing—the happiness that touches and gilds the humblest life, and makes it, what all life was to its Creator at the beginning, "very good," a blessed dispensation, an ordinance of love.

GOD'S TREES

"The trees of the Lord."—PSALM civ., 16.

THIS is the season of the trees. Many elements go to make the spell of the Spring landscape—the fresh green of hill and meadow, the bravery of the flowers, the glint of the stream—but most of the magic is wrought by the trees. Their beauty at this Springtime is one of the greatest delights that Nature has in her storehouse. Their foliage is young like the season, and with their every shade of delicate verdure there mingles the splendour of their many-hued blossom, gracious alike in achievement and in promise. The soul must indeed be dead that does not thrill in response to the call of the trees in these halcyon days.

The quick souls of our ancient fathers heard and answered the call. The Bible is full of the wonder of the trees. For its poets and preachers they had a message whose eloquence never failed. For them they were the "trees of the Lord," either because the giants of the forest, planted by no human hand, seemed to have been rooted by God Himself, or because their lofty stature and enormous girth entitled them to be regarded as the especial property of the Omnipotent in a world which was "full of His possessions." For them the trees, which far outlived not only the transient flowers, but man, with his three-score-years-and-ten—the trees, which lifted their heads proudly to the sky and stretched their arms confidently afar, were types of prosperity and well-being, of the well-being, in particular, of the righteous flourishing like the stately palm, or the evergreen planted by the water-side. The trees, casting a grateful shade in the summer heat, bearing fruit for human sustenance and delight, are favourite examples in the Bible of the Divine goodness extended to all living creatures, both great and small. They are the coverts of the beasts, the home, the music-room, of the birds. Without the trees, Nature would have been half empty for the old Hebrew poet; his song, his sweet speech about God, would have lost half its force and graciousness.

And we of a far later day would be unutterably poorer too. How much delight should we lose if the vision of loveliness that greets the tired eyes even of the town-dweller on such a morning as this were denied us! Here in stony London a frequent paradise meets us, which, like a veritable oasis in a veritable desert, the trees have made possible. The very poorest can claim these bright spots as their domain; the saddest may revel in them. They are God's free gift to all—given " without money and without price "—given to the poorest to make their poverty richer than the riches of the wealthy, given to the saddest to make their joy greater than the gladness of the joyous. For is not contrast the secret of all pleasure? Is not the capacity for happiness stronger in those hearts that are visited by only rare gleams of it? " Mine, mine! " cries the poor man, in an ecstasy born of his indigence; " Joy, joy! " cries the sorrowing, with a fervour heightened by his trouble. Such are some of the compensations of the Divine scheme!

Gratitude to God for having made His world so beautiful—this is the first feeling that the trees awaken in us, next to the delight created by their beauty. Gratitude and reverence—the same feelings which the trees aroused centuries ago in the poet-shepherds feeding their flocks on the olive-crowned hills of Palestine, or in the seers

GOD'S TREES

beholding their Creator in the twilight of the cedar forests of Lebanon. For the human heart is as unchanging as the world outside it. Science may add more and more to our knowledge of the workings of Nature; but it can only deepen, not enfeeble, our wonder at her marvels. Man's wisdom grows from year to year, but only to make ever clearer the infinitude of God's wisdom. The life of the tree, the subtle processes which constitute it—the rising of the sap, the stir of the bud, the colouring of the leaf—nay, the health which the trees exhale with their purifying breath—this is disclosed to us in a way which our fathers knew not. But the fundamental mystery of it all remains unsolved, and will remain unsolved for ever; for it is the mystery of life, the secret of God. And so, like our fathers, we must go on our knees, in our turn, and reverence and thank the Hand that made the trees so wondrous and so beautiful.

It is no superfluous lesson, though we have been taught it again and again. Not only must knowledge know her place, and, so knowing, exalt herself by her humility—not only must we remember that science can never dethrone Religion, but, on the contrary, more firmly establish her kingdom—we must reaffirm our covenant with the simpler duties which meant so much for the men of olden time. Again and again, as the Spring comes round, must the Spring in our own hearts be renewed, the fresh, childlike feelings of thankfulness and reverence create a new and a joyous world within us. Old as we may be, we must remain young to the end—young in feeling. Heirs to the intellectual riches gathered by the centuries, as we may be, we must keep a place in our minds for the faith and the lowliness of spirit that marked the world in its childhood. Evil will the day be when too much knowledge, too much worldliness, have made men old—robbed them of their power of wonder, of their reverence for a wisdom transcending their own, of their gratitude for blessings which retain their blessedness despite their familiarity.

"The trees of the Lord"—it is an apt description. God has made them, as He has made us. They are one with man, the summit of creation. This mystic thrill which the trees, in common with all plant-life, impart to us as they robe themselves in the waking-time of the Spring—whence does it come if not from the common bond of life that binds us to them? Speechless, immovable, they stand in field or wood, but they are one with us; those thrusting, expanding leaves of theirs, that silent growth of theirs, year after year, show it. That is why we are drawn to them, why we love them. With us they share in the great totality of life which fills the world, and for which the world lives. In a recent story a man is shipwrecked with a companion on an uninhabited island. In a fit of unreasoning frenzy he kills his comrade; and then a sense of his utter loneliness grips him. The sand beneath his feet, the coral reef below it, the imprisoning circle of the sea around him, are his foes, mocking his solitariness, and increasing its misery. One only stay, one only friend he has—a tree. To that he clings as to a human being, and his wretchedness is lightened. For it is one with himself—one through the mystic bond of life.

"The trees of the Lord"—His, but ours too—*our* trees, our kith and kin, made by the same Hand, given to us by that Hand to be our solace and our delight, to keep our hearts fresh and our memory green, to make us humble as children, gratefully mindful of all the mercies that make our daily portion. "Open Thou mine eyes," cries the Psalmist, "that I may behold wondrous things out of Thy law. I am a sojourner in the earth; hide not Thy commandments from me." But

Nature, too, unrolls a Bible before us; earth and sky and sea are manifestations of God to the open-eyed soul. May we be of those to whom the revelation is given! Let us pray for insight, so that we may look with new eyes, nay, with the old eyes of our fathers, upon God's world, and behold the wondrous things it may disclose to us. For then our sojourn on earth will be all the nobler, all the happier, seeing that God has not hidden His commandments from us, nor hidden Himself, with all the peace and the joy and the blessing that come with the vision of Him.

THE HALLOWING OF KNOWLEDGE*

"And thou shalt speak unto all that are wisehearted, whom I have filled with the spirit of wisdom."—Exodus xxviii., 3.

THE text is to be found in the lesson from the Pentateuch appointed to be read on this Sabbath. It speaks of a band of "wise-hearted" men who, at the command of Moses, are to make the priestly garments "for glory and for beauty." The work is to be done, it is true, for God; it is to lend grace and splendour to the sanctuary. But the wisdom and the skill that are to achieve it are earthly; they are the wisdom and the skill of the artist. And yet they are said to come direct from the Supreme, and their possessors to be filled with His spirit. At the head of this company of old-world artists is, as we read further on in Exodus, Bezalel, whose name signifies "in the shadow of God." And truly he is happily named. For Art both ennobles and consoles; it reveals to its elect the divine secret, and divinely shields them from many an evil. Secular though it is, it is holy, and he whom it inspires has the Spirit. And yet, like all sacred gifts, it must be used sacredly. The wise-hearted band of old dedicate their powers to the service of the Sanctuary. They fashion things of "glory and beauty"; but the glory is for God, and the beauty for His holy House. But Art is only one phase of many-sided wisdom. Every intellectual endowment is a patent of nobility, and all nobility is an obligation, a pledge binding us to the service of the Highest.

Thus I strike the keynote of this address. The

*Preached to Jewish members of the University of Cambridge.

THE HALLOWING OF KNOWLEDGE

sanctification of knowledge is surely no inappropriate theme upon which to speak to a congregation such as this. For a splendid enterprise, my brethren, has brought you to this ancient seat of learning from various parts of the land, nay, from various lands. In a sense the ancient company of workers, who toil to provide a fitting Sanctuary for God, live again in you. Like them, you are intent upon building a noble fabric—the fabric of the intellectual life—and filling it with "glory and beauty." It rests with you to make the parallel closer still. This fabric which you are fashioning may be, if you will, a Temple to the living God—one consciously dedicated to His service, and designed for His honour. But to you my theme appeals with heightened force. For, more than simple students, you are Jewish students, and your very religion binds you to the duty of reverencing and hallowing knowledge. All the associations of this historic University give dignity and sacredness to the intellectual life. "The stone cries out from the wall, and the beam out of the timber answers it." The strenuous story of six hundred years breathes its inspiring message to you, and spurs you to that self-sacrificing love of learning which distinguished your forerunners. But this impulse Judaism powerfully reinforces with its own special appeal. For what are six centuries compared with the thousands of years that Israel has lived, and lived for knowledge? We have seen how, in the very beginnings of their national life, our fathers did honour to the intellectual worker, how the artist and the thinker were placed on a level with the religious teacher, were held to be inspired, in organic contact with God Himself. But this indeed is only one example of Israel's reverence for the things of the mind, only one illustration of the impressive truth that, in your devotion to the tasks that are filling your happy years, you are faithfully obeying the call, showing yourselves loyal to the traditions of your historic race.

Have you ever thought how eloquently the Bible, in itself, by its very existence, witnesses to that truth? We are apt to regard the Hebrew Scriptures as a religious monument only. But, in sooth, they are more even than that. Deriving its chief value and significance from its divine story, its sublime patterns of human conduct, the Bible is yet full of absorbing interest as a revelation of the mind, as distinct from the soul, of the people who gave it to the world. As a piece of literature it compels unstinted admiration; so that even those who cannot accept all its doctrine are fain to own the magic of its external beauty. Where, among the writings of the ancient world, can you match the mingled simplicity and grandeur of the opening chapter of Genesis, or the rugged eloquence of Isaiah, or the tender appeal of the great "Prophet of the Captivity," or the picturesque imagery of Ezekiel, or the poetic inspiration of the Psalms? Nor is this all. Putting aside literary power, think of the knowledge displayed by the Scriptural writers. Think of the hygienic science of Moses, still the wonder of our age; think of the Prophet's acquaintance with contemporary history, of the familiarity with the wonders of earth and sea and sky shown by Job in common with all the old Hebrew poets. If the Bible were our sole literary treasure, it would suffice to demonstrate the sympathy that has ever attracted Israel to intellectual pursuits. But the Bible does not stand alone. It is the starting-point of a vast and varied literature, to which every age has made its contribution, and every land witnessed the growth. Need I cite the Talmud, with its keen discussions and its daring speculations, with its store of information on every topic under the sun? Need I speak of Ibn Gebirol

THE HALLOWING OF KNOWLEDGE

and Halevi, Israel's sweet singers ; or of Maimonides, the philosopher and physician ; or of Duran, the astronomer ; or of Ibn Ezra, the mathematician ; or of Chisdai, the statesman ?

But from men let us turn to ideas. "Learn," "know," "teach"—how often do these words occur in the Pentateuch ! They are an exhortation to get the highest form of knowledge—Religion—but also to ponder and to master the whole science of living. That the Lawgiver meant his hearers to cultivate their thinking powers as well as their emotions, to reason about Religion as well as to feel it, is certain. For the Pentateuch is the champion of enlightenment. It denounces superstition ; it would have us possess an intelligent, a reasoned creed. Alone, then, among the religious codes of antiquity it is the friend of the intellectual life.

Consider again the Book of Proverbs, the typical example of a series of works which, from their leading characteristics, have been styled the "Wisdom Literature." The wisdom there extolled has the fear of God for its base and crown, but the writers evince an æsthetic appreciation of the very grace that knowledge confers upon its happy possessors. "Wisdom is the principal thing ; therefore get wisdom ; yea, with all thou hast gotten get understanding. She shall give to thy head a chaplet of grace ; a crown of beauty shall she deliver to thee." Equally glowing is the panegyric pronounced by the author of the apocryphal *Wisdom of Solomon*. For him, too, wisdom is the ideal good. "When I am come into my house I shall find rest with her, for converse with her hath no bitterness, and to live with her hath no pain, but gladness and joy." Nay, wisdom has the widest connotation. Solomon, the impersonation of wisdom, is a sympathetic student of Nature, and makes its wonders the theme of his songs. "He spake," we are told, "of trees, from the cedar that is in Lebanon even unto the hyssop that springeth out of the wall; he spake also of beasts, and of fowl, and of creeping things and of fishes." And a later writer assigns to his knowledge a yet larger scope. "He knew"—so we read—"the constitution of the world and the operation of the elements, the circuits of years and the positions of stars, the violences of winds and the thoughts of men, the diversities of plants and the virtues of roots—all things, either secret or manifest."

Even the Rabbins, though for them the study of the Scriptures was the highest of all joys, could keep a place in their affections for secular learning. "He is a low man," they say, "who lacks knowledge, yes, even though he be learned in the Torah." For the Torah needs to be studied with intelligence; it is, to use their notable simile, like the sea; only the swimmer, who knows how to guide himself through the waters, can plunge into it safely. "If," they ask, "thou lackest knowledge, what hast thou gotten; if thou hast gotten knowledge, what does thou lack?" They lauded the study of science,—of medicine, astronomy; loving Hebrew, they praised the beauty of Greek. Nay, knowledge is but the means, and its end is that sane and intelligent application of it which alone is wisdom. Both are needed to make the complete man. It is possible to have knowledge and yet to lack the power of using it; it is possible to be ignorant and yet to have a counterfeit, a dangerous wisdom. The one, the Rabbins says, is to have bread without condiment, and the other to have the condiment without the bread.

Thus it is that one of the most important prayers in the Jewish liturgy—the *Amidah*—includes a supplication for the gifts of the intellect. The pious Jew offers the petition thrice daily, thus setting the hall-mark of religion

THE HALLOWING OF KNOWLEDGE

upon knowledge and understanding, and declaring them to be among the most desirable things. Nor has it been an unmeaning petition. There have doubtless been times when the Jew has been plunged in the darkness of ignorance, when a narrow religiosity has constituted for him the sum-total of the higher life. But far more often he has evinced an insatiable passion for intellectual joys. Nay, there have even been times when he stood almost alone as the torchbearer of science, when, but for his loving offices, knowledge and culture would have all but disappeared from the world.

As Jews, then, you are bound to the intellectual life by special obligations. All the incentives that keep you true to Judaism should make you earnest, conscientious students. For that is not true Judaism from which the intellect is divorced, and Israel's whole life-story is the story of battle for the truth, for the rights of the intellect as well as for the soul's freedom. All the voices of the past, then, bid you God-speed in your work. But those voices admonish as well as encourage. Intellectual power they bid us remember, is the gift of God, the manifestation of that divine spirit which worked so mightily in the artificers of the ancient Sanctuary. It calls for reverence. In what does that reverence consist?

In the first place, knowledge must be pursued for its own sake. Even the gentle Hillel could denounce the man who uses the "Crown" for sordid ends. And though the Crown is the beautiful title he bestows upon the highest of all knowledge, he would not, I am sure, have refused it to secular learning. At any rate, if he could revisit the earth, he would exhort us to set study far above the prizes it may gain for us, whether they be won in the university or in the world outside. The grace, the dignity, the strength which knowledge imparts —for these he would bid us reserve all our homage. It is an ideal which every student may well keep before him. I am not insensible to the conditions under which the intellectual toiler is compelled to work in these times. I know that the scholarly habits and enthusiasms of former days, when men would give themselves utterly to the quest of knowledge, regardless of the world and its joys, are becoming rarer because they are becoming more difficult. The old " way of the Torah "—" eat bread with salt, drink water by measure, lie on the earth, and live the austere life, and thus find thy happiness "—this is out of fashion in an age marked by an exacerbation of the struggle for existence, and by the increased significance of knowledge as the weapon of victory. The current flows so strongly that one needs to be a giant to swim against it.

And yet, while we cannot altogether ignore the value of intellectual gifts as the passport to worldly success, we may still preserve some of the ancient spirit, and prize them far more for the true self-realisation of which they are the instruments. Wealth, social influence, material comfort—these things it is not necessary to despise. But higher than them all let us set knowledge itself, with the discipline and the strength and the self-development that are yielded by its pursuit. To every student the thrilling words placed by the old Biblical Sage in the mouth of Wisdom come with mighty appeal: " Whoso findeth me findeth life "—life, which is something ampler and nobler than mere livelihood—" but he who sinneth against me sinneth against his own soul." For, my brethren, we cannot trifle with our higher powers—we cannot basely use knowledge—without a certain degradation.

Give yourselves, then, to study with single-hearted devotion, if you would live the worthy, nay, the happy life. For just because you think not of reward, it will come in abundant measure; it will come in joy—in the joy that knowledge jealously keeps for her true lovers, for those who woo her for herself alone. And since that joy is independent of all else, it will always be yours while health and strength endure. It will be beyond the reach of life's vicissitudes. Success will not eclipse it, nor failure corrode it. Next to your faith in eternal Goodness it will be your chief antidote against sorrow. You will have the calm mind of the student. And if there go with it the fixed heart that trusts in God, what can the world do unto you?

For even the intellect needs to be chastened and sanctified by union with the heart. " Man doth not live by bread alone "—no, not even by intellectual bread. Recognize your mental gifts; realize them to the full. But realize them under a deep sense of responsibility to Him who has given them to you. Use them; but use them well—for all good and seemly ends, in a manner befitting the sons of God, dowered with immortal souls. Cultivate, then, the virtue of self-reverence—self-reverence which, so far from being akin to self-worship, to vanity, is the cure for it. Respect your endowments because of their Divine origin, and so you will gain that spirit of humility which has ever been the mark of the true seeker after knowledge from the days of Joseph, with his cry, " It is not in me; it is God that will answer." " Not unto us, O Lord, not unto us, but unto Thy Name be the glory "—it is the prayer of every great soul, great because it is lowly. Whatever we are, whatever we achieve, let us acknowledge that all is of God, and that we are but His humble instruments. Let no pride taint our success; let only gratitude to the Almighty for having chosen us as His workers fill our hearts, and put the seal on our triumph.

Remember, too, that you have your powers and your

opportunities in trust, and that you must give a strict account of your stewardship. The divine compact with your fathers is renewed for you. God has led you into a goodly land flowing with milk and honey, and you, bound by your father's obligations, must fulfil your part of the covenant by hearkening to His voice. For intellectual gifts are a bond, and they contain all the potencies of the religious life. You can serve God with them; you can worship him through them. Amiel, the philosopher, went to his desk, we are told, as to an altar. In a like spirit of dutifulness and pious self-surrender go you to your work, striving through it to hallow yourselves and to glorify God. For this, as we have seen, was the spirit in which the great intellectual toilers of our race have ever worked, from that far-off age, when the company of artists lovingly wrought for the Sanctuary, down to this day.

And this brings me to my final word. You are here, I have said, as students, but also as Jews. What does that manifold character suggest but the duty of devoting some of your intellectual strength to the specific tasks with which your people is identified? If you are true lovers of knowledge, worthy representatives of your race, you will spare some of the leisure left you after your secular work is done to reverent study of the language and the literature and the history of Israel. Perhaps you have already anticipated this suggestion. If so, I shall rejoice. But if not, ought you to perpetuate the anomaly that, though there are Jews at this seat of learning, enthusiasm for Jewish studies is chiefly to be sought for elsewhere than in their ranks?

My brethren, I have finished. Let me indulge the hope that the affectionate counsel I have ventured to offer may find acceptance at your hands. It is because I number you among " the wise-hearted " of the text that

I have given it. And in addressing you on this subject I feel that I, in my humble fashion, have been fulfilling a solemn command—a command which the text also breathes: "And thou shalt speak unto all that are wise-hearted, whom I have filled with the spirit of wisdom."

May the Divine blessing attend your noble labours! May true "glory and beauty" crown them! Amen.

THE CHILD

"A heritage of the Lord."—PSALM cxxvii., 3.

THIS is the day of the Child. The wellbeing of the men and women that are to be is one of our chief preoccupations in these times. It fills a large place in our individual thought, our legislation, our social effort. Children are now seen to be the greatest of our national assets, the essential guarantee of strength and stability for the State in the years to come. They cannot be too well-cared for, or too happy ; nor can there be too many of them. We did not always think so. It is not so long ago that we thought the very opposite. For too many well-meaning persons children were of an importance commensurate only with their size and stature. They were children, and nothing more ; they were to be trained, of course, but their training had little significance for anyone but themselves or their parents, and it was to be narrow in scope and carried on by the sternest methods. Instead of a source of potential strength to the State, children might be a danger if they were too numerous, seeing that, according to old Malthus, population always tended to exceed its means of sustenance. The advent of the present war, destructive alike of human life and many an unsound theory, has emphasized the falsity of such ideas. We are going back, not for the first time, to some old Biblical conceptions which, in our short-sightedness, we deemed to be obsolete. The child is coming by his own once more, and with him Holy Writ, too, is being more justly appraised.

THE CHILD

In a delightful essay Dr. Schechter has indicated the considerable place assigned to children in the Rabbinical Literature. But, in this respect, the Fathers of the Synagogue merely follow earlier examples. The Child is a conspicuous figure in the Bible ; he meets us on almost every page. All the life of the people, domestic and public alike, is ordered with partial reference to him. He is to rest, equally with his elders, on the Sabbath Day, and to share in the joyous celebration of the great Festivals. Together with his elders, he is to attend the solemn reading of the Law in the ears of the assembled people, which is to take place every seventh year on the Feast of Tabernacles. His training is one of the inspired legislator's gravest concerns. The father is to teach the Divine Commands diligently unto his children, and to recount to them great historic events like the Exodus, which have exerted a profound influence upon the national life. For the Child is both the father to the man and the future citizen, and his training and character will largely determine not only his own fate, but the destinies of the Commonwealth.

Especially significant is the Biblical valuation of Child-life. In all the glowing pictures of happiness to come, drawn by Lawgiver, and Prophet, and Psalmist, the children are present ; they crowd the canvas, for there is always a multitude of them. The " fruit of the body," as well as the fruit of the ground, is Moses's promised reward to an obedient people. " The Lord God of your fathers make you a thousand times as many as ye are "—the Lawgiver's prayer, which we repeat every Sabbath morning, inevitably recurs to us. " As arrows in the hand of a mighty man, so are young children. Happy is the man that hath his quiver full of them ; they shall not be ashamed when they speak with the enemy in the gate." Thrice-armed is he who has a goodly progeny; father and sons, numerous and united, will victoriously maintain their cause in the courts and on the battle-field. And then there is Zechariah, with his delightful picture of a regenerated Jerusalem, " full of boys and girls, playing in the streets thereof " and Job's description of the typically prosperous people, who " send forth little ones like a flock; their children dance; they sing to the timbrel and the harp, and rejoice at the sound of the pipe," and Jeremiah's prediction of a better day for Israel when " their children shall be as aforetime "—as many and as happy, and when, as a consequence, " the congregation shall be established " before God. In the view of the Biblical writers the Child is truly a gift of God—" a heritage " from Him, as our Psalmist phrases it. " Who are these? " asks Esau of Jacob when they meet after years of estrangement. " The children that God hath graciously given thy servant," is the reply. Who shall say how vast a part those silent peace-makers may have played in reconciling the adversary brothers? Thus it comes about that, in the Bible, the promise of a Child is the promise of coming blessing, and nothing less than a divine or angelic voice is fit to communicate it. The story of Isaac, of Samson, of Samuel, are examples. Even before the child comes his training is carefully planned, for the heavenly gift must be reverently cherished. Nay, the training is to begin while the child is yet unborn, to begin with the discipline of the mother's own life. " What shall be the ordering of the child? " asks Manoah of the angel who announces the coming birth of Samson. " Of all that I have said unto the woman let her beware," is the reply. Here, surely, is the germ of the twentieth-century school for mothers, actual or expectant.

What is the use of children? Mindful of the teachings

both of the Bible and of modern sociology, we answer at once " to become men and women—good citizens, generous contributors to the accumulated store of human goodness." But the answer is not exhaustive. Have not children an immediate use—a use *as* children ? We think of them exclusively as learners ; but are they not teachers too ? How much wholesome instruction may we not get from them. For what are the chief characteristics of a child ? The first is sincerity, genuineness, simplicity affecting both thought and life. May we not see in the attribute a reproof to our own artificiality —our want of candour—our palterings with truth, our hollow flatteries. Does it not rebuke the wastefulness and the luxury which, always sinful, is particularly odious, peculiarly indecent, in the hour of a nation's stern ordeal ?[1]

Another characteristic of children is their patience. In small things fretful and rebellious, in big things they are strangely calm and self-restrained. If you go into a Children's Hospital and find one of the tiny sufferers especially quiet, not even a sob telling of the distress of that small heart, it will probably be because he is desperately ill. That lack of protest or self-pity is an ominous sign ; but it is also a wonderful bit of heroism, full of instruction for us grown-up people. Let us heed the admonition. That " strength to endure " which we ask for in one of our war-prayers is our great need, not only in war-time, but in normal days. How often do we cry out against the cruelty of life, forgetful of life's countervailing beneficence, unmindful of our duty to be strong and of good courage. Let us learn fortitude from these little folk, at once the weakest and the mightiest of mortals.

Another characteristic of the Child is loyalty. How

[1] Preached in War-time.

faithfully it clings to its old nurse, resenting new faces! Are we as leal? We drop our friends simply because we are tired of them, or are ungrateful to those who have done us faithful service. The old books, so full of precious lore, are given up for the new ones, however vapid and misleading; new voices, just because they are new, are permitted to drown the old ones, like Rehoboam's youthful counsellors. The Child, with no eyes for its nurse's grey hairs or homely face, clasping to its bosom its shabby doll, may teach us a better way.

Lastly, children are full of faith, especially of faith in God. Cynicism, distrust of life, are specifically adult defects; no child ever exhibits them. Let us be children, then, feeding our optimism, keeping a good word, a kindly thought, for others, believing the best, and not the worst, about humanity. Let us believe the best about God—about His rectitude, His goodness, the loving purpose that underlies His ordinances, whether they make for peace or war, for life or death. For, in so doing, we shall fulfil the precept of our Bible, which would have us not only teach our boys and girls, but learn from them. What is it that the old Prophet says? "When they see their children, the work of My hands, they shall sanctify My name"; for are not all children, like those of that same Prophet, "signs and wonders"—preachers of God, with hands held out to lead us back to Him from whom they have so lately come? And the modern seer echoes the old, gracious truth. For him, too, the Child is a "trailing cloud of glory," descending "from God who is our home," and "heaven lies about us in our infancy." Happy they who keep that celestial atmosphere with them through the after-years, who make the holy intuitions of childhood "the fountain light of all their day, a master light of all their seeing."

THE CHILD

Then
>In a season of calm weather
>Tho' inland far we be,
>Our souls have sight of that immortal sea
>Which brought us hither,
>Can in a moment travel thither,
>And see the children sport upon the shore,
>And hear the mighty waters rolling evermore.

Yes, the Children! For it is the Child-spirits, pure, lowly, loving, true, that people the heaven above—come from it, and return to it—even as they make the lower heaven that transfigures the workaday world about us.

PARENTS AND CHILDREN

> "Moreover He said, I am the God of thy father, the God of Abraham, the God of Isaac, and the God of Jacob. And Moses hid his face, for he was afraid to look upon God."—
> EXODUS iii., 6.

"THE God of thy father," as well as the God of the three great Patriarchs. Upon this the Midrash, in a delightful legend, says that, in that wonderful revelation, the story of which our Bar-mitsvah lad has read to us this morning, the Supreme began to speak to Moses in the voice of his father. His heart went out to the beloved accents. "My father, my father," he cried. "Nay," said the Voice, "I am thy father's God." No strange deity was speaking, but the God whom his father had taught him to reverence, the majestic Being who, despite his majesty, was endeared to him by all the tender memories of childhood. And so he was prepared for the momentous communication, for the solemn call to his life-work. He hid his face in awe; but he listened. For the love that dictated the call cast out his fear; it was answered by the filial love that lived on, even in manhood, in his own breast.

Of how many of those who are standing on the threshold of their career could the same be said in these days? They, too, like Moses, are about to take up their work in life; for them, too, the flaming bush—the wonderfulness of the world—excites their curiosity and their love of adventure. They would explore and investigate its marvels; they would turn and see this great sight, and find out why the bush is not consumed.

But it is with little thought, I fear, of the old home, with but scant heedfulness of the old voices, that they go forth. It is the absolutely new that they seek; to be told that very often the new is the old because rooted in it, and safeguarded by it, would not re-assure and encourage, but alienate and chill them. No; the reverence and humility, the noble self-distrust, of the greatest of the Prophets, are getting rarer. Young people nowadays are sufficient unto themselves; they must go their own way, and live their own lives. The ideas of their elders, painfully gathered from years of experience, are obsolete; the God of their fathers, just because He is theirs, just because He has been the hope and the stay of times other than the present, is discredited. They belong to a new age which has no use for any save " new gods, lately come up."

What I am saying is true, literally as well as figuratively. Youth affirms its right to choose its own God, its own religion, untrammeled by consideration for the past. The late Dr. Schechter was accustomed to deprecate the modern Jews' mechanical adhesion to their Judaism. They worship God, he said, half jestingly, half seriously, with their fathers' hearts, not with their own—not with their own, because they have none to worship with. But of our young men and women of to-day the very opposite must be said. If they worship at all, it is with their own hearts, or rather their own minds. Their fault is not that they do not think about religion, but that they think about it wrongly. Early teaching and old-time associations count for little or nothing with them; their religion must be brand-new —the newness is its main attraction—or they will have none of it. That the old folks cherished certain kinds of religious ideas, and lived a certain kind of religious life, is an all-sufficient reason for rejecting them. And so, too often, the spiritual life is undermined, and even perishes altogether.

Let us be just to these young people. The blame is not to be laid entirely upon them. The lure of the new world, now in the making, is all but irresistible. Ours is an age of freedom—of freedom of thought above all ; how can religion claim to be immune ? There is swift progress everywhere—in the domain of knowledge as well as in the material sphere ; why should spiritual values alone escape its effects ? What was good enough for a past generation is, by common consent, not good enough for ours ; surely it is mere common sense to apply the rule all round—to the higher as well as the lower things. So youth is not altogether unjustified. And then again if it is impatient, and just a little arrogant and contemptuous, age is not always wise. Are all parents fully deserving of the authority they claim ? What of their personal example ? And have they always driven with a rein that is neither too tight nor too slack ?

And yet let youth be wise. The new in religion is tempting ; but the new, equally with the old, must be scrutinised and carefully weighed. Freedom is good in itself ; but it must be used in a sober spirit, or it may lead to dangerous licence, as the political state of the world at this moment warns us. Better even a cast-iron religion that never yields to the impact of new-time thought and needs, than religious anarchy, with its formula of "Neither God nor law." I have known children grow up irreligious because of the excessive religiosity of their parents, their over-exacting demand for conformity. But I have also known young men and women spiritually shipwrecked because they have turned a deaf ear to all religion as something essentially antiquated, something incompatible with freedom. I would plead with the young on this question. I would ask them for sanity of thought. I would ask them to consider whether the past is not always the nursing-mother of the present, whether every new order, political, social, intellectual, must not, for very safety's sake, be built on the old, whether true progress is not always gradual evolution rather than revolution, with its violence and destructiveness. And, if this be so, I would further ask whether Religion ought not to advance on the same lines, whether the God of the past, the God of our fathers, ought not to remain the object of our allegiance and our worship, seeing that trust and belief in Him has been our salvation through the centuries.

But there is something besides Religion in question. There is the general outlook on life, the very way of living. In this respect also the cleavage between parents and children seems to be growing. Home-life is losing its old sentimental appeal. Young people, however insufficiently equipped for the grim battle outside, turn their backs on the family roof-tree with undisguised eagerness. *They* know best, they say, how to order their own lives. Sometimes the question turns on that most momentous of all ventures—marriage. It is a difficult problem. When the emotions are concerned reason stands a poor chance of a hearing. But it is not always the emotions that are concerned; cold calculation often enters into the matter. It is the very yearning for freedom, for self-determination, which is the dominant influence. And we all know how often this self-will, this blind revolt against authority, however mild, just because it *is* authority, helps to overshadow the after life. How many tears have been shed in bitter regret for the disdain of counsels which were as tender and loving as they were wise! The story of Rehoboam is eternally true.

For, after all, parental affection, the daily self-sacrifice so sustained, often so hidden away as to pass unnoticed, is a real thing, which cannot, in common justice, be ruled out of the discussion. I am old-fashioned enough to affirm it. Because it is the paternal voice that speaks in some great moment of life it must needs deserve the listening ear, the response of the soul's deference and affection. Or are we to say that humanity, to attain its crown, may rightfully be as the brute animal, which turns from its parent when, its primal needs duly satisfied, it is old and strong enough to forsake the lair in which it has been reared? An old Rabbi, in his ethical will, tells, for the instruction of his children, how, whenever he was at prayer, the memory of his dead mother would rise up in his mind, and he would picture her as she used to teach him to pray when he was a child. Did he not pray then, as an old man himself, all the better for the memory? And shall all this affectionate piety disappear in the name of progress? I cannot believe it. A re-fashioning of the new ideas, of the new relations between parent and child, is one of the crying needs of the age. Deeper filial love, more willingness to listen, a greater inclination to abate the claims of the present for the sake of the respect due to the past, is what the world requires if it is to be a regenerated world. This, at least, is the old Jewish idea. The Messianic age, says the last of the Prophets, is to be marked by the turning of the heart of the fathers to the children and the heart of the children to their fathers lest—such is the significant warning—God come and smite the earth with a curse, lest destruction light upon society. For a stable social order must needs be based upon the home and the family. And what is their sure foundation, in their turn, but self-sacrifice and reverence and love?

PARENTS AND CHILDREN

You, my young friend,[1] are indeed happy; for you have been blessed with good and wise parents, who find their greatest happiness in safeguarding yours. Some of their wisdom will assuredly have been imparted to you; and so you will keep, for their sake and your own, your affection and gratitude for them to the end. You will cherish the thought of them always as an inspiration to all that is good and worthy; like Moses, in the portion you have read this morning, you will let their voice—their teaching—make you brave, keen to answer God's call, when, under the Divine blessing, you have grown to manhood.

They stand for you as the symbol and the embodiment of great family traditions—traditions that bind you to loving zeal for Judaism, to outspoken defence of its cause, to faithful service of your community and your synagogue, to that best championship of Israel which lies in living the good life. This solemn day, when you enter upon your great spiritual inheritance, joins its appeal to that of your dear ones, both living and dead, to emphasise the obligation. Keep the memory of it always in your heart. Be a good Israelite, and then you cannot fail to be a good man—a worthy citizen of this England of ours, a true child of God, the Father in Heaven. May He be with you now and through all the coming years!

I give you the priestly blessing:—" The Lord bless thee and keep thee; the Lord cause his face to shine upon thee and be gracious unto thee; the Lord lift up His face unto thee and give thee peace." Amen.

---

[1] Spoken to the Barmitsvah.

MANLINESS

"And Moses spoke unto the Lord saying, Let the Lord, the God of the spirits of all flesh, appoint a man over the congregation."—NUMBERS xxvii., 16.

"A *man* over the congregation"—one is tempted to emphasise the word, and suggest that in the very choice of it Moses indicated his desire that his successor should be characterized by the manliness that distinguished himself. The Hebrew is Ish, which corresponds to the Latin *vir*. Both terms connote the male in his finest aspects, the strong, courageous, virile male. Knowing his people only too well, knowing that lawlessness and disintegration would follow for them upon slackness in their leader, Moses would have a *man* take his place—a vigorous, brave, resolute man, not a coward or a weakling. We recall other passages of Holy Writ in which manliness is held up as the ideal. "Quit yourselves like men"—so cry the Philistines one to another; "Be a man," is David's call to his son Solomon. And, like an echo of that call, there comes the summons of a far later day and a far different voice—the day and the voice of Hillel—"In a place where there are no men strive to be a man." It is a notable utterance, this last, seeing that it issues from the lips of a Talmudic Rabbi, and is set amid seemingly incongruous surroundings, amid exhortations to the gentler virtues, to piety, to the study of the Torah, to the temper and practice, apparently so little akin to manliness, which are known as quietism.

Certain it is that Moses wanted not only a leader for

Israel, but a manly leader, one who, in his own words, would " go out before them and come in before them." But what is manliness according to the old Hebrew interpretation ? What is a true man ? If, for Israel, Moses was the type of the true man, then the answer is not far to seek. Three characteristics of the great Lawgiver are held up to our admiration by the Pentateuch. He is faithful in all God's house ; he is meek above other men ; to him alone God speaks face to face. Let us understand these three statements, and we shall understand what manliness meant for our remote fathers, and what it may safely mean for us.

Moses was faithful—call him staunch or stedfast, and you will get nearer still, perhaps, to the meaning of the Hebrew. He had character, by which I mean, of course, that he set before himself certain principles of action, and sacrificed everything in order to be true to them. He was, then, a strong man—a morally strong man. Hence Michael Angelo was right symbolically to picture him, in the famous statue, as a man physically strong, with flowing beard and mighty sinews ; and Heine was right to speak of him as the builder of "human pyramids," far surpassing in impressiveness the granite erections that record the life and death of Israel's first oppressors. Moral strength was one of Moses's outstanding attributes. Only a strong man—only a *man*—could have defied Egypt, taken her slaves from her, delivered them not only from the shame of slavery, but from the dangers of freedom—transformed them not merely into a nation, but into a unique nation, with God for their King and religion for their constitution—laid the foundations of a religious polity which, outliving nationality, triumphing over time and chance and deadly peril, should exist, with force unabated, for more than 3,000 years. We have need of such men to-day, or of men made, however faintly, in the Lawgiver's image, so that it may be well with the nation, well with the community—so that " the congregation of the Lord may not be as sheep which have no shepherd." But the desire for strength, or any excellence, in other people, is a virtue which even the weakest find it easy to practise. What we have to strive after is to be men ourselves—strong, staunch, stedfast. How rare these qualities are ! How few *men* there are among Britain's millions of males—men who know how to rule, not a people or a community, but themselves, who formulate definite rules of conduct and cleave to them, who, choosing aims of which their conscience approves, march straight on to the goal, turning neither to the right hand nor to the left ! How few there are who put duty before expediency, who have a clear idea of what they are living for, apart from the satisfaction of mere animal needs and the acquisition of more or less material goods !

> Most men eddy about
> Here and there—eat and drink,
> Chatter and love and hate,
> Gather and squander.

Few indeed are they

> . . . whom a thirst
> Ardent, unquenchable, fires,
> Not with the crowd to be spent,
> Not without aim to go round
> In an eddy of purposeless dust.

These are the *men ;* who of us will be of them ?

But manliness is not strength only ; it is strength and something besides—strength tempered by gentleness, compassion, humility, by a host of qualities at first sight irreconcileable with it. Moses, the resolute man, is also the meekest of men. He is great, but he disclaims his greatness ; he is reviled, calumniated, but he says never a word. Moreover, he can listen patiently to the pleadings of mere women, and learn his duty from them. He is strong enough to be yielding, brave enough to confess his shortcomings. He knows his own mind, but can listen to others; he is firm but not obstinate, self-confident, but not self-conceited. Nor does he stand alone in this respect. Is it an accident that the author of the saying, " In a place where there are no men strive to be a man," was Hillel, the meek and the patient? No; for meekness and patience are signs of strength, not of weakness. Here is a lesson for the would-be man. Not one set of qualities, not the masculine only, will suffice for his outfit. The real man is made by borrowing something from woman—her gentleness, her pity, her power of renunciation. We know the poet's question: " Who is the happy warrior? Who is he That every man in arms should wish to be?" We know his answer too: " More able to endure As more exposed to suffering and distress; Thence also more alive to tenderness." Strength, yes; but the greater strength that forgoes its exercise, that spares the weakness, that respects the rights of others. " It is excellent to have a giant's strength, but it is tyrannous to use it like a giant "— Shakespeare's saying is worth a thought to-day. The conventional idea of manliness—that which is especially commended to the young—gives the chief place to physical prowess, to the mere assertion of men's superiority, without any worthy attempt to make that assertion good. The prevailing devotion to athletics— excellent in moderation—is responsible for this mistake. It is answerable, as many a public schoolmaster warns us, for a *superfcial* conception of honour, for the exaltation of a certain class of virtues to the exclusion of others. The Olympic Games, fine as the qualities were that they fostered, did not save ancient Greece from disruption.

She perished because her moral outlook was narrow, because she needed her worship of physical, of masculine excellence to be tempered by the cult of the feminine attributes of sympathy and love. But why do I draw these distinctions between the sexes? Are they not artificial? Is gentleness, is pity, a feminine virtue? Are courage and fortitude masculine ones? Do not all the virtues rightly and essentially belong to both sexes? Is not the difference merely one of manifestation and opportunity? A woman is compassionate by nature to the sick and the sorrowing; but equally natural is it for a man to be compassionate to those who are at his mercy. A man is brave in facing difficulty, in defying a hundred foes; is a woman less brave who gives her life for her child or bears the pain of giving him life? Different physically—morally, men and women are one. Their proper task is so to use their moral equipment that it may fashion as large a part as possible of their everyday life.

But Moses, strong and meek, communes with God face to face. The crowning element of his manhood is his power to realise the Unseen, to transfigure the daily life with the consciousness of God. To say that this is the crown of manliness may seem a paradox to many. Religion is commonly deemed the negation of manliness, which is defined as essentially self-reliance, contentment with this world, and indifference to the next, a preference for the real and the actual, a contempt for the visionary and the ideal. And yet the most manly of men have been the religious men, if by manliness we mean self-mastery, stedfastness, and the capacity for solid achievement. The men who have written their names deepest on the history of the world are the men of faith —those who, because they felt themselves in the grasp of a Higher Power, submitted to its behests and its direction, and who, because they believed themselves called to a mission, set themselves with single mind to fulfil it as a sacred charge. Moses was one of them. All the wonders he wrought were made possible only by his implicit belief in the Divine commission and guidance. In that sense the story of his miracles is true to the letter.

Religion—you will get little moral good—you will get no true manliness—without it, for you will get no moral stability, no certainty of self-control, without it. It is not usually thought so. It is becoming more and more the fashion, especially under the influence of a decadent literature, to hold that self-restraint and renunciation are proofs of weakness, that such acts, for example, as that to which Joseph was invited in the hour of his greatest temptation, if not proofs of manliness, are at least not incompatible with it. Religion teaches the direct contrary. The true man, it says, is the pure man—the man who subordinates the solicitations of his lower nature to the appeal of his higher self, of the Divine in his own soul, who cries, with Joseph, " How can I do this great wickedness and sin against God ? "

Well, the dispute is an old one ; it is the age-long dispute between Paganism and Hebraism, between the false idea of self-realization which limits self to the sensual, at best the intellectual, and the true one, which includes in self the whole man, spiritual as well as intellectual and physical. The religious side in that conflict we hold to be the nobler. Those who take it are doing their best for the world and for their own souls, blessing others by their example, quitting themselves like men.

I especially bring home this truth to you, my youthful hearers. You are young ; life is all before you, and it is for you to settle the principles which are to guide you in living it. Chief among them set religion, the fear of God, trust in Him, submission to Him, belief in Him. Do not think that this trust and belief is out of date. The notion might have had some plausibility thirty or forty years ago, when physical science, usurping an authority to which it was not entitled, declared that, after ransacking the Universe, it had found no trace of Deity and, with the editor of a French dictionary, who had refused to admit into his work an article on "God," protested that the idea of God "lacked actuality." We are living in different times. Physical science has learnt to know her place; she recognizes that there are boundaries even to *her* kingdom, and that there is a vast domain of experience which she cannot explore because it is inaccessible to her. We are listening now not only to the teachings of the intellect, but to the testimony of the soul, with its witness to its Master, the God of the spirits of all flesh. New prophets have arisen in these latter days to carry on, in a new language, and with new arguments, the old doctrine of the ancient Seers, to deepen the consciousness of the Divine in the hearts of men, to reaffirm the truth and the supremacy of the religious idea, to postulate God as the one adequate explanation of the Universe, the one source and effective sanction of men's moral conceptions. An Oliver Lodge in England, a James in America, an Eucken in Germany, a Bergson in France—these men have taken the place of the preachers of materialism who had the ear of the world three or four decades ago—have taken that place, —may we not say?—to the certain uplifting of the thoughtful sections of mankind.

And so I say to you in all affection, but in all earnestness too: Keep your hold on God; strengthen it; give it greater power over your lives, if you would show that you understand the forces that are at work in your generation, if you would prove that you have caught the spirit that is beginning to dominate your age. For so you will show yourselves men—alert, living men—men, just because you feel God within you and are strong enough to yield yourselves to Him. And you will have your reward. You will have the joy and the dignity that religion bestows upon its adherents, the stability it gives them in the hour of moral stress, the victory it ensures them in life's battle, the solace it offers them in life's sorrows.

THE ETHICS OF WORK

"Seest thou a man diligent in his work? He shall stand before kings."—PROVERBS xxii., 29.

WHEN, according to the Talmudic legend, Adam, expelled from Paradise, was told "thou shalt eat the herb of the field," he wept. "Shall I," he cried, "and the brute beast eat from the same manger?" But when he heard the rest of the Divine decree: "in the sweat of thy brow thou shalt eat bread," he was comforted. He was to be punished, but not degraded. The Divine fiat, though stern, was merciful. For work, far from being a curse, is a blessing. It is the salt of life, which gives it health and savour, the antidote to its cares, the magic stone that transfigures the daily task, and "makes drudgery divine."

This wholesome truth is preached by the Bible again and again. Enforced in a score of texts, it is inculcated more effectively still by that indirect doctrine which is taught without words. The Hebrew Scriptures, in this respect unique, perhaps, among the great religious books of antiquity, are a panorama of worldly activities, a series of living pictures whose common note is industry. For an example we need not go outside the lesson read from the Pentateuch this morning. It shows us Jacob, the progenitor of God's chosen people, toiling with unremitting energy, if with excessive shrewdness, at his prosaic occupation. And so it is throughout. The French painter, Millet, delighted to convey by his canvas the mingled pathos and nobility of the peasant's

THE ETHICS OF WORK

calling. The old Hebrew historians were beforehand with him. No worldly occupation is too humble to be glorified by their pen, none too lowly to be worthy even of their heroes. For what matters it how commonplace a task may be? All the distinction lies in doing it nobly, and such distinction may well be the aim of Patriarch and Lawgiver, of Prophet and Sage, of everyone who would live his life well.

It is an everlasting truth, and one which the world, for ever conning it, has not yet fully grasped. Nay, it would seem as though the world were further off than ever from its complete apprehension. The dignity of labour is just the one time-honoured verity which the modern spirit is most inclined to dispute. The ancient myth which made work the primeval curse seems, by a strange paradox, to be almost the only remnant of ancient legendary lore which retains its vitality in this age of doubt. Certainly, the number of persons who regard labour as a blessing is diminishing fast. Men's best energies are spent not upon work, but upon the attempt to escape from it. Never has steady toil fallen into such disrepute. The mania for speculation and gambling, which is eating away the heart of latterday morality, owes nearly all its origin to a contempt for patient industry. Men would get wealth without being at the pains of working for it. And too many of those who do work submit to the necessity in a grudging spirit. Their occupation yields them no delight. They go to it late and leave it early. They add week-end to week-end; they cry "let Bank Holidays come round!"

I am very far from undervaluing the need for recreation. A man may make himself a slave to work, as he may to pleasure, and suffer all a slave's degradation. But there is a golden mean in all things. If we ought not to give ourselves to toil, body and soul, to the detriment of the physical health and to the injury of the intellectual and the spiritual life, we ought also not to despise it as a necessary evil. The many holidays that people manufacture for themselves in these days are not so much the outcome of a need for recreation as the result of a distaste for steady and sustained labour. Men lose all pride in their work. Instead of making it their life's task, in the fulfilment of which they may find true ennoblement, they regard it as the mere means of living. And so, having degraded it, is it any wonder that they dislike it and evade it ? How can that be aught but an irksome burden which has long since been robbed of every attribute of dignity ?

Nor is the mischief confined to any one class ; it permeates the entire social structure. If it infects the man in the city, it takes hold also of the day-labourer in the workshop. He, too, is fast losing that joy in his work, that proud sense of creation which transforms the artizan, however humble his task, into the artist. Once work was something more than a means of subsistence ; it was a delight, a fount of honour, a challenge to the worker to throw into it his whole self.

>   The hand that rounded Peter's dome
>   And groined the aisles of Christian Rome
>   Wrought in a sad sincerity.
>   Himself from God he could not free.

This is the temper in which the humblest workman toiled in olden times. It was the temper praised by the Rabbins. "Choose life," God commands us ; "and what," cry the Rabbins, "is life, but work, yea, even handwork ?" But to-day, thanks, partly, to minute sub-division of labour, what a different spirit animates the toiler ! Spaek to the modern working-man of the dignity and the joy of labour, and you speak to him in

THE ETHICS OF WORK

a strange tongue. There are many honourable exceptions; but the average toiler is not so much a workman as a working man, an automaton bound by a hard fate to go through a monotonous round of toil as the alternative to starvation. He works like a machine and, alas! allows himself to be used as a machine. And the result is the same as it is in the case of his betters. He dislikes his work and flies from it as soon as he can; and what he does he does half-heartedly. At the stroke of twelve he throws down his hammer, though the nail be only half driven home. And since his whole heart is not in his labour the quality of his work suffers.

Some of you have been reading about the matter in your newspaper of late. A few years ago a bricklayer, we are told, would lay a thousand bricks in a day; now he will lay only three or four hundred. This is what is known as restriction of output. The less work a man does, the more there will be for others to do, and the fewer, therefore, the unemployed. Whether the statement about the bricks be literally true matters little. To limit production is admitted to be an unwritten law of organised labour. Well, it is a beautiful contrivance; but it has one obvious drawback. If more men are required to do the same quantity of work than of old, the cost of production will necessarily be greater, and England seriously hampered in her fierce struggle for an industrial foothold with foreign competitors. Let the workman persist in his policy of diminishing the output and he will find sooner or later that the output has been reduced to vanishing-point by forces other and mightier than his own. Then, instead of limiting his work, he will have no work to limit. His occupation will be gone.

The national prosperity, then, is involved in this matter. But something else is involved that is more important and more solemn still—it is national morality. This is an economic question, of course, but, like every such question, it has its moral side. Nay, economics, I make bold to say, is rooted in ethics. No industrial principle can be sound that is morally unsound. And is there not something radically unsound in the notion that a man may take pay for a fair day's work and give less than a fair day's work? The old moralists knew how to characterise such conduct. Maimonides warns the workman against denying the master his rightful service, against working by fits and starts, or idling away odd moments. To do so, he says, is to spend the day dishonestly. The shortcomings of the master may be urged in defence of modern industrial policy, and possibly not without some show of reason. But no unrighteousness can justify unrighteousness. The workman who does less work than he has agreed to do, or does it negligently, commits an immoral act. No extenuating circumstances can alter its character. And where do such practices take their rise except in that low conception of the nature of work of which I have spoken? Let a man rejoice in his toil, prize it as a blessed heritage, and he cannot stoop to such meanness.

You will object, perhaps, that all this would be better if said to a congregation of working-men. Well, as a matter of fact I propose to say something of the sort to an East-end audience to-morrow night. If I say it here first it is because the question is one which vitally concerns not the working class only, but every section of society. We are all deeply interested in national wellbeing; we ought all to be as deeply interested in national righteousness. And what is to become of national wellbeing when the worker, who is the backbone of the nation, is morally out of health in regard to the great business of his life, when he has an endless quarrel

THE ETHICS OF WORK

with his work, when, instead of being a source of real happiness to him, it breeds a sullen sense of wrong, of resentment against his master, of angry revolt against the entire scheme of things? What is to become of national wellbeing when, as a consequence of this temper, the nation is being beaten out of the markets of the world? And how will national morality fare—national morality, which is the one guarantee of national wellbeing—if the labourer deems himself justified in working with only one hand when he is engaged to render the service of both hands?

Even more deeply concerned are we to find the remedy. Perhaps it lies side by side with the disease. Perhaps one day the workers themselves, gaining a firmer grasp on economic and moral truth, may see the fallacy they are cherishing in its real proportions. Or perhaps some industrial catastrophe will have to bring its rude awakening. Either of these things may happen. But I prefer to turn my gaze in another direction. There are the children in the schools of the nation, whom it is the nation's business to equip for the battle of life. It is for you and me, as citizens, to see to it that, as part of that equipment, they are imbued with right ideas on this momentous question. Of late years the ordinary subjects of elementary education have been supplemented by technical training. The workshop has been made an adjunct to the schools. This is assuredly a step in the right direction. But it does not cover the whole ground. For it is of little use to arm a lad for the industrial fight if afterwards he turns his tools into weapons with which to attack the national stability, both industrial and moral.

What is needed is that, with this technical instruction, the teaching of sound economics and sound ethics should go hand in hand. Teach a boy to handle the chisel and the saw, but teach him so to handle them that he may carve out for himself a happy, because an honourable and a dignified life, and help to fashion a worthy national life. In short, what the children of the industrial classes have to learn more than all else is the true significance of labour in its relation both to capital and to the worker himself. Labour, he must be made to understand, is neither the slave of capital nor its master. They are co-ordinate; they are not rivals, but partners. The two combined make the wellbeing of a people, the wellbeing of the world. Their interests, then, are identical, and they are equal in dignity. But their dignity can only be upheld by the worth of those who represent them. "Seest thou a man diligent in his work? He shall stand before Kings." The veriest day-labourer is royal, if he behaves royally, if he honours his work and does it bravely and faithfully, in a spirit of noble self-denial. Whereas let him degrade it by indolence, by neglect, by narrow insistence on phantom rights, and it will revenge itself by degrading him.

This, I say, is what the workmen that are to be, nay, the capitalists that are to be, must needs be taught. For only by learning the lesson—the lesson of self-respect and mutual respect—and obeying it, can they win wellbeing for themselves, and help to build up on a firmer foundation the sacred fabric of national happiness.

ABOUT "WHISPERING"

"Be not called a whisperer."—ECCLESIASTICUS v., 14.

BY "whisperer" the Wise Man means the backbiter, the collector and distributer of defamatory gossip. He is thinking of the social bravo who, using words for his dagger, stabs his victim in the back. Secrecy is of the very essence of his trade. He says of another what he dares not say to his face. He prefers hint and innuendo to open speech. "Whisperer" is a good name for such stealthy cowards.

This sort of sinner has existed since history began, so fascinating is detraction for the speaker—and the listener too. The Bible is full of warnings against it. There is Leviticus, for example, with its command, "Thou shalt not go up and down as a talebearer among thy people." There is Proverbs, with its solemn reminder that "death and life are in the power of the tongue." And there is the Psalmist, too, with his striking picture of the backbiters who sharpen their tongue like a sword, and bend their bows to shoot their arrows, even bitter words." And Ben Sira, our author, fulminates against it no less energetically again and again. "Hear ye, my children, the discipline of the mouth. There is a manner of speech that is clothed about with death; let it not be found in the heritage of Jacob. . . . Be not called a whisperer, and lie not in wait with thy tongue. For as upon the thief there is shame, so there is an evil condemnation upon him that hath a double tongue."

More than twenty centuries separate Ben Sira's world from ours; but it cannot be said that we are more free from the sin he denounced than were the men of his time. The tongue is as unruly a member as ever it was. It is just as rebellious—works just as much mischief—as of old. Unbridled speech is a note of the age. There is too much talk everywhere—in Parliament, where legislation is impeded by excessive loquacity, in the Law-courts, where Bench and Bar forget, in unseemly jesting, the solemnity of justice and the anxieties of the litigants—also, some may be inclined to add, in the pulpit. But in these instances morality is only remotely concerned, and it is not difficult to find a remedy. It is otherwise with the individual's sins of speech. They directly impinge upon morals; they exert a profound effect upon the moral life. They are, moreover, hard to cure—all the harder because by most people they are not recognized as sins. But they are all the more insidious on that account, and cry out, all the more urgently, for a warning word. It is just against those acts of which we are inclined to say, " Oh, there is no harm in them; everybody does them," that the moralist needs especially to raise his voice.

" Be not called a whisperer." A whisperer!—how many there are to-day who answer to the description. To speak ill of others, to set them in an unfavourable light, is the commonest of offences. It is not necessary that the speech shall be false in order to constitute the offence. The conscious slanderer is a miscreant whom I prefer to think of as being non-existent among average men and women; and it is of average men and women, and *to* them, that I am speaking. It is a truism, of course, that scandal grows as it passes from mouth to mouth, and that the defamer may be a liar without knowing it. But the kind of talk that I have in my mind is not false talk, but true. The truth, we all know, may be a libel; and, in like manner, the telling of it may be, and often is, a sin—and a cowardly sin. The

ABOUT "WHISPERING"

sinfulness of detraction lies in its power to lower the subject of it in the estimation of the hearer. Sometimes it fastens upon positive wrongdoing, sometimes only harmless peculiarities. Now it takes the form of condemnation, now of ridicule. Consult your experience and you will see how large a place such talk occupies in ordinary, everyday conversation, how often the whisperer is on the war-path.

You will say, perhaps, " What does it matter ? The absent do not hear and therefore suffer no harm." Do they not ? Just reflect for a moment. Let an absent person be talked against, or merely laughed at, in your presence, and you will never think of him in quite the same way again. Your mental attitude towards him will be subtly changed. You may struggle against this effect, but it is a thousand chances to one that you will not succeed. That word of depreciation or of ridicule will colour your opinion of him henceforth. Whenever you meet him or think of him you will recall the unfavourable picture which his critic drew of him, perhaps years ago—drew of him perhaps in all thoughtlessness.

In all thoughtlessness, I say. For, as a rule, there is little or no spite in this disparaging talk. It is indulged in more or less idly, from a desire to amuse, or from a foolish ambition to tell the hearer something he does not know. And since people are more interesting than things, it is about people that one prefers to have news. But the results are none the less deplorable. I knew a man who, in bygone years, had done a discreditable act, the only one in his record. He made what amends were in his power, and his friends were determined to forget that dark chapter of his life, and never to allow it to affect their relations with him. But one day someone, by no means an unworthy or unkind person, spoke to another, in casual conversation, of that old lapse, raked up that forgotten scandal. It was done without good reason, but also without malevolence. But it was a cruel act all the same—cruel to a fallen man, who had bravely tried to live down his offence, and whose fall had been published to one hitherto ignorant of it. *There* is the pity, the tragedy of it all! We mean no harm by our idle talk, yet we *do* so much. A mere word lightly spoken, without malice or any evil intent, simply to fill up an empty moment or two, and the mental attitude of one human being to another is radically and irreparably changed for the worse.

And remember that the person disparaged is not the only sufferer. Evil speech is a boomerang. It injures, as the Rabbins point out, not only the absent subject of it, but the hearer, and even the speaker himself. The hearer, because to listen is to be an accomplice, and almost inevitably to yield to the temptation of capping one good or bad story with another. It is to be degraded. I consider it an insult to myself when somebody comes and talks to me against a third person, for he shows that he has a low opinion of *my* character as well as of the other man's. Nor does the speaker get off scot free. You cannot talk against another, or laugh at him, without a loss of moral tone. But, indeed, character must have been vitiated already to make such speech possible. There is no surer clue to a man's moral condition than the way in which he talks about other people. Let him be a "whisperer," and there must be something narrow and arid—yes, even vulgar—in his nature. The man of fine character disdains all this petty tittle-tattle. His outlook is too broad to admit of his busying himself needlessly with other people's ways or doings. He remembers, moreover, that he is not perfect himself, and he deems his moral judgment best employed when turned upon his own shortcomings.

Free from malice as detraction may be, there is still something in it peculiarly detestable to the healthy mind. It does its work in secret. The whisperer, as I have already pointed out, is well-named, for he says under his breath what he would not venture to say aloud. He speaks, or hints, in private, of the blot on A's past; will he speak of that blot to A himself? He makes fun of B's peculiarities; will he make fun of them to B? But there is something else in it, equally odious. We talk against others—often our bosom friends—and then go straightway to meet them with a smile on our face and fair words on our lips. Jeremiah put his finger on this foul blot centuries ago: "One speaketh peaceably to his neighbour with his mouth; but in his heart he lieth in wait for him." Ben Sira, in Ecclesiasticus, says of such offenders that they have "a double tongue." It is treachery itself.

How excellent it would be if we could come to look at the matter from this point of view! But there is something more to be said. By all means let us keep the immorality of the thing steadily before us—the injury we do to others, the moral wrong we inflict upon ourselves. But we may well think of it, too, as a sin against good manners. Let us come to see that it is, in colloquial phrase, as truly "bad form" to indulge in this depreciatory tittle-tattle as it is, for example, to talk loudly or loud, and there would be some prospect of its dying out. The Rabbins seem to have got this point of view. A good man of unbecoming speech, they say, is like a palace built next to a tannery. Just that one drawback spoils all his excellence. That is an effective way of looking at it. We pride ourselves on our education, our culture, our good breeding; and the pride is praiseworthy. But how inconsistent are we when we stoop to ill-natured gossip for our pleasure, and are not above extracting amusement from another's shortcomings! The hardest word in the English language to define is the word "gentleman." But surely in any satisfactory definition of it a place must be found for that genuine respect for ourselves, and for human nature generally, which finds expression in kindly judgments and kindly speech. And it need hardly be said that what is true of the gentleman is equally true of his counterpart among the other sex.

If the defamer could only see the matter in this light—see all the meanness of it—there would be some chance of his sin being stamped out. But its best chance of perishing lies in another direction. If there were no receivers, there would be no thieves. "If nobody," it has been aptly said, "gave calumny a lodging, it would starve, and die of itself." The old Jewish Sage in Proverbs said much the same thing: "As the north wind bringeth forth rain, so should a backbiting tongue an angry countenance." Yes; the real remedy lies with you and me. Let us refuse to listen to the scandalmonger, and his occupation will be gone. *There* is the whole matter in a nutshell. Depreciation thrives because we let it thrive by listening to it. Who are the popular people in ordinary society? Is it not the "snappers-up of unconsidered trifles," the busy-bodies who fetch and carry the latest intelligence about other people's affairs and shortcomings? Whereas, I am afraid, those who have no such choice morsels to retail are voted dull and unsociable. "Eh, but you're a puir creature," cried Carlyle in broad Scots across a dinner-table to a fellow guest who had distinguished himself by particularly inane talk. And it is these poor creatures—the whisperers of the text—who find a ready welcome in homes that pride themselves on their refinement.

Well, I say, we can help to put an end to it all. We

have, as the Rabbins remind us, our defence against evil-speaking, and our cure for it, in the soft lobe of the ear. Insert it, and the detractor charms in vain, charm he never so wisely. And then who knows?—perhaps one day he will desist from gossiping for higher reasons. Perhaps he will come to see that life has troubles enough —inevitable troubles—and that it is a sin and a shame gratuitously to add to them. And, perhaps, too, he will come to see that charity and loving-kindness are the imperious need of all men, with their chronic heartache, himself not excluded. And then he will begin to spare others because he feels the need of being spared himself— by men, and by God also. The old familiar prayer will come home to him in all its meaning : " That mercy I to others show, that mercy show to me."

ILL TEMPER

" Surely anger killeth the foolish man, and resentment slayeth the simpleton."—JOB v., 2.

So Eliphaz, one of Job's comforters, admonishes the sorely-tried Patriarch. It is useless, he says, for mortal man to get into a passion with destiny, to cry out angrily against the painful discrepancy that exists between fortune and merit. The wise will submit themselves to a Will that they have neither the power nor the right to question. Nay, wrathful protests and indignant murmurings, are not only useless but foolish. They recoil upon him who utters them. They are the senseless act of the enraged captive who hurls himself against his prison walls. They bruise; they kill.

The text, however, may serve to teach another, though a kindred moral. Our quarrel with fate, if we have one, is happily intermittent. As a rule, it is pleasing to think, we pursue the even tenor of our way either unconscious of a grievance or forgetful of it. It is about the spirit in which we ought to face, not life itself, but its petty difficulties—not the everlasting problem, but the passing ones—that we may profitably regard the text as speaking to us. For in too many of us that spirit leaves not a little to be desired. We allow everyday worries to put us out far more than they ought. More common than the anger with the general scheme of things, upon which Eliphaz pours his scorn, is the irritableness produced by small and transient troubles. And, as we shall see, it is no less futile and foolish. It has many victims; but, chief among them, is the mind that nourishes it.

Ill-temper—it is almost as common a defect as the tendency to disparaging speech about others, concerning which I spoke a little while ago. And, like that failing, it has become thus common owing to our faulty perspective. We fail to take its true measure, to see all the mischief of it. We recognize the need of correcting it clearly enough if other people manifest it. Then we shake our head, or our finger, at it, according to our temperament or our opportunities. Irritableness and bad temper are ugly things to look at—that we feel; we forget that others feel it too, and that our own irritableness and bad temper are not exactly beautiful to look at. There is no failing which we strive more earnestly to cure in children. We fully realize its gravity in their case; we see that, if it be allowed to weave itself into the growing character, it may become the root of many evils and of much unhappiness. The pity is that we do not turn the microscope more often upon ourselves, and get the benefit of the keen analysis which we apply so industriously, and with more or less justification, to others.

That ill-temper is a species of cruelty, we shall all admit. Some of the kindest persons in the world seem to be hard at work creating a minor martyrdom for those about them. Now it is an angry word, now an impatient gesture, now a frown—little things in themselves, but productive of the infinitude of pain which little things have such a wonderful knack of causing. Evil, according to the old proverb, is wrought by want of thought as well as want of heart. And here we have an illustration of its truth. Most of the unhappiness that bad temper occasions is wrought by good people. They would not consciously hurt a fly; but here they are making others miserable without intending it—others, most probably, whom they would sacrifice themselves to shield from visualized harm or suffering. This is the natural history of everyday ill-temper. Its bad effects are unintended. No one would deplore them more than the ill-tempered person himself if he could only realize how serious they are. There are people, of course, who are wrothful from choice, who are never happy unless they are angry, and who take a morbid delight in seeing their victim writhe and squirm. But these are exceptional monsters, to be put into a Chamber of Horrors, not into a sermon. We will leave them out of consideration, if you please.

Let us restrict our attention to the average man and woman. All the mischief they do by their irritableness is done thoughtlessly, and the brunt has to be borne by those nearest to them. The Rabbins explicitly exhort us to be gentle and long suffering towards those of our own household. It is a strange exhortation. Why should those of our own household be specified ? Is not consideration due to everyone ? But the saying is based upon a knowledge of human nature. It is just those with whom we come into daily contact—our dependents, our dearest, alas !—upon whom we chiefly visit our dissatisfaction—dissatisfaction, not always with *them*, but with *things*. If affairs have gone wrong, if we have an ache or a pain, if the weather is not to our liking, they have to suffer for it. To our friends and acquaintances we are more tender ; we *do* see the injustice of making them responsible for bad markets or meteorological eccentricities. We do contrive to put a curb on our temper in their case. Does not that very fact suffice to condemn all such angry manifestations ? We are able to keep a fairly tight hand upon ourselves in our intercourse with those who are more or less strangers ; is it not, then, a real, because a preventable sin to let ourselves go in our attitude towards those who share our

ILL TEMPER

lives with us, to whom we are debtors for constant kindness, perhaps for daily acts of self-denying love, and who consequently have the very first claim upon our patience and consideration. What an anomaly the whole thing is! Convention, politeness, social law call for our self-restraint, and we exercise it; but when it is demanded by a sense of the forbearance due from the superior to the inferior—nay, when it is claimed by love—we fail to respond. The hearts we cherish—hearts in which we would not wilfully plant a thorn—these suffer at our hands; the hearts that are indifferent to us spur us to self-mastery, get from us a calculated tenderness. Why, my friends, our action ought to be exactly the reverse. If some outlet is really necessary for our vexation, let us seek it abroad, not at home. It would at least be more courageous, as well as less unjust.

But, in truth, there is no need to vent our ill-temper upon anybody. This mental blood-letting may well go the way of the old phlebotomy. That we can rule our spirit if we will is proved by the most convincing of all facts—the fact, namely, that, as we have seen, we actually do it. It is simply a matter of discipline. I am quite sure that all irritable persons could be much more amiable if they tried. Only they don't try. They have got into the way of thinking, when they are angry, that they can only feel better by making other people feel worse. Suppose they tried another method. Suppose, when they were out of temper, they retired to their room, and had it out with *themselves!* We cannot, I admit, always be in a good temper; it is often a matter of health, of nerves; and then, too, people *are* just a little trying occasionally, and things do sometimes go askew. But the wrong lies not in *feeling* out of temper, but in showing it—for *that*, at least, we *can* help. Nor is even the yielding to angry impulse always a sin.

It may be a virtue. All the past wrongs of the world, all its extinct evils, have been slain by a healthy anger. I do not know what would become of humanity if there were no such things as a passionate sense of injustice, a hot rebellion against superfluous suffering. But we must discriminate. Moses, moved by righteous indignation, strikes down the cruel taskmaster, and he is implicity justified by the sacred story; under deep provocation he cries, " Ye rebels," and he loses the Promised Land. In the one case he vindicates the sanctity of justice; in the other he sins against his own dignity.

And so I reach my final point. Senseless anger wounds no one so cruelly as the angry man himself. It is quite pathetic to think of the number of worthy people who are spoiling their lives by their irritableness. They allow the tiniest worries to vex them; they get out of temper with others when in reality they are angry with themselves. The misery that these unfortunate people suffer is incalculable. They are the prey of self-reproaches. They know that they have made themselves disagreeable, and that they have fallen below the moral standard they normally set themselves. It spoils their lives, I say—wears them out—slays, as the text tells us. When thinking of this topic one inevitably remembers Hillel, the notoriously good-tempered man. A common fellow, we read, once laid a wager that he would rouse the Sage out of his studied calm. So he goes to him on a Friday, when he is busily preparing for the Sabbath, and plies him with a whole string of stupid questions, all of which Hillel answers in turn with imperturbable gravity and patience. " But," says the man, " I have many more questions to ask, but I fear to weary thee." " Ask them, my son," answers the Sage. The man feels himself beaten. " Thou art Hillel," he cries; " I wish thou hads't never been born, for through thee

I have lost a hundred pounds." "Better that thou shoulds't lose thousands," replied Hillel, "than that I should lose my temper." Of course; how he would have despised himself if he had! What peace of mind, what inward satisfaction, what enviable happiness would he not have missed!

And so the lesson comes closely home to us. We are all self-lovers; and there is no harm in it, if ours is the higher self-love. We hold an effective and no unworthy incentive to good temper before us when we think of the joys we may get from it—the tranquil mind, the satisfied conscience. And there is a lower consideration still, which, however, we need not therefore despise. We like to look well, and for others to think that we do. What pains, what money, do not some of us expend in order to attain this desire. But surely one of the secrets of good looks is a placid spirit, one that is at rest in itself, and is filled with loving kindness for others. The newspapers print effusions from time to time styled "Hints about Beauty." To their favourite nostrums—their powders and washes—the writers forget to add the most effective specific of all—good temper. It is a serious omission. For just as anger killeth, so an equable mind gives life. It ensures that health of mind and body without which, in the last resort, true beauty —the beauty which will not wash off—is impossible. Here, then, we have *gratis* a prescription for one of the most coveted of human possessions. Let us give it a trial. None of us will regret it, I am sure.

GIANTS

" And all the people that we saw in it are men of great stature; and there we saw the giants."—NUMBERS xiii., 32, 33.

THE tendency to exaggeration seems inborn in the human mind. The calmest and least romantic natures are not altogether free from it. To report a fact is almost inevitably to magnify it. Travellers' tales are proverbially suspect. It is not surprising, then, that exaggeration should be the note of stories coming down from remote ages, when men fed on wonders. " There were giants in the earth in those days "—the words in Genesis sum up the early story of mankind. It is full of the marvellous. The nursery-tales, crowded with big men and big doings, which are the delight of the modern child, are old-time romances upon which the imagination of the full-grown man was wont to nourish itself in the world's childhood.

This love of the wonderful, and the tendency to exaggeration which is born of it, are illustrated in the narrative from which the text is taken. The spies have seen some tall men in Canaan; by the time the scouts get back to camp those tall men have grown vastly in number, perhaps also in size, and the land is full of them. " All the people that we saw in it are men of great stature." Here is legend in the making. There never have been races of giants; at most there have been only families of them. The old popular notion that primitive man was of gigantic proportions, and that the human race has gradually deteriorated in stature through the ages gets no support from anthropology.

The legend manufactured by the spies found only too ready credence. The love of the marvellous not only creates the myth, but provides a public for it. In the story before us the consequences are disastrous. The giants that exist only in the fancy of the spies keep Israel out of Canaan for forty years. "Fear not the people of the land," cry sober-minded Joshua and Caleb ; "the Lord is with us, therefore fear them not." The only reply of the panic-stricken people is, "Stone them." And so the fictitious giants overcome the living proclaimers of the truth. A little calmness, a little courage, would prick this bubble. But these qualities, at the moment, are far to seek.

Giants!—they belong essentially to old-world story. And yet not entirely. There are giants still, as the greatest of English allegorists, with his tale of Grim the Giant and Giant Despair, knew full well—giants looming large in the modern man's mind and working evil in his life—giants, big and formidable enough in themselves, but made a hundred times bigger and more formidable by the common man's own terrors. We all know those giants! The dread of them paralyses the springs of effort and turns the joyousness of life into mourning, just as it did in the case of the Israelites of old. Giants!— one of them is Difficulty. In itself it is a manageable, an inspiring, I had almost said a benevolent sort of giant ; but unfortunately we endow it with monstrous proportions, with a fictitious strength and hostility, and we quail before it. There is no tonic more bracing than Difficulty ; health, physical and moral alike— life itself—would be impossible without it. But for the need and possibility of conquering it there would be no Promised Land for any of us. "Three good gifts," say the Rabbins, "God gave to His people—the Law,

Canaan and Life Everlasting—and the condition of winning them all was tribulation." The saying is eternally true. No boon worth having is won without struggle, without a grim tussle with the giant Difficulty. The boon itself is naught compared with the struggle itself—with the glad pain of effort, the ecstasy of conquest. What but difficulty has made the discoveries possible that have enhanced the world's knowledge and wealth, enlarged the sum of human well-being? A dark continent invites the explorer—invites him by its very darkness, with its cry, " Come and be the first to light me up "—invites him by the prospect of hard physical toil, by the thought of the rivers he will have to ford, the peaks he will have to scale, the heat, the cold he will have to endure, the enemies, animal and human, he will have to fight. A new world of knowledge and achievement calls to the man of science, to the chemist, the engineer, the bacteriologist. Them, too, the giant Difficulty confronts ; what labour, what thought, what baffled efforts, again and again renewed, are not needed to overcome it! The very difficulty is the allurement. But for that who would give himself to the task of discovery? Verily it is a kindly giant after all. Men fight him, but love him—love him just for giving them something to fight. There was a great social reformer once,[1] to whom the thought of a Golden Age lying in the future was a positive trouble. What a dreary place, he argued, this world would be if there were no wrongs left to redress! The theoretically perfect state of society is something to be sought after, not attained. The Golden Age, like every other ideal good, is always to be. A world without a wrong to be righted, without an obstacle to be surmounted, without a temptation to be wrestled with, would be a dying world.

[1] John Stuart Mill.

The facing of difficulty is the making of man, the making of character. All our duty lies in fighting the giants, in overcoming the tendency to run away from them. The Promised Land takes various forms for each of us; but the giants always effectually bar the way, if they do not draw us on. If we take up their challenge, we conquer; if we slink away, we are beaten. Our hope is to succeed in the worldly life. We would succeed, too, in the moral life—something more momentous still. But we shall never do either unless we take the measure of the foe calmly and without panic. It is a bad thing to despise one's enemy, but it is a far worse thing to overestimate him. If so many go down in the great battle of life it is because they commit this latter mistake, because they see a lion in the path when there are only a few rough stones; because, instead of a giant or two, they fancy that they have to deal with a whole tribe of Anakim. Or, to put it in another way, they undervalue their own strength. Like the Israelites in our story, they are as grasshoppers in their own sight as well as in the sight of the enemy. But let them stand up to the redoubtable foe, and his formidableness vanishes. I daresay you know what it is to wake up in the night and think with hot dread of the morrow's work. It seems utterly beyond you. But when day comes, and you are at close grips with the monster, how his proportions shrivel! It is so always—in the worldly fight, and in the moral fight also. Keep your giant at arm's length, and you can do nothing against him; close with him, and you bring him to his knees. "Let us go up at once and possess it," cries stout-hearted Caleb, though he, too, has seen the giants; and his brave words should be the motto of everyone who could do something in the world, but for the young especially, to whom the great Canaan of life is for ever calling out, "Come up and take me."

Yes, come up *at once*, before fear has made the giants the formidable creatures they are not.

Giants!—Difficulty is one of them; Trouble is another. What son of man has not looked upon it? But the thing is to face it. Let us shrink in terror before the enemy, and our Promised Land—peace of mind, energy, faith—is lost to us. Is it not true? If sorrow has dominion over us, if reverse, pain, the ingratitude of hearts we have cherished, the loss of our dearest, rob us of all the light of our life, it is because we do not marshal the forces that are at our command—the thought of the blessings that are left to us, our trust in everlasting rectitude and goodness. It is because we do not grapple with our trouble, saying, "This is a bitter root, but I will extract its virtue; it shall help me to heal the far worse hurt I have done myself." For cannot sorrow rebuild character? May not our struggle with adversity and pain yield us increased strength with which to essay the larger duties of life, a quicker sympathy for those with a yet greater sorrow than ours? "It would be," says a modern writer, "a poor result of all our anguish and our wrestling, if we won nothing but our old selves at the end of it; if we could return to the same blind loves, the same self-confident blame, the same light thoughts of human suffering."

And another giant there is that bulks largely in men's vision; it is the fear of death. For some of us it hardly exists at all, so absorbing is the masterful present, with its work and its pleasures. But, for others, for those, in particular, whose feet are already set on the downward slope of the years, it is a very real giant indeed, one that has attained in their thoughts to colossal proportions. If we analyse this fear it usually proves to be either a dread of going into the Great Beyond alone, or the shrinking from nothingness, from the thought of the entire cessation of thought, of consciousness and feeling. But is it not a needless terror? For if death be the end of consciousness, then, when it comes, we shall feel and know nothing, not even the nothingness of death. And so, because there will be nothing to fear, we need fear nothing. But if, as religion tells us, and as we believe, there *is something;* if death is but the gateway of another life, then why should we be afraid to enter it alone? God will be in that realm, and to be with Him is to be with a friend. And surely the goodness that has made this life worth living will not fail us in the life to come. It is because we do not contemplate death with placid gaze, because we steal shy, timid glimpses of it, that it is a King of Terrors. You remember Doré's popular picture representing Daniel in the den of lions. The Prophet, his hands bound behind him, stands quietly confronting a crowd of gaping, snarling brutes. But it is they who stand at bay. They dare not touch him; they are vanquished by the stedfastness of his gaze. It is the human story writ small. The monsters are the work of our own hands; let us believe in them and they overcome us with our own fears. On the other hand the giants are real; but we have only to believe in ourselves, believe in God, and they are as naught. "The Lord is with us; therefore fear them not."

It is to help the toiling pilgrim to battle with at least two of the giants—Pain and the Spectre of Death—that the hospitals carry on their merciful work.[1] For none of us can altogether fight our battle alone; we need the help of our fellow-men and the courage that comes of the very thought of it. And if this is true of everyone, it is true, above all, of those who have to bear the double handicap of poverty and suffering. The hospitals

[1] Preached on Hospital Sabbath.

appeal to-day to the first instincts of our common humanity—love for our kind, pity for those whose lives are pitiful. Help these hapless fellow-workers of yours to fight their formidable antagonists; and be sure that, in the hour when you are wrestling with your own giant foes, the memory of your aid will help you to victory in your turn.

For Product Safety Concerns and Information please contact our EU representative GPSR@taylorandfrancis.com
Taylor & Francis Verlag GmbH, Kaufingerstraße 24, 80331 München, Germany